2-16-60

INDUSTRIAL EVOLUTION OF COLUMBUS, OHIO

INDUSTRIAL EVOLUTION
OF COLUMBUS, OHIO

By

Henry L. Hunker

Assistant Professor of Geography
The Ohio State University

Bureau of Business Research Monograph Number 93

Published by

BUREAU OF BUSINESS RESEARCH
COLLEGE OF COMMERCE AND ADMINISTRATION
THE OHIO STATE UNIVERSITY
COLUMBUS, OHIO

COLLEGE OF COMMERCE AND ADMINISTRATION
WALTER C. WEIDLER, *Dean*

BUREAU OF BUSINESS RESEARCH STAFF
VIVA BOOTHE, *Director*

JAMES C. YOCUM, *Marketing*   PAUL G. CRAIG, *Economics*

MIKHAIL V. CONDOIDE, *Economics*   RALPH M. STOGDILL, *Personnel*

OMAR GOODE, *Tabulations*

Research Assistants

MARY PRIEST MARTIN   MARTHA N. STRATTON

WILLIAM D. OYLER   DIAL M. SHAHANI

MARTHA MOUNTS, *Assistant to the Director*

FOREWORD

There is presented in this monograph an account of the factors both external and internal which have influenced the retardation or the accelleration of the industrial evolution of Columbus, the effects of these forces upon changes in the industrial pattern of the city from time to time, and the shifts in industrial location within the city as growth and expansion have occurred.

Since no period in a city's history is ever completely static, changes were occurring in the industrial complex of Columbus even as this study was being made, and many have occurred since its completion. Thus, a few firms included in this study have ceased to operate, others of substantial importance have been established or have moved into the city, and some have changed their locations within the city. However, the broad outline of factors influencing the industrial life of the area, the general direction of major trends, and the pattern of industrial location within the city remain substantially as presented.

Viva Boothe, *Director*

ACKNOWLEDGMENTS

It is not possible to recognize individually all of the persons who have contributed something to this study. The more than 220 representatives of the various Columbus manufacturing plants which were visited during the Summer and Autumn of 1952 contributed time and ideas as they attempted to answer thoughtfully the questions of the writer. Their ideas, and the facts they presented, have been incorporated in this study but if there are errors in interpretation, they are the writer's.

Mr. Grover Clements, of the Franklin County Regional Planning Commission, was especially helpful with his offers of information, maps, and interest. Mrs. Rosemary Martin, of the Industrial Bureau, the Columbus Chamber of Commerce, discussed phases of the study in the light of the Chamber's interest in manufacturing in Columbus. To these, and to the other members of their organizations, the writer offers his appreciation.

Professor Alfred J. Wright of the Department of Geography, The Ohio State University offered critical advice and valuable suggestions during the progress of the basic research. Professor Eugene Van Cleef of the Department of Geography, The Ohio State University, aided by his willingness to discuss any questions that pertained to urban or industrial planning in Columbus.

And to Dr. Viva Boothe, Director of the Bureau of Business Research, The Ohio State University, who has helped mold the final form of this study, appreciation is expressed.

HENRY L. HUNKER

TABLE OF CONTENTS

ix

LIST OF TABLES

LIST OF CHARTS

LIST OF MAPS

ILLUSTRATIONS

CHAPTER I

THE RISE OF A COMMERCIAL CENTER

Columbus, Ohio, on the relatively flat Ohio till plain near the western edge of the Appalachian Plateau, was the first state capital in the Northwest Territory and the first planned state capital in the United States. The geographic position of the site, near the center of the state, was the principal reason for its selection for the capital of Ohio.

A Planned Political Center

In March 1803, the General Assembly of Ohio met in Chillicothe with the purpose of organizing the state government. The Assembly divided the state into counties with Franklin the first among the new counties created. Franklinton, then a thriving town on the lowlands west of the Scioto River, became the county seat. Franklinton had been first settled in 1797 when Lucas Sullivant, engaged in a survey of the Virginia Military District, laid out the plans for the settlement on the low banks of the Scioto River near the point where it meets with the Olentangy (Whetstone) River.[1]

State Capital—The General Assembly continued to meet in Chillicothe until 1810, after which it met briefly in Zanesville. The desire for a permanent capital increased and the advantages of several sites in central Ohio were considered by the Assembly. Zanesville, Lancaster, Newark, Worthington, and Dublin were prominently mentioned until a group of men from Franklinton, including Lyne Starling (brother-in-law of Lucas Sullivant), Alexander McLaughlin, John Kerr, and James Johnston, offered the General Assembly a tract of about 1,200 acres of land on the east bank of the Scioto opposite Franklinton. In addition, they offered to give the state 20 acres of land in this tract on which a capitol, a penitentiary, and other buildings would be constructed.

[1] "If there is wonder that he located on the lowlands, instead of the now more desirable lands east of the river, the answer is to be found in the fact that he had nothing to do with the latter lands. The limit of the tract he was surveying was the river." [Hooper, Osman C., *History of the City of Columbus, Ohio* (Columbus: The Memorial Publishing Co., 1920), pp. 11-12.]

The permanance of the site was not settled upon but it was agreed that the capital would remain at Columbus until May 1, 1840. Only an act of the legislature could then change the site.[2] Joel Wright, of Warren County, was appointed the State Director in charge of the actual development of the capital. His city plans influenced the pattern of settlement and growth in Columbus.[3] The sale of the first city lots took place on June 18, 1812.

Central Ohio had few cultural attributes in 1812. Self-sufficient agriculture dominated the economy but even its advance was slow. The people were primarily engaged in clearing the land of its extensive hardwood forests so that agriculture could succeed.

County Seat—It has been suggested that ". . . the selection of the site for Ohio's capital must have been more for what it might become than for what it was at that time."[4] And yet, it was near the center of the state, it was more accessible than the other places proposed, and the donations of the proprietors were very desirable. As the capital of the state, Columbus increased its population through immigration; commercial activities were expanded as the needs of the growing population developed. In a matter of a few years, the town outdistanced Worthington (which had been founded in 1804) and Franklinton. By 1824, the County Court was moved from Franklinton. With this move, Columbus assumed the additional local importance of a county seat.

Settlement of Central Ohio

When it was created the capital of the state, Columbus had neither the physical nor economic qualities that presaged important developments. There were no outstanding raw materials evident, no important trade routes of wide scope, nor did the town serve more than local markets. Columbus possessed, however, the *geographical position* which led to economic growth and stability.

[2] Peattie, Roderick, Editor, *Columbus, Ohio: An Analysis of a City's Development* (Columbus: Chamber of Commerce, 1930), p. 1. In the early 1840's, there was some agitation to move the capital from Columbus to some other town more centrally located and less "metropolitan."

[3] Wright, Alfred J., "Joel Wright, City Planner," *The Ohio State Archaeological and Historical Quarterly*, Vol. 56, No. 3, July 1947, pp. 290-291.

[4] Hooper, Osman C., *op. cit.*, p. 27.

Land Grants

Original land grants and surveys have upon occasion served to unite and promote settlement in virgin areas. This was true in several parts of Ohio. Many of the early settlements in the state can be attributed to the various grants. The Congress of the United States provided for a survey of the western lands in May 1785; on July 13, 1787, the Ordinance for the Government of the Northwest Territories was adopted. A number of chartered companies left eastern states to take up settlement in the new territory but their influence did not extend immediately into central Ohio.

Military Grants—Three major military grants were made in the central Ohio area, primarily to reward men who had fought in various United States' wars. A major division was the United States Military Lands set apart by Congress in 1796 to satisfy the claims of participants in the Revolutionary War. This tract lay east of the Scioto River, north of the present Fifth Avenue, in Columbus (See Map 1). To the south of these lands for four and one-half miles and extending eastward 48 miles was the Refugee Tract.[5] This tract was appropriated by Congress for the benefit of Canadian and Nova Scotian persons who had espoused the cause of the Colonies in the Revolution. A third division was the Virginia Military Lands west of the Scioto River that Virginia reserved for her soldiers in 1790.

Congress Lands—Finally, the Congress Lands were set aside in 1796 to be sold directly to the settlers. They lay south of the Refugee Tract and east of the Scioto River.

Settlement

These subdivisions opened the Ohio country to surveying teams and to settlers. Lucas Sullivant first visited central Ohio in 1795 as a surveyor and, recognizing the qualities of the area for farming, purchased land to which he returned in 1797. Others, learning of the fine Ohio soils, came to the area and took up holdings.

Among the early settlers were some of the best blood and brains of New England, Pennsylvania, and Virginia. These new settlers brought their native cultures with them into Ohio and organized

[5] The present Refugee Road in South Columbus formed the southern edge of this tract.

MAP 1—Ohio Land Grants in the Columbus Area

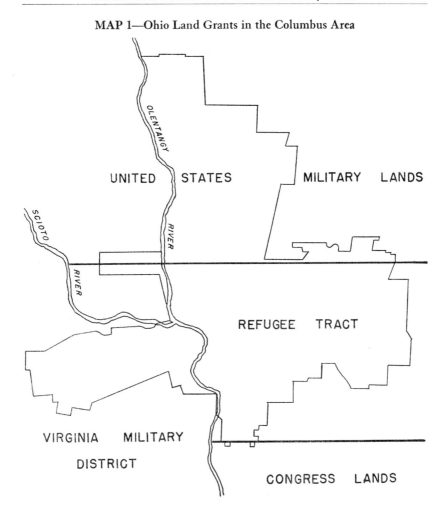

AFTER- O.C. HOOPER, "HISTORY OF THE
CITY OF COLUMBUS, OHIO" 1920 P. 9

active communities. An early member of the local community wrote
of the diverse geographic backgrounds of her neighbors: she received
pumpkin from Vermont neighbors, corn hominy from the Virginians, and sauerkraut from Pennsylvania Germans. One writer notes

that ". . . with Puritan leadership from the north and Cavalier leadership from the south, Ohio could not fail to produce a versatile and energetic whole."[6]

Routes into Ohio

The Indian trails that traversed the Ohio country, and the waterways of the Ohio system jointly provided the early access to the state. It is not the purpose here to debate which route was more important. The point is clear—the route which was most conveniently available at the time was utilized by the settlers.

Appalachian Mountains — The Appalachian Mountains, although a barrier to the settlement and development of the Ohio Country, provided the corridors through which the early settlers from the south and east passed to reach the western lands. These corridors gave access to Ohio both by land and by water routes. The lowland route through western Pennsylvania, and the Wilderness Road through the Cumberland Gap in eastern Tennessee, were the first routes traveled.[7] Later, the Mohawk Valley and the Erie Canal gave direct and easy access to the lake plains of Ohio. There were other corridors, as well, that carried settlers and commerce to Ohio: the fact remains, however, that the state did not experience economic growth until this mountain barrier was penetrated.[8]

Trails—Hulbert asserts that it was by the trails that crossed central Ohio— ". . . the keys to the central West . . ."—that many settlers reached their destinations. He suggests that the Indian trails were the primary routes followed by the early settlers into the interior of Ohio. Certainly, the following trails, which generally penetrate the gaps in the Appalachians, were of special significance:

> *Warrior's Path*—Through the Cumberland Gap streamed many
> southern farmers who followed this trail north through the
> Scioto Valley to Lake Erie. It was also a major route for armies.

[6] Zimmerman, Carrie B., "Ohio, the Gateway to the West," *The Ohio Archaeological and Historical Quarterly,* Vol. 40, 1931, p. 140.

[7] Brown, Ralph H., *Historical Geography of the United States* (New York: Harcourt, Brace and Company, 1948), pp. 184-186.

[8] See Wright, Alfred J., *Economic Geography of Ohio* (Columbus: Division of Geological Survey, 1953), pp. 1-3.

Sandusky-Richmond Trail—This passed through central Ohio (the home of the Shawnee), through the Hocking area, and to the Great Kanawha River Valley. It was an important fur route and it brought settlers to central Ohio from the eastern and south-eastern seaboard.

Monongahela Trail—This trail connected central Ohio with south-western Pennsylvania and the Monongahela River valley.

Moravian or Scioto-Beaver Trail—From the Beaver River valley of Pennsylvania westward by way of Steubenville and Coshocton came the settlers from Pennsylvania and New England.

Many of these same trails later became the courses of the first roads that crossed Ohio.[9]

Waterways—The Ohio-Mississippi river system was central Ohio's contact with the outside world. Extending northward from the Ohio River, the Muskingum, Scioto, and Miami rivers were among the principal means by which new settlers reached into the heart of the state. It was in these river valleys that some of the earliest settlements were established.

This river system was also the chief means of carrying incoming merchandise and outgoing produce for central Ohio. As early as 1810, Lyne Starling and others built flatboats on the Scioto River and ventured with their cargoes of agricultural products down the Scioto, Ohio, and Mississippi, eventually to reach New Orleans.[10] The New Orleans market was a great one for the Ohio farmers, but it was a buyer's market and the farmer suffered frequently as a result.

The economy of the agricultural south was based upon its two cash crops—cotton and tobacco. A lively exchange took place between southern markets and northern farmers with food crops, especially cereals, exchanged for the cash crops of the south. The flatboats, and later the steamboats, carried corn, wheat, oats, flour, pork, bacon, and whisky, to the down-river market. The cash obtained from these sales bought the much desired manufactured goods of New England and Pennsylvania which could not be had in the trans-Appalachian country.

[9] Hulbert, Archer B., "The Indian Thoroughfares of Ohio," *The Ohio Archaeological and Historical Quarterly*, Vol. 8, 1900, pp. 260-273.

[10] Hooper, Osman C., *op. cit.*, p. 131, and Unstad, Lyder L., *A Survey of the Industrial and Economic Development in Central Ohio with Special Reference to Columbus, 1797-1872* (Unpublished Manuscript, The Ohio State University Library, 1937), p. 50.

Local Transportation Facilities

Communities in central Ohio were reached either by trails or by river until a program of local road construction was initiated. The earliest roads of central Ohio connected the small towns with the county seat or a river town. A few such roads had been opened prior to the founding of Columbus—from Franklinton to Lancaster, Newark, Springfield, and Worthington. Roads were little more than trails until the War of 1812 prompted the construction of military roads. In 1814-1815, the Assembly authorized the money to construct a road between the capital and Granville, as well as to improve other roads.

"The great work, however, was left to individual enterprise. In 1816, the Franklin Turnpike Road Company was incorporated to build a road from Columbus to Newark . . . It was the first of an almost innumerable throng."[11] Other toll roads were undertaken with a 106-mile road between Columbus and Sandusky the most ambitious effort. The roads were poor, generally, with transportation slow and expensive, but the change from pack train to freight wagon and stage coach did much to accelerate the commercial development of central Ohio.

The Development of Inter-Regional Transportation

Up to 1833 the principal means of transportation in central Ohio were the Indian trails, the natural waterways, and the limited turn-pikes constructed by the legislature and by private concerns. The year 1833 marked a turning point: the National Road reached Columbus, and the Ohio and Erie Canal was opened along its full route. These events played a major role in shaping the commercial growth of Columbus during the next few decades; they also exerted a strong influence upon the growth of population in Central Ohio.

From a town of 700 in 1815, Columbus had increased in size to only 2,435 by 1830. This fifteen-year period was one of relatively slow growth characterized by a poorly developed transportation system. In the following decade, the city more than doubled in size reaching a population of 6,048 by 1840. This increase can be attri-

[11] Hooper, Osman C., *op. cit.*, p. 132.

buted to the city's growing importance as a political center, to its role in commerce in central Ohio, and to its greatly enhanced position with respect to major inter-regional transportation facilities.

The movement of new settlers into the Ohio country and beyond continued in the mid-1800's. By 1850, 17,882 persons were permanent residents of Columbus. However, the opening of the Illinois and Iowa lands for settlement had the effect of disrupting or retarding the growth of population in the city. In the decade between 1850-1860, only 672 persons settled in the city. Immigration into Columbus was low; emigration from Columbus was relatively high at this time. The continuing westward migrations reached their peak in 1857, after which Columbus resumed a steady growth.

The National Road

The concentration of population in Columbus was stimulated by the juncture of the National Road with the Scioto River. The importance of the city as a junction was reflected in the marked crossroads pattern which evolved.

The National Road was the culmination of earlier attempts to link central Ohio with eastern markets. While the Indian trails and waterways carried the settler and pack animal into the state, it was not until roads and canals were established that eastern trade "invaded" Ohio.

The projection of the National Road into Ohio in 1825 offered the first opportunity for inter-regional trade by overland carriers. The Road originated in Cumberland, Maryland, crossed the Ohio River at Wheeling, and continued westward through Zanesville to Columbus.[12] The system of highways that centered about the National Road provided ". . . the first great division of internal improvements, by which Ohio was opened to the outside world . . ." and the time involved in travel—about 49½ hours between Wheeling and Columbus—was a marked improvement over earlier efforts.[13] Built at Federal expense, the Road reached Columbus in 1833, and

[12] Brown, Ralph H., *op. cit.,* p. 106.
[13] Stoddards, Paul W., "The Economic Progress of Ohio: 1800-1840," *The Ohio Archaeological and Historical Quarterly,* Vol. 41, 1932, p. 177.

later continued westward through Springfield into Indiana. The route in Columbus followed Friends Street (now Main) west to High Street, thence north to Broad, and west out of the city.

Columbus reflected the opening of the Road with a growing population and increased commerce and industry. The Ohio Stage Company, with headquarters in Columbus, was one of the largest transportation companies to utilize the new road. Carrying passengers, mail, and light freight, this line gave Columbus an important place in the expanding transportation network of the state. It connected the city with points throughout central and southeastern Ohio.

More important, perhaps, the National Road was the means by which commercial freight and livestock reached the eastern markets. Moore gives an account of this activity:

> From the east there were caravans of wagons, many of them drawn by four and six horses, conveying the products of the shops and mills to the frontier, and from the west they were transporting the products of the fields and farms. . .[14]

A major part of Columbus' business, however, was centered directly and indirectly about emigrant trade at this time. Jordan gives the example of one traveler, with a wagon-load of household goods, who stayed in Columbus only two hours—long enough to eat, drink, and have a shave. This traveler was no exception, for hundreds more thought of Columbus as a stopping-point only.[15] But, while these travelers stopped, felloes were tightened, harnesses mended and repaired, horses shod, and local merchandise purchased. The commercial gains resulting to Columbus merchants were appreciable.

The National Road never proved as beneficial to the farm population of central Ohio as did the Ohio and Erie Canal. The Road proved inadequate for the large-scale movement of agricultural surplus, other than livestock. Consequently, tolls on the National

[14] Moore, Opha, *History of Franklin County, Ohio* (Topeka: Historical Publishing Company, 1930), p. 147.

[15] Jordan, Philip D., *The National Road* (New York: The Bobbs-Merrill Company, 1948), pp. 126-127.

Road were but a fraction of the tolls collected on the canal. Tolls were based upon the injury done the road by the movement of people, wagons, and livestock; they were made to provide income to be used for repair purposes.[16] In 1840, one of the most prosperous years for the National Road, tolls amounted to $51,364.35 in Ohio. While this figure was three times the total collected in Pennsylvania, it was still small when compared with the Ohio and Erie Canal.[17] Canal tolls, amounting to $452,122.03 in 1840 reflect the greater commercial traffic in agricultural products that the canals carried.

The National Road, never a profitable venture, was turned over to state control in 1831—two years before its extension to Columbus. By 1859, travel was almost entirely local with practically all benefits confined to local areas. The road soon fell into disuse and the costs of repair became prohibitive. As railroad activity increased and as the road continued to handle only local traffic, the state gave up its control and care to the counties through which the road passed.

Turnpikes

In addition to the National Road, the turnpikes, which were first established in the early 1800's, were extended considerably from 1845 to 1855. They were limited in mileage but connected Columbus with Harrisburg, Portsmouth, Pomeroy, Worthington, Mt. Vernon, and dozens of other communities. As a consequence of the expanded overland accessibility afforded by the turnpikes, Columbus' shops turned out wagons in increased numbers both for the westward-moving settlers and for the adjacent farm population. The Ohio Stage Company had its wagon shops as well as its offices in Columbus. The wagon and buggy industry developed around the activities associated with the stage company and with the improved transportation system.

[16] Representative tolls for the period 1843-1844 showed that each passenger on a coach paid ten cents at each toll gate. A horse and rider paid three cents at each gate and a cart or wagon with two horses paid twenty cents. Individual animals and herds were charged, based upon the damage done the road. A score of sheep cost five cents, hogs ten cents, and cattle twenty cents. For further information relating to tolls, see the *Eighth Annual Report of the Board of Public Works,* Columbus, 1844, pp. 28-30.

[17] Hulbert, Archer B., "The Old National Road: The Historic Highway of America," *The Ohio Archaeological and Historical Quarterly,* Vol. IX, 1901, pp. 455-457.

Canals

Even with the greater overland accessibility, there remained many towns in central Ohio which could not economically market their agricultural products. As early as 1816, Governor Ethan Allen Brown, called the "Father of Ohio Canals," discussed the possibilities of canals in Ohio with Governor DeWitt Clinton of New York. In 1818, the General Assembly was urged to consider canals as one way to increase the industry and develop the resources of the state. It was believed that the canals would also provide a cheaper route to markets for the surplus of Ohio farms. Other proponents of canals argued that eastern merchandise could be brought into the state more cheaply. The Act of February 4, 1825 marked the beginning of the canal-building period in Ohio's history.

Routes—Five routes were considered: by way of the (1) Mahoning and Grand rivers, (2) Cuyahoga and Muskingum rivers, (3) Black and Muskingum rivers, (4) Scioto and Sandusky rivers, and (5) Maumee and Great Miami rivers. A through route was not the first consideration of the planners: the primary object was to insure the maximum development of the state. A compromise to satisfy politics and economics established two routes—The Ohio and Erie Canal, following a wandering route from Cleveland to Portsmouth by way of the Scioto Valley, and The Miami Canal, to follow the Great Miami River from Dayton to Cincinnati. The former route was chosen to aid central Ohio since the interior of the state had no easy access to market (Map 2).

The Ohio and Erie Canal was begun on July 4, 1825 when ground was broken at Licking Summit, but the 307-mile canal, which cost almost eight million dollars, was not completed until 1833.[18] Columbus was not on the main canal. On April 30, 1827 work was begun on a branch canal connecting Columbus with Lockbourne. This 11-mile stretch, the Columbus Feeder, was opened in 1831.

Effects of the Canal—The relatively cheaper transportation afforded central Ohio communities by the development of the Ohio

[18] Huntington, C. C. and McClelland, C. P., *History of the Ohio Canals: Their Construction, Cost, Use and Partial Abandonment* (Columbus: The Ohio Archaeological and Historical Society, 1905), pp. 31-32.

MAP 2—Ohio Canal Routes

AFTER - HUNTINGTON AND MC CLELLAND
"HISTORY OF THE OHIO CANALS"

and Erie Canal had repercussions both in the exporting and import-
ing of goods. The canal opened wide new markets to the farmers
of central Ohio by way of Lake Erie and the Ohio River. The value
of Ohio farm products in the markets of the east and south was
increased tremendously. The canal also had the effect of providing
the settlers of central Ohio with easier access to the manufactured
products of the east. Naturally, the water route resulted in lower
transportation rates so that eastern merchandise reached Ohio com-

munities at more reasonable prices than had been possible by overland trade. The following comparisons of prices for a period before the canal was in full use and for one of its peak years, reflect the changes in prices that were to benefit the central Ohio farmer so much.

	Wheat	Corn	Sugar	Coffee
1829	50c bu.	25c bu.	9c lb.	15c lb.
1858	$1.08 bu.	70c bu.	7c lb.	12c lb.

Not only were the prices higher on domestic goods but the bushel of wheat which had doubled in price bought three times as much goods in 1858.[19]

Actually, the Ohio and Erie Canal never developed as an important through route. This was due to an economic force—the absence of a market along the Scioto Valley and at the terminal city of Portsmouth—and to a physical one—the wandering course of the canal and its insufficient supply of water at certain times of the year. But the canal ". . . stimulated industry, developed the great resources of the State, increased the value of the land and property along its courses, and invited new capital."[20] Along the northern part of the canal, industries developed; the southern section, along the lower Scioto Valley, carried considerable agricultural trade; central Ohio gained the least.[21]

The principal exports of the canal counties included the surplus agricultural products of the Scioto Valley. The shipment of wheat, corn, oats, and other grains formed the basis of Ohio's trade. As early as 1842, Ohio led the nation in wheat production with 25,-387,439 bushels. New York state ranked second, producing 11,132,472 bushels. In the same year, Ohio farms produced nearly 40 million bushels of corn and 20 million bushels of oats.[22] This agricultural surplus provided Ohioans with the means whereby they could purchase a variety of goods from eastern centers. Pig iron, castings,

[19] Ibid., p. 129.

[20] Stoddards, Paul W., op. cit., p. 190.

[21]The so-called canal counties enjoyed considerably greater valuation of real estate and personal property than the non-canal counties. By 1859, the 37 counties adjacent to the canal had an assessed valuation of $87,700,000 greater than that of the non-canal counties (Huntington, C. C. and McClelland, C. P., op. cit., pp. 122-123).

[22] Annual Report of the Commissioners of the Canal Fund, Columbus, 1843, p. 10.

wrought iron, manufactured products, and merchandise of all sorts, were imported into central Ohio. The canals also provided the means by which considerable tonnages of salt and coal could be imported from southeastern Ohio. While the exploitation of these mineral raw materials was undertaken at this time, the area awaited the development of the railroads for maximum utilization of these resources.

Tolls on the Ohio and Erie Canal exceeded those of the National Road by as much as ten times. In 1833, the total exceeded $100,000 for the first time. Within a 25-year period, tolls fell below this figure and never again were as large.[23] It was in the decade between 1840 and 1850 that the Ohio and Erie Canal prospered most. The greatest single year was 1847 when tolls amounted to $452,530.76. In this same decade, Columbus enjoyed its greatest period of canal activity.

Throughout the history of the Ohio and Erie Canal, Columbus proved to be one of the least important commercial towns (Table I). Huntington states that ". . . many of Ohio's most flourishing towns and cities owe their early growth to the fact that they were favorably situated along the canals at places where breaks must occur in transportation, where products were to be shipped or reshipped, where men must be employed in handling the commodities, where elevators must be built, and where markets are established."[24] Columbus did not participate in many of these activities. Its position, off the through route (Map 2), is a partial explanation for the limited trade of the city, but a further factor was the absence of large, permanent businesses in the city to create or induce wealth. Many smaller communities along the canal route consequently experienced greater canal trade than Columbus.

The capital city attracted new settlers, however, so that the 1820 population of 1,400 had increased to 18,554 by 1860. In addition to encouraging and fostering settlement, the transportation systems

[23] The canals operated at a loss from 1856 until after the Civil War. Following a brief period of prosperity, losses again occurred (Huntington, C. C. and McClelland, C. P., *op. cit.,* p. 43 and Appendix F, p. 170).

[24] *Ibid.,* p. 121.

TABLE 1—The Amounts Received at Seven Ohio Canal Stations for Tolls, Fines, and Water Rents, 1835-1878

Year	Cleveland	Massillon	Newark	Columbus	Circleville	Chillicothe	Portsmouth
1835	$68,757.36	$13,518.11	$20,551.87	$ 4,291.16	$ 9,870.34	$11,857.92	$22,583.69
1840	86,851.89	37,011.71	97,877.76	15,525.72	32,777.31	31,613.25	33,110.97
1845	62,284.97	14,272.02	22,153.13	7,864.37	14,775.31	18,564.39	25,235.33
1850	90,874.20	44,143.74	35,975.06	12,620.90	17,440.28	22,669.56	32,000.92
1855	43,210.10	9,853.90	6,474.44	4,854.43	8,609.83	19,157.29	12,592.44
1860	16,156.94	6,627.76	4,051.35	4,190.25	6,670.93	10,753.55	5,425.88
1878	12,335.27	4,627.64	1,200.35	1,368.11	772.32	1,342.12	100.12

Source: The Annual Reports of the Board of Public Works, Columbus, Ohio. The data were taken from the reports published in 1837, 1841, 1845, 1851, 1856, 1861, and 1879. The year 1878 was used as the final year, since data on the five-year intervals between 1860-1880 were missing.

which centered upon central Ohio stimulated trade and industry. Cheap transportation provided greater access to market and permitted Columbus industries a wider choice of raw materials.

From 1850 on, the Ohio and Erie Canal rapidly declined in importance. By 1860, trade was limited to short hauls of bulk materials. With railroad competition increasing rapidly, the canal soon lost favor. Its only service in the latter quarter of the nineteenth century was in the movement of local commodities.

Railroads

As early as 1825, there was some agitation by citizens of central Ohio for the development of railroads. Nothing was done until 1830, when a number of local road companies were incorporated but construction was not planned.

The first rail line into Columbus was the Columbus and Xenia Railroad. The Little Miami road had been completed from Cincinnati to Xenia and there was great effort to continue this road to central Ohio. After many delays, construction was begun. "The rails (strap iron on hardwoods) for the road were bought in England and cost three cents a pound delivered here, the transportation charge being more than the original cost of the rails. A locomotive was shipped from Cincinnati by river and canal to assist in the track-laying." By 1853, the two roads operated as a unit and continued so until 1869.[25]

Canals and plank-roads soon gave way to the railroad enterprises which were supported enthusiastically. The Cleveland, Columbus, and Cincinnati Railroad Company began operations on February 16, 1851, and was a success from the beginning. Following this, the Central Ohio Railroad was completed to Zanesville in 1853, and a year and a half later reached Cambridge. Contact with the Ohio River to the east was achieved over the Baltimore and Ohio line. Almost at the same time, 1854, the Columbus, Piqua, and Indiana's first train traveled the route to Piqua; the entire line opened in 1859.

The desire for railroads was great, but frequently the companies were no more than paper arrangements; the financial structure was weak, and many failed before the planning stage. With the con-

[25] Hooper, Osman C., *op. cit.*, p. 226.

struction of the four lines noted above, the first era of railroad building in central Ohio was at an end. Columbus had contact with
Cincinnati, Cleveland, the Ohio River to the east, and Indiana; and
consequently served a larger trade area.

These roads, either originating or passing through Columbus,
were not enthusiastically backed by local business men, partly because the capitalists in the community did not realize the immediate
value of railroads, and partly because the powerful Ohio Stage
Company, a monopoly, was centered in Columbus. By 1852, however, the stage line had lost out to railroad competition; in 1854, its
equipment was sold and shipped to Iowa where it was used on the
new frontier.[26]

[26] Unstad, Lyder L., *op. cit.*, p. 292.

CHAPTER II

ANTECEDENTS OF MANUFACTURING IN COLUMBUS

The forces that were vital to the commercial growth of early Columbus were not necessarily the same ones active in the limited industrial development of the city. From 1812 until 1870, the growth of manufacturing in Columbus proceeded at a slow pace. Actually, there was little in Central Ohio at this time to encourage large-scale manufacturing. However, a variety of small industries were established, consisting primarily of firms processing agricultural raw materials, or selling directly to the farm market.

During the first 50 years of its history, Columbus was concerned primarily with political and commercial activities—activities that are common to a capital city set in the heart of a productive agricultural land. The pattern of industrial development reflected both the favorable and unfavorable aspects of the ties with agriculture that typified the area. The people who first settled central Ohio were farmers: it was natural that their main interests were in agriculture. The initiative and inventiveness necessary to manufacturing enterprises had to be supplied from these farm backgrounds. Unlike the Western Reserve and the Miami Valley where urban-industrial backgrounds dominated the settlement pattern, the rural backgrounds prevalent in central Ohio proved to be something of a handicap to manufacturing. In addition, manufacturers in central Ohio were limited to a farm market by inadequate transportation facilities, and the basic raw materials for manufacture were restricted to the products of the local farms. As commercial ties became stronger, it is true that each of these forces was modified, but the basic pattern was established and Columbus' manufacturing progress, for nearly a half century, was tied to agriculture and the implications of agriculture.

The close connection between farm and industry provided the manufacturer with certain distinct advantages: agricultural raw materials were readily available, an important local farm market was present, and competition from other manufacturers was absent in central Ohio since inadequate transportation facilities hindered the free movement of outside goods into the area.

The self-same advantages were, by their obvious limitations, disadvantages. Generally, they proved to be temporary handicaps although some of them—such as the absence of mineral raw materials—continue to the present day. From the founding of the city until 1870, no outstanding advantages were present to stimulate real industrial activity. Eighteen-seventy is a turning point, for at that time Columbus began to achieve greater accessibility. The immediate results were a wider market for a greater variety of products, more diverse raw materials, and increasing competition with other centers. It is apparent that identical forces take on a new significance with a change in time—*timing* is a factor to be considered in all phases of Columbus' history.

Retarding and Promoting Factors

The factors enumerated below are normally discussed when considering the localization of industry. The purpose here is to analyze their effects upon Columbus' manufacturing either as retarding or as promoting factors.

Limited Markets

Markets profoundly influence the character as well as the scale of industry. Columbus manufacturers were limited, until approximately 1870, both in the extent and the value of their operations to the farm trade of central Ohio. Such a market attracted neither the large-scale manufacturing operation nor provided the incentive to firms which produced goods for nation-wide sale. The limitations placed upon the market were the result, essentially, of two phenomena: the types of settlers attracted by the original land surveys, and the inadequate transportation facilities which prevailed in central Ohio until the latter decades of the nineteenth century.

Land Surveys—Central Ohio, made up of 13 counties (Table 2)[1]

[1] This division of counties is taken from Alfred J. Wright, *Economic Geography of Ohio*, Ohio Geologic Survey, Columbus, 1953, p. 16, Fig. 11. The counties include Highland, Fayette, Madison, and Union in the western tier; Ross, Pickaway, Franklin, Delaware, and Marion in the central tier; and Fairfield, Licking, Knox, and Morrow in the eastern tier.

was comprised of parts of three different surveys: the Virginia Military District, the Congress Lands, and the United States Military Lands (Maps 1 and 3). The surveys each attracted specific groups of people—people from different parts of the country and with different cultural backgrounds. It was central Ohio's fortune to draw a larger share of new settlers with agricultural backgrounds than did many other parts of the state. Thus, the initial impression made by the settlers was agricultural in nature. Long after these early settlers were gone, their heritage—the "impress" that they made, as Howe calls it—remained to influence succeeding generations and the growth and development of the area. By considering the backgrounds and the interests of these first settlers it is possible to explain, in part, the limited industrial market available to Columbus manufacturers during the first 50 years of the city's history.

Western Counties—The western tier of counties in central Ohio is entirely within the Virginia Military District; hence, settlement was by Virginians or by other persons, largely southerners, who had served with her armies. The majority of the early settlers of Highland County, the southernmost of the western tier, were from Virginia and North Carolina; the pioneers of Fayette and Madison counties came from Virginia and Kentucky. In Union County, as well, this pattern was repeated although a large number of Pennsylvanians were also to be found. Even as late as 1880, of those new citizens not Ohio-born, 28 per cent in Highland, 35 per cent in Fayette, 22 per cent in Madison, and 18 per cent in Union counties were Virginia-born. The influx of settlers from Pennsylvania was large and Irish immigrants had increased noticeably.[2]

These early settlers established grain and livestock farms similar to those characteristic of the eastern south. Their culture was, obviously, in no way related to that of the eastern city-dweller. Their agricultural holdings were frequently quite large. Normally, agriculture does not encourage heavy concentrations of people; extensive methods further limit the numbers of people who may settle the land. As an example, Madison County once had farms of thousands of acres which were generally sublet to tenants, most of whom were

[2] Cf. Howe, Henry, *Historical Collections of Ohio*, (Cincinnati: C. J. Krehbiel and Company, 1898), Vol. 1, pp. 125, 603, 912, and Vol. 2, pp. 164, 704.

MAP 3—Ohio Land Grants

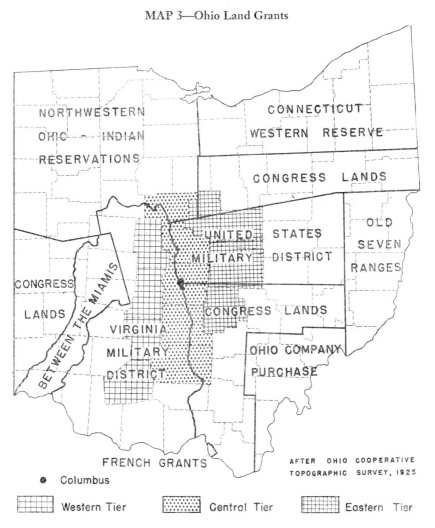

● Columbus

Western Tier   Central Tier   Eastern Tier

Irish. Indeed, the two factors of sparse populations on agricultural lands and the relatively low-income tenant farms on the land further reduced the market potential for manufacturers in Columbus.

Central Counties—The central tier of counties is divided by the Scioto River and is, consequently, included in three different land surveys. West of the river, the Virginia Military District has influenced settlement patterns in each of the counties; east of the river,

the Congress Lands and the United States Military Lands have
affected the patterns (Map 3). In every sense of the word, these
have been transitional counties. The southernmost counties, Ross
and Pickaway, and those parts of the counties west of the Scioto,
were characterized by Virginian settlements. The three northern
counties and the eastern half of the other counties, were settled
principally by peoples from the the Middle Atlantic and New England states. These divisions were apparent in the shape of holdings,
in the pattern of land tenure, in the types of agriculture engaged in,
and in the effects these settlements had upon manufacturing in
Columbus.

A traveler who passed through Pickaway County prior to 1840
noted the striking contrast in land use and tenure between the east
and west sections. His comments suggest why the Columbus market
was predominantly rural.

> Within the county, on the west side of the river, is a terri-
> tory of about 290 square miles, containing a population of
> 8,376, averaging a fraction less than 30 to the square mile;
> while the territory on the east side of the river, within the
> county, embracing only 209 square miles, sustains a popula-
> tion of 11,349, averaging about 55 to the square mile . . .
> To an observing traveler passing directly through the county
> from east to west, the contrast is very striking. While on
> the one side he finds the lands well improved, with fields
> of moderate size, well-fenced, with a good barn, and neat
> dwelling-houses to each adjacent field; on the other, he
> finds occasionally baronial mansions . . . with rarely a barn,
> and each field large enough for two or three good farms . . .
> The prices of the same quality of land on the east side are
> generally about double those on the west side. A part of
> this difference . . . results . . . from the different origin of
> the inhabitants. Those on the east side originated mostly
> from Pennsylvania; while those on the west side had their
> origin generally in the more northern slave states.[3]

According to Ralph Brown, the most enthusiastic reports of
Ohio came from the settlers and migrants who had visited the Pick-

[3] *Ibid.*, Vol. 2, p. 401.

away Plains. Settlement was so prompt that much of the area was in agricultural land-use even in 1806.[4] Here, again, the best market Columbus manufacturers could hope for was an agricultural one. The almost complete absence of urban centers in central Ohio must be considered as a detriment to the development of manufacturing.

Eastern Counties—The counties forming the eastern tier experienced their greatest growth in the period between 1820 and 1840 when population increased by more than 135 per cent (Table 2). The inhabitants of Licking County came from Pennsylvania, Virginia, New Jersey, New England, Wales, and Germany; those of Knox County were mainly from the Middle States, with some of New England origin.[5] Similarly, Fairfield and Morrow counties experienced heavy settlement from the east as well as scattered settlement from Virginia. The eastern groups were prominent in Licking County where the Welsh, from eastern Pennsylvania, established themselves in Welsh Hills, and settlers from Massachusetts founded Granville.

In these counties the land grants were of Federal origin and were open to those holding a military bounty from the federal government (as in the case of the United States Military Lands), or to any interested settler (as in the case of the Congress Lands). These counties provided an area in which the urban dweller of the Middle Atlantic and New England states merged with the agriculturist of the South. This sectionalism strangled trade since the people from the opposing areas did not trust the credit or the bank notes of their neighbors. Hence, there was no large outlet for manufactures: the limited market that Columbus faced to the west was extended to the east.

Inaccessibility for Settlement

Central Ohio was relatively inaccessible for settlers prior to the development of the National Road and the Ohio and Erie Canal. Brown states, in considering only a part of the surveyed lands of

[4] Brown, Ralph H., *Historical Geography of the United States* (New York: Harcourt, Brace and Company, 1948), p. 204.

[5] Howe, Henry, *op. cit.,* Vol. 2, p. 65 and Vol. 1, p. 981.

Central Ohio, that ". . . the Congress Lands were inferior to others only in one major particular: their inland position reduced accessibility."[6]

Table 2, which shows population increases in central Ohio counties for 20-year periods, provides a basis for considering the influence of the greater accessibility which was experienced after 1830. The coming of the National Road and the Ohio and Erie Canal in 1833 was an impetus to settlement. The eastern counties showed a population increase of 135 per cent in the years between 1820-1840; the central counties, an increase of almost 67 per cent; and the western counties, a gain of almost 80 per cent. This was the period of the greatest percentage increase in population for the central Ohio counties.

Actually, the counties bordering the Scioto Valley were settled much more slowly than those of the Miami Valley or those of the Muskingum Valley. Inaccessibility was the primary factor. The Scioto Valley did not possess some advantages that were inherent in the other valleys. The trading potential of towns along the middle Miami Valley was greatly enhanced by their position with respect to the earlier-settled Licking River valley of Kentucky. This valley, directly across the Ohio River from Cincinnati, was an important migration and trade route. It served as a funnel through which settlers traveled to gain access to Ohio.

In contrast, the Scioto Valley virtually is enclosed with only a narrow valley floor penetrating the hill country of Pike and Scioto counties. No trade route is open to the south: the trade territory opposite the mouth of the Scioto is practically sterile. Thus, the market that was available to Cincinnati and Dayton by virtue of geographic location had no parallel in the lower Scioto Valley or in the hill country where the Ohio and Scioto rivers meet.

Within a few years after its settlement, Ohio was the leading producer of wheat and corn in the nation, and central Ohio was a major grain surplus area. The attitude of the people here was to favor agricultural production and to ignore manufacturing. The

[6] Brown, Ralph H., *op. cit.*, p. 229.

advantages gained by the construction of roads and canals favored agriculture. The importance of these routes to manufacturing was not considered for many years.

TABLE 2—Population Increase in the Counties of Central Ohio, 1820-1880

Counties	Population				Per Cent Increase		
	1820	1840	1860	1880	1840 from 1820	1860 from 1840	1880 from 1860
Western Tier							
Highland	12,308	22,269	27,773	30,281	80.9	24.7	9.0
Fayette	6,336	10,879	15,935	20,364	71.7	46.5	27.8
Madison	4,799	9,025	13,015	20,129	88.1	44.2	54.7
Union		8,443	16,507	22,357		95.5	35.4
Total	23,443	50,616	73,230	93,131	79.9[a]	44.7	27.2
Central Tier							
Ross	20,610	27,460	35,071	40,307	33.2	27.7	14.9
Pickaway	18,143	20,169	23,469	27,415	11.2	16.4	16.8
Delaware	10,300	24,880	50,361	86,882	141.6	102.4	72.5
Franklin	7,639	22,060	23,902	27,381	188.8	8.3	14.6
Marion		18,352	15,490	20,565		−15.6	32.8
Total	56,692	112,921	148,293	202,550	66.8[b]	31.3	36.6
Eastern Tier							
Fairfield	16,508	31,858	30,538	34,284	93.0	−4.1	12.3
Licking	11,861	35,096	37,011	40,050	195.9	5.5	8.2
Knox	8,326	19,584	27,735	27,431	135.2	41.6	−1.1
Morrow			20,445	19,072			−6.7
Total	36,695	86,538	115,729	120,837	135.8	10.1[c]	4.4
All Central Ohio			337,252	416,518			23.5

[a] Based on 3 counties—Highland, Fayette and Madison; Union County not formed until later in 1820.

[b] Based on 4 counties—Ross, Pickaway, Franklin and Delaware; Marion County not formed until 1842.

[c] Based on 3 counties—Fairfield, Licking and Knox; Morrow County not formed until 1848.

Source: Howe, Henry, *op. cit.* This table was compiled by assembling data from various sections of Howe's volumes.

In addition, Columbus had little real opportunity to compete for markets in industrial products in its first 50 years. While the distance from urban markets was a distinct handicap to industrial growth, it must be remembered that it was the food production of central Ohio, not the mechanical inventions or manufactures, that reached and interested the urban markets.

Limited Raw Materials

Along with the limitations imposed upon manufacturing by the type of market that persisted in central Ohio for 50 years, had been the limitations resulting from the absence of any mineral raw materials upon which an industrial economy could be founded. What the enterprising artisan or mechanic could consider as local raw materials were the simple products of the forests and farms. These were sufficient resources, nevertheless, for the beginnings of small handicraft shops.

From the farms of the area came the wheat for the flour and grist mills and wool for the woolen factories that struggled for existence. Flax-dressing mills and small distilleries enabled farmers to dispose of their flax and grain. Soap and candles were made from animal products, and leather-working shops were established to use the hides. From the hardwood forests that literally covered central Ohio, came ash and hickory for wagons, implements, and tools, and walnut, cherry, maple, and poplar for furniture. These same forests supplied homes and industries with wood and charcoal for fuel.

Useful mineral raw materials were not close at hand. Coal and iron ore were known to exist in southeastern Ohio but Columbus did not benefit immediately from them. It was not until 1829 that John L. Gill, a hardware merchant, brought bituminous coal into Columbus by wagon from Nelsonville in Athens County.[7] The presence of this resource made no great impression upon local interests, however. Columbus' entrepreneurs were obviously not alert immediately to the advantages inherent in the coal reserves.

The iron ore of southeastern Ohio was put to use at an early date as the basis of the important Ohio charcoal iron industry. Lawrence, Jackson, and Vinton counties enjoyed a wide reputation as iron centers in the nineteenth century. Columbus interests made no real effort to secure and use the native southeastern Ohio ores until after 1870. Between 1812 and 1870, the foundries in Columbus secured their pig iron from sources beyond central Ohio.

[7] Lee, Alfred, *History of Columbus, Ohio* (Columbus: Munsell and Company, 1892), Vol. 1, p. 373.

Lack of Adequate Power

Prior to the development of the steam engine and the use of coal as a fuel, industry had to rely on either direct water power or animate energy to produce the energy needed in ordinary manufacturing operations. In Columbus, neither the Scioto nor the Olentangy rivers had sufficient fall or adequate sites for the development of power-operated mills. But even as early as 1813, a few saw-mills, distilleries, and flour mills had located on the relatively short but steep streams which emptied into the Scioto from the high banks of the river. Most of these mills depending upon water power, and all of those depending upon animate power, were short-lived. They were superseded by plants utilizing steampower. No large manufacturing plant developed in Columbus before the advent of steampower.

The first large manufacturing plant in Columbus and one which has frequently been called the first successful manufacturing establishment in the city, the Ridgway Foundry, converted to steampower in 1830. In 1831, the first steam saw-mill began operations in the city; from then on, steampower steadily replaced water power in the manufacturing plants of Columbus. With more extensive development of the Ohio coal fields, adequate fuel and power was practically assured to Columbus' manufacturers.

Transportation System Geared to Agriculture

The transportation system that developed in central Ohio was not one to encourage manufacturing. Because of the primarily agrarian interests of the early settlers, the principal purpose of the inter-regional transportation system was to move agricultural surpluses to market. Inducements for manufacturers did not lie in this direction, naturally. The routes by which materials moved were too slow and inconvenient to assemble cheaply the raw materials needed for industrial operations of a sizeable nature. It was much more economical to ship finished manufactured goods into Ohio than the necessary materials for manufacturing industries.

The canal, the principal means by which bulk commodities were transported between 1830 and 1850, provided Columbus with a limited exchange of goods. (See Table 1 showing income from tonnages on the canal). Certainly, the canal provided little opportunity for contact between urban areas. The canal's principal use was in the transportation of agricultural products.

The railroads which entered Columbus after 1850 did not relieve the inaccessibility to manufacturing centers. They brought the city commerce, but it was commerce limited, primarily, to farm surpluses. Contemporary thought emphasized this fact: "The railroads bring the farmers so near to the eastern cities that they are not much dependent on their neighboring towns or cities for markets for their production. The capital of the towns and cities principally made the railroads—the farmer profits by them."[8]

The Opening of the Hocking Valley—It was not until 1869 that railroads penetrated the Hocking Valley and the coal reserves present there. The construction of the Hocking Valley Railroad was discussed first in 1857 but the road was not chartered until 1867. In August of that year, the first train passed through Columbus bound for Chicago with 15 cars of the coal which had spurred the road's development. The line was soon extended to Toledo on Lake Erie; later a southern branch reached the Ohio River.

Entrepreneurs and capitalists in Columbus were decidedly interested in developing the coal reserves of the southeastern plateau. The demand for coal from such points as Cleveland, Toledo, and Chicago, stimulated activity in Columbus so that very shortly a growing *through commerce* developed in the city. It was hoped, by some local interests, that the coal, cheaply shipped to Columbus, would give the city a base for an iron and steel industry when used in conjunction with Ohio iron ores. These hopes did not materialize. The bulk of the coal trade remained as through trade and the iron ore was never much used beyond the ore-producing counties. Eventually, however, a fine railroad network centered upon Columbus and the city enjoyed a jobbing trade of considerable importance.

[8] Martin, William T., *History of Franklin County* (Columbus: Follett, Foster and Company, 1858), p. 55.

Labor

From the earliest period, the absence of a skilled labor force has frequently limited the type of manufacturing industry which has been attracted to Columbus. On the other hand, an available and stable supply of semi-skilled and unskilled labor was rarely missing. As a consequence of the availability of cheap labor, labor has played a significant role as an attractive force to industry.

A few skilled mechanics and artisans settled here in the early 1800's; their numbers increased by the late 1820's. Artisans from eastern cities migrated westward in these years primarily to avoid the effects of a series of economic depressions in the east. They looked to the west for opportunity. Many who came to Columbus stayed and organized handicraft shops. In such a way, Columbus began to assemble the basic skills of manufacturing.

There was a later influx of skilled workers when many German immigrants made their way into central Ohio in the 1840's. The immediate result of this was the establishment of new manufacturing activities and the enlargement of other operations. Prior to these two migrations, the basic settlement was by farm people from the south and east.

The German workers occupied the southern part of the city, and their small, but neat, story-and-a-half brick homes and well-kept gardens still characterize parts of South Columbus. The German laborer represented part of a labor force that was trained and reliable. These workers are known to have attracted plants to the southern section of the city .[9]

Low Wage Rate—The absence of skilled workers naturally resulted in the establishment of a lower average wage rate in Columbus compared with other large Ohio cities. The large number of low-wage workers on the various government payrolls helped to perpetuate this condition. From time to time, this factor of lower wage levels has attracted certain types of manufacturers to the city.

One other feature of the labor force was the availability of

[9] The influence of the German working force has waned but many firms now in operation in South Columbus indicate that it was one of the principal factors influencing their choice of site in the area.

rural workers. The rural population formed a stable supply of untrained but relatively cheap labor. Columbus was without competition for this labor.[10]

Influence of the Ohio Penitentiary Upon Labor—A last factor, but a very important one, which contributed to the prevailing low-wage rates historically associated with Columbus is the Ohio Penitentiary. The Penitentiary has been one of the most controversial operations in the city's industrial history. It has been both an advantage and a handicap to manufacturing. It attracted some manufacturing to the city by its system of contract labor, but by so doing, hindered the growth of the free labor force in the city. It was this latter force which opposed strongly the continuing use of convict labor for manufacturing purposes.

The Ohio Penitentiary was built in 1815 by the same men who laid out the city and erected the capitol. The convicts produced copper wares, hoes, axcs, chains, and nails, among other things, as early as 1817. The goods were sold in the city and the return from the sale was used to pay the warden's salary and to operate the institution. The majority of the citizens and the legislature favored this program since it attempted to make the institution self-sufficient.

The use of convict labor, however, posed a serious problem to the free workers of the city. The larger companies could employ prison labor under contract at wage of $37\frac{1}{2}$ to 50 cents a day.[11] With more than 500 workers employed at such wages, the position of the free worker was jeopardized. While there was strong opposition to the continued use of contract prison labor by the free workers and, later, by other manufacturers, it was continued for almost a century.

Without a doubt, many capable men left the city because of this discrimination. Because of its immediate benefits to the individual manufacturer (who enjoyed the low-wages paid) and to the tax-paying citizens (whose taxes were used to operate the institution), the system was upheld. Growing disfavor and aroused public sentiment with regard to the convict labor adversely affected industrial growth in the city.

[10] Many of these conditions prevail today. In addition, an abundance of cheap, female labor has proved to be an incentive to certain industries.

[11] Unstad, Lyder L., *op. cit.,* p. 479.

Typical German Homes In South Columbus

Capital and Initiative Not Encouraging

As Columbus grew to be more than a rural town, its prominent citizens included men with money to invest. Few of them, however, saw the advantages to be gained from investment in industry. Their interests were principally in land speculation and in transportation. *The Columbus Gazette* of 1857 noted this especially and editorialized that ". . . every dollar that can be spared, aye, and borrowed too, goes into the purchase of lands, that are to lie idle long years . . ."[12] Much local capital was also tied up in the Ohio Stage Company and, after its collapse, in the railroads. Beyond their interests in land and railroads, Columbus businessmen apparently were not speculative: their enterprise, energy, and businesss interests were tempered by a sort of "old-time" conservatism. Consequently, capital was cautious and not inclined to take risks that manufacturing involved.

Since no large-scale operations could be undertaken without considerable sums of money, small shops with limited assets dominated the city's manufacturing until after 1870. Occasionally, men with initiative and inventive genius were able to succeed in manufacturing enterprises in spite of the limited capital available to them. Until 1854, every industrial firm in the city was owned and operated independently. In that year, one of the first incorporated organizations in the city, the Columbus Machine and Manufacturing Company, was established.

Concern regarding the lack of manufacturing enthusiasm became a public issue with *The Columbus Gazette* the outstanding critic. An editorial in September 1858 considered the advantages of Columbus as an industrial site but it pointed out, also, that the lack of interest on the part of local capitalists had cost the city many new plants that subsequently went to Dayton, Springfield, Cincinnati, and other Ohio cities. Furthermore, the *Gazette* reflected, skilled mechanics were lost for lack of work. It noted, too, that the primary use made of the railroads by local intersts was ". . . to gape at the immense traffic which daily passes through the depot, and wonder why people go abroad to buy."[13]

[12] *The Columbus Gazette,* February 13, 1857, p. 2, col. 1.
[13] *Ibid.,* September 17, 1858, p. 2, col. 1.

Passive Opposition to Manufacturing

Lack of interest in manufacturing endeavors has been one factor in understanding the limited industrial growth that occurred in Columbus between 1812 and 1870; opposition to manufacturing is another. The opposition that evolved in the city was essentially passive but it has persisted from the early 1800's to the present day, in some quarters. It has taken the form of opposition from the citizenry, disinterest by the capitalists, and sectional opposition on the part of the State Legislature.

Columbus was, first of all, a political center. Manufacturing not tied directly to the immediate demands of the community usually met with some opposition. On the other hand, it was natural that *commerce* should develop, since agriculture dominated the surrounding countryside; and, with the crossroads pattern formed in 1833, the natural trading activities inherent in such a situation were accepted by the residents.

The leading capitalists expected to reap a profit from trade and from land sales to new settlers who arrived in the city in increasing numbers in the middle 1800's. They were unwilling to risk the uncertainties and low initial returns of manufacturing, however.

Some of these men controlled the Ohio Stage Company which operated until 1852. They, and the men who supplied them with equipment, actively opposed the railroads in the 1840's and 1850's. Most writers agree that the late arrival of railroads into Columbus can be attributed to their strong opposition. Only when outside capital was invested in the railroads did the city secure the facilities it needed. Local businessmen were unwilling to back roads that might be through roads only: they wanted the business common to a terminus or junction point.

Those industries dependent upon the services of railroads were handicapped by this delay. Firms which would have been attracted to central Ohio because of the accessibility to coal and iron ore in the southeast either failed to materialize or were established elsewhere.

In addition to the position taken by local citizens and local capitalists, the influence of the State government upon the growth of manufacturing in Columbus must be considered. It has been both beneficial and detrimental. The presence of the capitol and other state institutions did give impetus to local business. But because of the strong sectionalism of the legislature, they ". . . retarded progress in an almost equal degree. They excited a jealousy and a prejudice against her (Columbus), as though she were a parasite living and growing at the expense of the rest of the State."[14]

A few firms expanded their operations because of government contracts but this was not a common practice. Printing firms, binderies, and blank-book publishers found the city an excellent location, of course. The sectional interests in the legislature demanded, from time to time, an equal distribution of expenditure among all parts of Ohio. Thus, Columbus' manufacturers received no more consideration than others. What may appear to have been an advantage in location—the fact that Columbus was the capital of the state—actually had very little influence on the early development of industry.

Summary

A market limited to central Ohio by inadequate intra-regional transportation, discouraged the develpment of manufacturing in Columbus prior to 1870. Not only did agriculture form the basis of the market, but it also supplied industry with its raw materials. The local manufacturer was distinctly handicapped by the absence of mineral raw materials and adequate power sites.

Venture capital was extremely limited, but men of initiative, and often with inventive talents, tended to offset this. The scarcity of experienced labor and the demoralizing effect of the Penitentiary upon free labor further affected industrial growth. These factors were countered, in part, by the presence of an ample supply of unskilled workers.

Out of these conflicting forces an industrial community emerged slowly.

[14] Studer, Jacob H., *Columbus, Ohio: Its History, Resources, and Progress* (Columbus: J. Studer, 1873), pp. 565-566.

Status of Manufacturing, 1812-1870

1812–1835—Simple and small-scale manufacturing operations date back almost to the first settlement of Columbus. The first shops —mills for grinding grain and for cutting logs—were organized more out of necessity to serve the community than for personal gain or as profit-making ventures. But by 1817, handicraft shops making watches, compasses, and surveying instruments, were already in operation and their numbers were on the increase. In response to the activity of the state government, a book bindery was opened. The many products of the farms found a ready market in the shops, breweries, and wool-carding and blending mills.

TABLE 3—Manufacturing in Franklin County, Ohio, 1820

Articles	Value	Raw Materials	Quantity	Employees	Capital
Boards and scantling	$ 1,770	Logs		2	$ 1,700
Boots and shoes	5,376	Leather, upper and sole		28	
Broadcloths, cassimeres, sattinets, etc.	12,000	Wool and cotton	7,500 lbs. W 250 lbs. C	12	16,000
Flour	—	Wheat, corn, rye	26,640 bus.	3	13,200
Furniture, cabinet	500	Cherry, walnut boards		1	75
Hogsheads, barrels, tubs	1,500	Lumber		8	600
Leather	9,060	Hides, skins, bark		5	12,500
Nails cut, farming utensils	19,000	Iron nail rods	40 tons	26	2,200
Saddles and bridles	6,200	Leather, hardware		3	2,800
Whiskey	13,825	Corn, rye, barley	13,330 bus.	11	
Wool, carded	—	Wool	4,500 lbs.	1	750

Source: *Digest of Accounts of Manufacturing Establishments in the United States and of Their Manufactures,* Washington, 1823. (Facsimile reproduction of the original.)

Table 3, Manufacturing in Franklin County, Ohio, 1820, gives an indication of the types of manufacturing carried on within the first decade of the founding of Columbus. Two points stand out: the dependence upon agricultural raw materials in the manufacture of finished products and the dependence upon a farm market, as evidenced by the types of finished products. With capital invested in manufacturing at $55,000 and approximately 100 men employed in the shops, Columbus' industrial development was under way.

The requirements of the farmers for tools, agricultural implements, and household items were reflected in the growth of small metal-working concerns. The Columbus Foundry of Joseph Ridgway & Company began operations in 1822. Its principal product was the Jethro Wood patented plow. Since it was considered the best plow in use at the time, the market was large and Ridgway made and sold ". . . an immense number." The plow was not cast in one piece as were most others of the day, but had interchangeable parts which could be substituted in the field. It was one of the first examples of the application of the principle of standardization and interchangeability of parts in agricultural machinery.[15]

The first carriage and wagon shop began operations prior to 1819 using native hardwoods. Three years later, a second shop was in operation and, by 1826, J. W. White opened a business to make a variety of coaches, wagons, hacks, and gigs. He made many coaches for the Ohio Stage Company and is often considered to be the pioneer in the great carriage-making industry that eventually developed in Columbus.[16] Other manufacturers made saddles, harnesses, chairs, and wheels for this growing industry which aptly reflected the commercial importance of Columbus at a natural intersection of trade routes.

Blacksmith shops were an integral part of the community and there were copper, tin, and iron smiths, many of whom were dependent upon such distant sources as Baltimore for their basic raw materials. Rope, leather, furniture, and edge tools for agriculture and manufacturing were made. In 1827, Gill and Greer came to Columbus from Pittsburgh and opened a sheet metal shop and foundry. This became the Franklin Foundry, of later importance. In the same year, the Ohio Penitentiary, which had already gained a reputation as one of the largest manufacturing units in the city, brought out a "new patent plough" in competition with the Ridgway plow but it did not last long.

The principal handicaps to increased industrialization in the 1830's appeared to be the limitations of capital and the absence of manufacturing skills and experienced entrepreneurs. Steam power, which had earlier proved itelf, began to replace the inadequate power

---

[15] Bidwell, P. W. and Falconer, J. I., *History of Agriculture in the Northern United States, 1620-1860* (Washington: The Carnegie Institution, 1925), pp. 209-210.

[16] Cf., Hooper, Osman C., p. 219.

that had handicapped the earlier operations of flour and textile mills. With an enlarged local market and the reliance upon agricultural raw materials, the small shops were able to succeed.

1835–1845—The foundry of Gill and Greer expanded considerably in 1838 when it began the production of stoves, plows, and mill irons. Corn shellers, threshing machines, and clover machines were invented or improved upon by local firms and these products reached an expanding agricultural market. Papermaking, soap and candle production, and the manufacture of a variety of household goods increased considerably. The Hayden Iron Works was large but the majority of the more than 100-man working force was prison labor. Hayden's success was attributed, by some of his contemporaries, to the low wages paid to the prison labor.[17]

1845–1860—Ridgeway's Columbus Foundry began the manufacture of steam engines in 1848. A year later a car factory was built to produce railroad rolling stock. Without Ridgway's interest and enterprise these shops probably would have gone to Cincinnati. Ridgway's company was successful in all of its ventures but with the death of Joseph Ridgway—perhaps the leading manufacturer and entrepreneur in the city—it was sold to Peter Hayden in 1854. Hayden, in addition to his iron operations, employed more than 200 workers, most of whom were convicts, in the manufacture of saddletrees and coach hardware. The "Birmingham Works" of his company produced iron bars and rods. Hayden's operations expanded in 1857 to include the Columbus Iron Works in which wire, wire cloth (screen), pumps, springs, and axles were made. It was one of the largest concerns in the city. Coal from southern Ohio and local scrap were utilized in its operations.

The Franklin Foundry of Gill and Greer continued to expand. In 1855 a steel plow was introduced and by 1858 the company was selling more than 4,000 of these in a year's time. Other local foundries made a variety of products for the home, farm, and industry.

Three tool companies were organized between 1850 and 1851. The Ohio Tool Company, incorporated in 1851 with a capital stock of $190,000, employed 200 workers in the manufacture of carpenter's

[17] Cf. Unstad, Lyder L., pp. 262-264.

planes. It was one of the first incorporated plants in the city. The Ohlen, Drake Company, later famous as the Ohlen and Bishop Company, began the manufacture of quality saws.[18]

The carriage industry continued to grow although railroad competition threatened its success. The boot and shoe industry enjoyed some success in Columbus so that by 1849 approximately 200 persons were employed. The ordinary shops producing anything from copper and tin ware to furniture were numerous.

Civil War Period—The Civil War was the first national conflict to affect Columbus. With the camps and prisons of the Union Army here, manufacturing, trade, and business in general, increased. Few important manufacturing concerns actually began functioning during the war, but the expansion of established firms was common. Metal and machine shops increased in number. The M. C. Lilley Company, bookbinders at the outset of the war, emerged as manufacturers of regalia in 1865. The Columbus Bolt Works grew to a place of importance in the pattern of manufacturing that evolved out of the war. The city began to think and act more like an industrial town as the impetus of the war caused it to consolidate its activities on firmer ground.

Summary

With the end of its first 50 years of growth, Columbus emerged as a commercial-political center. The relatively insignificant manufacturing activities of the community were over-shadowed by its commercial functions. The limitations of transportation restricted the city's markets as well as its choice of industrial raw materials. A new "industrial system" was said to have been established at the end of the Civil War. Actually, Columbus awaited the inter-regional railroads for its first burst of true industrialization: this came in the latter quarter of the nineteenth century.

[18] The Ohlen and Bishop Company, later the Rockwell Tool Company, was responsible for the importance of the saw industry in Columbus. The Ohlen and Bishop Company sold out to Rockwell Tool Company in 1951. Both firms have now left Columbus.

CHAPTER III

THE WIDENING INDUSTRIAL HORIZON: 1870-1952

The changes in the economy of Columbus and central Ohio during the first 60 years of the city's history were based primarily upon the improvements that took place in transportation. Not until the National Road and the canal provided cheap transportation for agricultural commodities were the farmers liberated from the restrictions of a non-industrial market. The manufacturing interests had to wait longer before they experienced the benefits of a wider market and a greater variety of raw materials. The year 1870 marks a turning point in Columbus' history.

Factors in the Evolution of Industry, 1870-1900

Three major groups of factors were involved in the evolution of industry at this time: population growth, expansion of railroads, and utilization of the raw materials of southeastern Ohio. Columbus experienced a consistent increase in population following the Civil War decade. Not only did numbers increase but the quality of the working force improved considerably. The expansion of the railroads affected all phases of the Columbus economy: the effect of this expansion upon industrial development was significant. The nature of market and raw material accessibility changed appreciably during these 30 years from 1870 to 1900. An outstanding manifestation of the changing source of raw materials was the *planned* shift from agricultural raw materials to mineral raw materials as the basis for industry. Although a complete shift never emerged, the enthusiastic support given to those industries which would utilize minerals was an important factor in stimulating local industry at this time. Here the close ties between Columbus and southeastern Ohio, with its coal, iron ore, timber, and natural gas, proved profitable. Utilization of these resources not only helped stabilize local industries, but it proved an attractive force to firms of national reputation which began, for the first time, to locate in Columbus.

Population Growth

Between 1812 and 1900, Columbus expanded from a handful of settlers to a city of approximately 125,560. The percentage increase in these years was frequently great although numerically the increase was small. The greatest period of growth occurred between the years 1840-1850, when an increase of 195 per cent was experienced. The following ten years offered a sharp contrast, for less than 1,000 persons were added to the community. These years, 1850-1860, found the migrants moving west as the railroads opened the rich farm lands of Iowa, Missouri, and Kansas to settlement. Columbus lost many of its own citizens and gained few new settlers.

TABLE 4—Population Growth in Columbus, Ohio, 1820-1910

Year	Population	Per Cent Increase
1820	1,450	
1830	2,435	67.9
1840	6,048	148.3
1850	17,882	195.6
1860	18,554	3.7
1870	31,274	68.5
1880	51,647	65.1
1890	68,150	70.6
1900	125,560	42.4
1910	181,511	44.6

Source: *United States Census Reports, 1860–1910* (Washington: United States Department of Commerce, 1864-1913).

Following the Civil War and a short-lived boom, the city reached a population of 31,274 in 1870. With an increase of 65 per cent or to 51,647, Columbus ranked as the thirty-third largest city in the nation in 1880. It continued to grow in size during the remainder of the nineteenth century. Between 1880 and 1890, Columbus experienced an increase of 70 per cent in population growth whereas the state of Ohio gained by less than 15 per cent (Table 4).

The quality of the working force improved materially during the latter part of the century. With the influx of a large number of Germans in the 1840's and an additional group in the 1880's, a more reliable and experienced type of industrial worker was available to manufacturing interests. Skills garnered through the years within the manufacturing community were put to better use by new industries. As a consequence, Columbus possessed a much more experienced and adaptable labor force in the last 30 years of the century. It cannot be doubted that industry was affected by this.

An increasing number of persons were engaged in some type of manufacturing in Columbus during these years. In 1870, about 5,150 persons were employed in manufacturing. This number increased to 17,000 by 1900. At no time, however, did the manufacturing payroll in Columbus compare with that of Cincinnati or Cleveland.

The percentage of native-born persons in Columbus towards the end of the nineteenth century was high. Whether valid or not, local groups used this fact in an attempt to encourage industry to locate here. Both in the 1890's and in more recent years, promotional literature published by such groups as the Board of Trade, the Chamber of Commerce, and the newspapers, emphasized the high percentage of native-born workers. By 1880, about 82 per cent of the people were native-born; this proportion increased to more than 90 per cent by 1900.[1] Only Springfield had a higher percentage of native-born in the state. It is evident that the problem of a "troublesome foreign element" was not present in Columbus as it was in Cincinnati and Cleveland.[2] Negroes have resided in Columbus since the early 1800's, but their relative numbers have been small. In 1900, when very few Negroes were employed in any type of manufacturing, they accounted for less than 7 per cent of the total population of the city.

Expansion of the Railroads

The increase in population experienced in the last three decades of the nineteenth century reflected, in large measure, the growing importance of railroad activity in central Ohio. Columbus was provided with accessibility to the resources of southeastern Ohio and of other parts of the nation; the greatly expanded railroad network provided wider markets; and new opportunities were opened for

[1] *United States Census Reports, 1880–1900* (Washington: United States Department of Commerce, 1883-1901).

[2] In 1900, approximately 82 per cent of Cincinnati's population was native-born but in Cleveland less than 68 per cent was native-born.

investment by Columbus interests. The combination of these factors proved attractive to new manufacturing organizations as well as to new settlers who sought employment.

In the decade prior to the Civil War, Columbus was a terminal for a north-south railroad and for an east-west line. The Ohio and Erie Canal was still an important commercial carrier and the stage coach had not yet lost its fight to the railroads. But by July 1870, when the Hocking Valley Railroad reached Athens, Ohio, Columbus entered a new era of inter-regional transportation. Railroads, controlled by local capital, developed quickly to provide the city with easy access to the resources of its tributary area, southeastern Ohio.

To supplement the activities of the Hocking Valley road, other railroads were readily subscribed to. The Columbus & Ferrara, which was backed by Columbus capitalists, established contact between the city and the coal and iron fields of Perry County. A railroad from Columbus to Portsmouth and one north to Toledo were supported vigorously. The former, the Scioto Valley and New England, reached Chillicothe in 1876 and was extended to Portsmouth the following year. Its principal freight was lumber but tonnage in iron ore and pig iron was heavy. The Columbus & Toledo, completed in 1877, carried coal, primarily, to Lake Erie. All of this railroad activity added a new incentive to the manufacturing interests of central Ohio.

In addition to the roads that were distinctly local, the Baltimore & Ohio Railroad was credited with opening up central Ohio. Studer noted: "For some years, it held the key to this splendid western country, inducing emigration to, and settlement in Columbus, its terminal western point, thereby contributing largely to the prosperity and wealth of the city."[3] It served the important purpose, as well, of linking Columbus with the major markets to be found in New York, Philadelphia, and Baltimore.

The railroads gave impetus to increased trade and commerce and, in turn, created investment possibilities for local and foreign capital. The city soon became a jobbing center. Within a few years after the opening of the Hocking Valley Railroad, Columbus merchants were doing more business in supplies with southeastern Ohio

[3] Studer, Jacob H., *op. cit., p.* 489.

than with any other part of the state. By 1885, there were more than 67 firms engaged in wholesale trade: hardware, groceries, saddlery, furniture, dry goods, boots, shoes, and other items, were sold in the mining communities. Columbus, with no rivals for this trade in southeastern Ohio, experienced rapid commercial development between 1880 and 1890.

By 1887, the railroad interests alone had a business capital of approximately $150,000,000. The amount of tonnage in freight in Columbus was greater than for any other city of similar size. The city benefitted directly from the use of the coal reserves in local industries but it benefitted far more indirectly through the transportation of the coal to other parts of the country. A great amount of coal was shipped to Cleveland, Toledo, Chicago, and other communities north of Columbus.

The railroads afforded employment for large numbers of men in the shops they built in Columbus. The Pennsylvania Railroad had its second largest shops here and all of the offices of the Hocking Valley Railroad were in Columbus. The shops, in turn, attracted manufacturing establishments which were suppliers to the railroad industry. With 15 rail lines entering the city in 1890, the Board of Trade believed ". . . the business man and manufacturer find the success of their enterprises unexcelled. . ."[4] in Columbus.

Resources of Southeastern Ohio

More than any other resource, the coal from southeastern Ohio provided the spark for the rapid expansion of railroads and for the increase in manufacturing which occurred in Columbus and central Ohio after 1870. Timber, iron ore, and natural gas, each played a part in attracting industries to Columbus and in giving the city a new basis for manufacturing.

Coal—Coal was the cause of the rapid increase in railroad activity after 1870. In turn, the mining communities of southeastern Ohio gave Columbus its first large market for manufactured products. Industries developed and expanded in the city to take advantage of the trade that coal and the railroads had generated. The trade

[4] *Annual Report of the Directors and Secretary of the Columbus Board of Trade for* 1890, Columbus, 1891, p. 59.

relations that were developed during the latter years of the nineteenth century persist, more or less, to the present day (See Maps 6
and 7).

Ever since John Gill brought coal to Columbus from Nelsonville
in 1829, it has influenced the economic growth of the city. The coal,
easily mined, seemingly inexhaustible, and of good quality, was
delivered in the city by relatively cheap rail transportation.

The coal fields were controlled, for the most part, by local
capitalists. The Hocking Coal and Iron Company, a Columbus-
owned organization, was the largest company. It employed approximately 3,000 of the total of 10,000 employees at work in the fields
in 1887. There were more than 55 retail coal dealers in Columbus
at that time.

Of the four and one-half million tons of coal shipped through
Columbus in 1890, less than 10 per cent remained in the city for
commercial or manufacturing use.[5] Columbus was a center for the
large coal-hauling railroads and, as such, benefitted indirectly from
the through trade. The accessibility to good quality coal, however,
was sufficiently important to attract a number of coal-consuming
industries to the city.

Iron Ore—From the time of the first charcoal furnace in southern Ohio, which utilized native ores, until the introduction of the
higher quality Lake Superior ores, the development of an iron and
steel industry was anticipated by enthusiastic Columbus citizens.
Although a large iron and steel industry never materialized in Columbus, the coal and iron ore of the southeastern counties served
the purpose of attracting rolling mills, foundries, and other metal
consuming industries to Columbus.

Perhaps interest in a local iron and steel industry ran high
because Columbus capital controlled at least 15 extensive furnaces
in the Hanging Rock iron district of southern Ohio.[6] These furnaces,
which remained competitive until World War I, had developed
because the forest products, iron ore, and limestone were immediately
available.

[5] *Ibid.*, p. 59.
[6] These furnaces were judged to have a capacity of approximately 200,000 tons
(*The Industries of Columbus: A Resume of the Mercantile and Manufacturing Progress
of the Capital City of Ohio,* Columbus, 1887, p. 19).

Columbus did not possess this combination of favorable factors nor was the iron ore of Ohio of sufficient quality or quantity to provide the basis for an extensive steel industry. And yet, it was believed locally that ironmasters in the Columbus district could produce iron as cheaply as anywhere else in the country. Optimism was high in 1873:

> A new impetus was given to the manufacturing industries of the city by the establishment of the blast furnace of the Columbus Iron Company in the year 1870. . . . The location of this furnace in our city soon induced our own and foreign capitalists to invest in various other manufacturing enterprises into which the consumption of iron entered. . . . Rolling mills, foundries, furnaces, pipe works, etc., are springing up.[7]

These most enthusiastsic hopes were not realized but the city did experience increased industrial growth, partly dependent upon its location adjacent to the iron fields of the southeast.

Timber Resources—In contrast to iron ore, the timber resources of southeastern Ohio played an important role in the development of manufacturing activity in Columbus. Lumber was one of the principal exports to Columbus from the southern counties, greatly influencing local manufacturing in the nineteenth century, although it is of little significance today.

More than 1,500 workers were engaged in the lumber industry of Columbus in 1890. It was estimated that no industry had so increased in importance in the preceding decade. Local interests observed that Columbus was becoming one of the great hardwood lumber markets in the country. Lumber was one of the principal items shipped by the Scioto Valley and New England Railroad, which had a terminal in Columbus.

New manufacturing plants came to the city to make use of the lumber secured from southeastern Ohio forests. The great carriage and wagon industry used the wooden products of the wheelwrights and manufacturers of bent-wood products. With the location of these parts suppliers in the city, Columbus became a center for this industry. Showcase manufacturing plants became prominent

[7] Failing, Henry M., *First Report of the Business and Prospects of the City of Columbus* (Columbus: The Ohio State Journal Commercial Printing House, 1873), p. 5.

in the city before the end of the century, and companies making furniture increased in number. Each of the wood-consuming plants tended to strengthen the bonds between Columbus and southern Ohio.

Natural Gas—The last of the natural resources of southeastern Ohio to be developed was natural gas. Natural gas attracts industry to its source. The discovery and utilization of natural gas in the fields of Hocking and Knox counties influenced the localization of industry in Columbus in the last decade of the nineteenth century.

The Columbus Natural Gas Company was organized in 1886 to pipe the gas from eastern fields to Columbus. The Board of Trade, in 1891, noted that the ". . . striking of natural gas wells the past year within easy reach of the city, has added an impetus to manufacturing pursuits . . . natural gas is being used as fuel, both for domestic and manufacturing purposes."[8] Perhaps most affected by the use of gas in manufacturing were the glass firms of the state. Many moved to Columbus and central Ohio at this time to utilize the natural gas in their operations. Of these older companies, only the Federal Glass Company continues to operate in the city.

With the industrial use of natural gas, Columbus anticipated enlarged manufacturing activity. The new fuel, together with coal and iron ore, gave the city a combination of resources for manufacturing such as it had never previously known.

Industrialization, 1870-1900

The manufacturing establishments that began operations in Columbus between 1870 and 1900 followed one of three lines of development: (1) they were a continuation of the types of manufacturing industries that had been established in the previous decades, (2) they were new firms whose development was based upon the increased importance of Columbus as a transportation center, or (3) they were firms which located in the city because of the presence and possible utilization of the natural resources of southeastern Ohio.

The first group represents organizations which started at a time when local transportation facilities were limited. These companies

[8] *Annual Report of the Director and Secretary of the Columbus Board of Trade for* 1890, p. 62.

were limited both in their supply of raw materials and in the extent of their markets to the agricultural economy of central Ohio. The inadequacies of labor and the shortage of risk capital further restricted their growth. Included in this group are machine shops, foundries, tool shops, flour and grist mills, textile mills, and the like. Their continuation as manufacturers must be regarded as a sign of their earlier success.

Those industries whose development was based upon the contemporary transportation systems were the first to give Columbus a national name as a manufacturing center. Out of the operation of certain of these plants, Columbus gained a reputation and prestige in manufacturing which it had never before known. Carriage and wagon shops, coupled with the small supply shops that made seats, wheels, dashes, and bent-wood products, gave the city a reputation as a leading carriage center. There were local firms which produced iron rails, railroad cars, and equipment for the passenger and freight services of the railroads which had shops and offices in Columbus.

The third group of firms was established as a consequence of the various raw materials of southeastern Ohio. Even before these resources could be profitably utilized, the potential that they held was sufficient to attract new firms to Columbus. Coal was both a potential and realized resource—its presence and utilization attracted firms to Columbus which need coal for power. Iron ore held a greater potential for industry than was ever to be realized. A number of large engineering and foundry operations were located in Columbus anticipating the use of the iron ores of the Hocking area. While the use of these ores was never large in Columbus, the city profited by having the new firms locate here. The easy access to the natural gas field of east-central Ohio also played a role in bringing gas-consuming industries to Columbus. To meet the specific needs of the growing manufacturing and mining industries, inventive genius and capital responded enthusiastically in the thirty years between 1870 and 1900.

1870–1880—In this decade, the small shops of the local craftsmen dominated the industrial structure of the city. The Columbus Car and Wheel Works, which appeared to be the biggest establishment, employed about 400 workers and used more than 9,000 tons of pig metal and 1,800 tons of wrought-iron in its operations in 1872.[9] Its growth was due directly to the expanded railroad facilities in central Ohio.

The foundries and iron shops of earlier days remained active. The Columbus Bolt Works grew to a place of prominence with the coming of the carriage industry and the Ohlen Saw Company continued to prosper. The Franklin Iron Company, with a large blast furnace, yielded about 50 tons of pig iron daily. With the manufacture of iron and steel finally accomplished, the value of the coal and iron ore resources in the neighboring counties was realized.

It now seems odd that the rise of the agricultural implement manufacturing industry had so little direct effect upon Columbus' manufacturing but the agricultural "revolution" that struck Ohio in the middle of the nineteenth century almost completely missed Columbus. There were but two implement manufacturers in the city in 1872: the industry was not as important as the location and resources of central Ohio might seem to justify. The successful operations of the Ridgway shop and of other implement shops of an earlier period were not duplicated. Consequently, the city lost the manufacturing experience that was Springfield's and Cincinnati's. A skilled working force that might have resulted from such an industry did not materialize to benefit later industries.

Columbus did profit by the transportation "revolution" that occurred in the 1870's and continued until the 1900's. Two results were the establishment of the carriage and wagon industry and the growth of the Columbus Rolling Mill Company which produced more than 100 tons of rail per day. The firms engaged in producing materials for the railroad industry, included with the supply firms, had the largest capital investment of any industry in the city with more than one million dollars by 1875.[10]

The peak in the carriage industry was not reached until the following decade but new plants came to Columbus as the industry continually moved towards the central states from the east. The reasons were many: land was cheaper, suitable lumber was abundant,

[9] Unstad, Lydor L., op. cit., p. 406.
[10] Failing, Henry H., op. cit., pp. 6-8.

markets were at hand, prices were favorable, and the developed railroad system afforded an excellent means of transportation. By the later 1870's, local products were reaching the national market.

By 1887, there were 18 companies employing about 3,000 workers in the city: Columbus led the nation in the production of high-class carriages. The Columbus Buggy Company, organized in 1875 but an outgrowth of an older firm, was the largest in the city. It was here that mass production of carriages took place with assembly-line techniques in vogue—one buggy was made every eight minutes. About 1,100 men were employed in this plant and more than $2,000,000 worth of goods was sold in 1890.[11]

1880-1890—The Columbus Board of Trade actively encouraged new companies to locate in Columbus. Competing cities of similar size attracted new industry through a sponsorship program. In contrast, the Columbus Board believed that it ". . . should extend every courtesy and encouragement to parties seeking a location in our city . . . but measures contemplating financial aid . . . are impracticable."[12]

Local initiative and capital were responsible for the development of two firms whose histories are now synonymous with the city's growth. In 1877, the Lechner Manufacturing Company (now the Jeffrey Manufacturing Company) began the production of coal-mining machinery and rotary drills for the coal industry market in Ohio. Four years later, the Kilbourne and Jacobs Company was organized to serve the mining industry with supplies.

Even though the iron industry was a leading one in the city, the Columbus Rolling Mill was forced to close its operations in 1884. When the change from iron to steel rails took place, the company could not obtain the necessary raw materials and the business gradually failed. Foundry products, structural steel, railroad cars and castings, anvils, bolts, and other items continued important, however.

The boot and shoe industry, basically a local one, expanded its operations and entered national competition for markets and raw

[11] Hooper, Osman C., *op. cit.,* p. 221.

[12] *Annual Report of the Directors and Secretary of the Columbus Board of Trade for* 1890, p. 5.

materials. This "revitalized" action was due, in large part, to the emergence of the H. C. Godman Company as one of the major shoe companies in the nation. Columbus was soon recognized as a leading shoe center in the mid-west.

1890-1900—With the enlargement of the national scope of local companies, Columbus began the slow process of maturation as it became a part of the manufacturing economy of the nation. There were more than 900 factories in the city making everything from carriages and foundry products to jewelry and watches. While enlarging the national market, local industry remained stable and diversified.

Columbus supported a large foundry industry although not on a level with Cincinnati and Cleveland. An early survey showed that the major advantage for the foundries in Columbus was the excellent transportation system. A reasonable freight rate gave the manufacturer a wide market for his castings. Skilled foundry labor according to Alvin Ketcham was available in Columbus and at low wages— wages somewhat lower than those paid at competitive points as shown below:[13]

	Yearly Wage		*Yearly Wage*
Columbus	$536.00	Pittsburgh	$561.00
Cincinnati	$537.00	Chicago	$564.00
Dayton	$539.50	Cleveland	$566.00

What is now the Buckeye Steel Castings Company was organized in 1886 and the Columbus Steel Works and Furnaces of Carnegie Steel were built in 1894-1895. The Works had an annual capacity of 160,000 tons.[14] These firms responded to the combination of raw materials and market when they located in Columbus.

The A. K. Rarig Engineering Company, manufacturer of steam engines, compressors, pumps, and other products, was brought to the city largely through the efforts of the Board of Trade. Other iron and steel consumers came here at this time. Products ranged from elevators to laminated tubing for bicycle frames.

[13] Ketcham, Alvin, "The Foundry and Machine Shop Industry in Columbus," *Columbus Manufactures,* (Columbus: The Ohio State University Library, Unpublishsed Manuscript, 1906), pp. 18-19.

[14] Excerpts from a letter from W. Everett McLaine, Director of Public Relations, United States Steel Corporation, 1953.

The shoe industry continued its growth. There were four large firms in the city by 1900 and many smaller ones. Columbus followed St. Louis and Cincinnati as a leading shoe center in the mid-west. It had excellent transportation facilities for finished products and for raw materials. While the local market was not well-developed, local firms reached the national market with ease. Labor was satisfactory, especially since partially trained male and female workers were abundant.

By the turn of the century, Columbus had reached a degree of industrial maturity unknown in the past. While still not a major manufacturing city, its national reputation had been enhanced by the carriage, foundry, and shoe industries.

Factors in the Accelerated Growth of Industry, 1900-1952

There was no stimulus to industry after 1900 comparable to that provided by the utilization of the raw materials of southeastern Ohio after 1870 and by the transportation system which assumed its inter-regional character in the late 1800's. These two factors were of prime importance in establishing Columbus as a manufacturing center. By 1900, there were no new natural resources to be developed in central Ohio; the effects of the realized resources were declining. The railroads remained a *permissive* factor in the expansion of manufacturing, but they did not directly influence the location of industry in Columbus as they had in the previous quarter century.

Between 1900 and 1914, the city and the nation experienced a minor depression with the result that few new industries came to Columbus. World War I brought little manufacturing activity to the city but an expansion of manufacturing facilities occurred in the post-war boom period. This prompted considerable optimism and the continuing industrial development of the city seemed assured. The serious depression of the 1930's had a sobering effect upon Columbus as well as the nation, however. While Columbus fared better than many other Ohio cities because of the diversification and stability of its factories, there was no significant increase in manufacturing at this time. The second World War, and the accompanying post-war boom, resulted in the greatest increase in industrial growth in the city's history.

It is necessary to review these events in order better to understand the continuous but irregular development of industry between the years 1900 and 1952. In retrospect, it would appear that three factors, especially, influenced the location of industry in Columbus in these years.

The revolution which took place in transportation between 1900 and 1952 gave the city a great advantage—greater than it had had in the era of the railroads. The position of Columbus was modified by the opening of land and air routes, and by the concentration of the major automobile centers within a few hundred miles of the city. The famous carriage industry declined rapidly in these years but it was replaced by an expanding automobile industry and a short-lived aircraft industry. Columbus became an important parts supplier as a mid-way point between the steel centers and the automobile assembly centers. Thus, the changing market became a primary factor in the industrial growth of Columbus in the twentieth century.

Plants were attracted to the city by a second factor—a good labor force. Unions were not active in Columbus and strikes were rare. Columbus was advertised as an "American City"—one having a high percentage of native-born laborers. The labor force was stable, wages were relatively low, and some skills were present. The shoe industry and branches of the autombile industry increased their operations in the city partly because of these factors.

A third factor—and one of increasing importance—affecting the localization of industry has been the Federal Government. Either by direct or indirect means, the Federal Government has influenced the pattern of industrialization in Columbus in the past half century. This has been true especially during war-time emergencies. There was no evidence of direct government participation in manufacturing in Columbus during World War I, other than minor defense contracts. With the entrance of the nation into World War II, however, the city's industrial pattern was greatly altered by its participation in military preparations. The only large government-financed plant in central Ohio was built in Columbus in 1941 for the Curtiss-Wright Corporation. This was a major turning point in the city's industrial history, as will later be shown. Local firms received contracts and sub-contracts totaling millions of dollars. Dozens of small machine shops had their beginnings in this period and were able to continue operations into the post-war period. In this way, the government was an active force in creating industry and in effecting the expansion and maturation of already-established firms. Certainly, the Federal Government's program in central Ohio can be considered one of the major forces in shaping the city's emergence as a mature industrial center.

Industrialization, 1900-1952

1900-1914—The conservatism of local business interests continued to retard the growth of manufacturing early in the twentieth century. Risk capital for manufacturing operations remained scarce: for want of sufficient capital, a number of promising concerns overlooked Columbus. Within this period, a more active Chamber of Commerce made efforts to interest firms in the city. The Chamber tried to establish a $1,000,000 Guarantee Fund, the purpose of which was to aid new firms in setting up their operations in the city. Promotional literature was published, too, with the intention of interesting outside industries in relocating in Columbus. While these progressive steps were being taken, the Chamber assured its members that ". . . great care (was) used in the selection of prospects and in making offers . . . the city does not want new plants which have not good prospects of success."[15]

It was during this period that many plants were established on Marion Road. Just outside the city's limits, these firms enjoyed all the privileges and benefits of the city but they paid only a township tax which was 100 per cent less than the city tax. A conscious attempt was made to attract outside concerns either to the city or to the adjacent townships.

By 1914, there were over 800 plants in the city and Columbus ranked among the 40 leading industrial cities of the nation. About 35,000 persons were employed by industry producing $85,000,000 worth of goods yearly. The average wage for all types of labor was

[15] *Annual Report of the Columbus Chamber of Commerce,* Columbus, 1914, p. 28.

about $600 a year. Skilled labor received as high as $3.00 a day.[16] The relatively low wages and the excellent labor relations were added incentives to plant location.

The principal factories included the foundry, machine shops, and blast furnaces of the Carnegie Steel Company, the U. S. Steel Corporation (two blast furnaces and a billet mill), and the Columbus Iron and Steel Company.

Columbus also had seven "varied" firms, each the largest of its kind in the world: Jeffrey Manufacturing Company, Kilbourne & Jacobs, Wolfe Brothers Shoe Company, Capital City Dairy Products (butterine), M. C. Lilley and Company (regalia), Peruna Drug Company, and the Columbus Buggy Company. By 1914, the latter firm was no longer a leader; it was replaced by a member of the rapidly growing automobile industry.

In this transitional period in the transportation industry, there remained in operation in 1907 six large buggy manufacturing plants and more than a dozen suppliers. The Brown Manufacturing Company was known as the largest maker of carriage and electric automobile lamps in the world. While the carriage industry was not yet abandoned, this company was active in the automobile industry. The Midgely Manufacturing Company had, in Columbus, one of the largest factories in the country for the manufacture of automobile wheels and rims.

The shoe industry continued to expand. More than 5,000 workers were employed in 1904 and 7 large firms were in operation. The H. C. Godman Company and Wolfe Brothers Shoe Company were two of the largest in the nation. With an efficient, low-wage labor force, Columbus grew as a shoe center when other towns were losing this industry.

1914-1920—The beginning of World War I, following close upon a long period of depression, hindered industrial expansion. The threat of U. S. entry into the war limited new enterprises because investment was timid. It was characteristic of local capital to avoid investment: many of the efforts of the Chamber of Commerce to bring new firms to the city were consequently ineffective.

Some diversification of manufacturing activity occurred during

[16] *Ibid.*, pp. 11 and 16.

the war years, however, with the Belmont Casket Company, the Federal Chemical Company, and the Kilgore Manufacturing Company locating in Columbus in 1917. These firms came to take advantage of distribution facilities. Other small plants were established but no major organizations developed.

In 1916, the Chamber of Commerce tried to bring a Federal armor plate plant to Columbus. A brochure was published emphasizing the advantages of this location. Columbus steel plants were producing up to 350,000 tons a year and could easily satisfy the armor plate plant's required 20,000 tons of pig iron. Good railroad service and an abundant supply of low-cost but unskilled rural labor were favorable factors emphasized. Furthermore, the city had a diversified and stable type of industry which was relatively free from industrial competition.[17]

While this effort was unsuccessful, government contracts did benefit local manufacturers. By August 1917, ten firms were engaged in war-time production and late in the same year more than 50 firms were so engaged. A War Industries Board was set up as a branch of the Cleveland Division in 1918 with the purpose of getting all industry, large and small, coordinated in war production to speed up operations, allocate labor, and regulate supplies more satisfactorily. But even this program did not bring the city important war contracts.[18]

A lasting influence of the Federal Government was the erection of a $7,000,000 government depot here. This storage plant, one of three large ones in the country, was built in 1918. It has added to the government payrolls in Columbus and has become a stabilizing force in the economy of Columbus.

The ten largest industrial employers in the city in 1918 include:

Jeffrey Manufacturing Company
Buckeye Steel Castings Company
Federal Glass Company
H. C. Godman Company
Ralston Steel Car Company
Carnegie Steel Company
Ohio Malleable Iron Company
M. C. Lilley and Company
J. P. Gordon Company
J. W. Brown Mfg. Company

[17] *Determining the Location of the Government Armor Plate Plant; Brief for Columbus, Ohio.* (Columbus: Columbus Chamber of Commerce, 1916).

[18] *Monthly Bulletins of the Columbus Chamber of Commerce,* Vol. 4, August 1917, p. 1, and Vol. 4, October 1917, p. 12. See also the *District Manufacturers Commission of Ohio,* 1918, letters and data referring to the establishment of this commission.

Foundry products, railroad and mining equipment, shoes, glass, and automobile parts were the leading products. A year prior to this, the American Rolling Mill Company (Armco) took over all of the facilities of the Columbus Iron and Steel Company. The plant ranked seventeenth in size. The Ford Motor Company had a branch asssembly plant here which ranked as one of the twenty-five leading firms in the city.

Columbus gained new factories in the immediate post-war years. The Timken Roller Bearing Company of Canton built a $1,500,000 plant on nine acres of land at Fifth and Cleveland avenues. Approximately 1,300 persons were employed at the time. The location was due primarily to the fine transportation network which tied Columbus to Pittsburgh and Detroit, in conjunction with a stable, low-wage labor force.

By 1920, the Allen Motor Company moved here from Fostoria, the Henedrson Tire & Rubber Company from Bucyrus, and the Julian and Kokenge Company from Cincinnati. The American Zinc Oxide Company built a branch plant here. Smaller plants were also established. At this time, Columbus had a population of 237,000 of which 10 per cent was engaged in work in the 900 manufacturing plants.

1920-1940—The pace of industrialization slackened during the post-war depression which lasted from 1920 to 1922. Conditions were not favorable to industrial expansion but the city continued to seek stable and diversified industries which were suited to the community. The brief depression was followed by increasing activity. The Industrial Bureau estimated that the city's business payroll increased by more than 365 per cent between 1914 and 1926.[19]

The number of wage earners in industry is a criterion by which to gauge manufacturing activity in a city. From 26,751 workers in 1919, employment dropped in the early 1920's but picked up again to reach 26,576 in 1929. The effects of the depression are clear—in 1935 the number of wage earners in manufacturing had fallen to 17,516. Depression years are reflected clearly in the total carloads entering and leaving Columbus in 12-month periods: in 1929, 175,122

[19] *Columbus: A City of Men, Materials, and Management,* (Columbus: Columbus Industrial Bureau, 1928), p. 6.

carloads were recorded; in 1933, the lowest year, only 82,592 carloads were recorded. The value of manufactured goods dropped from an all-time high (up to 1934) of $212,227,751 in 1929 to the relatively low figure of $89,687,883 in 1933.[20]

In the 1920's, the leading concerns were closely associated with the field of transportation. Automobile parts had been made here since the first decade of this century. Commercial aviation was stimulated by the success of aircraft during the war. As early as 1916, Columbus was thought of as an aircraft center. There was the suggestion that the city, long a carriage center, could turn the buggy plants into aircraft supply plants where bodies, propellers, and other wood parts could be made. Five years later a 100-acre lot, five miles east of the city, was purchased for an airport. This was later abandoned and, in 1926, an $850,000 bond issue was approved to purchase a 543-acre site east of the city.

The first transcontinental airway in the United States involved train service from the east coast to Columbus where a tri-motor plane carried passengers to the west. The railroads had brought industry to the city at an earlier date; the aircraft industry did not immediately duplicate this. Two firms, Columbus Auto Brass Company and the Columbus Aircraft Corporation, tried to make aircraft but did not succeed financially. Both firms were backed by Columbus capital. Port Columbus eventually became an important Naval, Marine, and Army base. Commercial transportation grew considerably, as well, but it was not until World War II that a large-scale aircraft industry succeeded.

Meanwhile, other phases of manufacturing were undergoing changes. The Armco plant moved to Hamilton in 1928 to be near its main plant and the local facilities were taken over by the Columbus Coke and Iron Company which operated them as merchant furnaces.[21]

Two new hot-air furnace companies located here and increased Columbus' importance as a leading center for the warm air heating industry. The Armstrong Furnace Company came from London,

[20] The City Manual, Supplement to the City Bulletin, Columbus, 1932, p. 9, and 1934, p. 9.
[21] Borth, Christy, True Steel (Indianapolis: Bobbs-Merrill Company, 1941), p. 262, and Monthly Industrial Review, June 12, 1928, p. 4.

Ohio, in 1928, and at about the same time, the Midland Furnace Company built a large plant on Olentangy River Road. Five other large furnace companies had already been in operation.

The expansion by integration of local firms continued. The Jaeger Machine Company bought the Lakewood Engineering Company, its chief competitor, and the Jeffrey Manufacturing Company bought the Galion Iron Works. This was done so that Jeffrey could absorb a basic metal company into its organization.

By the end of these 20 years, Columbus had undergone a change in its industrial structure. The leading products included mining machinery, concrete-mixing equipment, oil-well derricks, oilcloth, shoes (19 per cent of the nation's total), and artificial teeth facings. The city was known as a center especially for the shoe, heating and cooling equipment, and mining machinery industries. Its national importance had increased.

1940-1952—The second World War had a great influence upon the further industrial development of Columbus. Its most obvious influence was the $14,000,000 Curtiss-Wright aircraft plant which was erected in 1941 at government expense to manufacture naval aircraft.

A less obvious result was the fact that a great labor pool was created. Men and women, Negro and white, from cities, towns, and farms, were attracted to Columbus by the high wages of the aircraft industry. The force was essentially untrained but the Curtiss-Wright organization provided on-the-job training as well as preliminary training in metal working at the State Fairgrounds. With fewer than 3,000 workers at its outset, the plant employed more than 25,000 during the war-time peak. Thus, an important labor pool was created not only for the war emergency but for use in the post-war periods, as well. This labor force proved to be an exceedingly important factor in attracting new industry to the community.

As the aircraft industry sought labor on the local scene, it created hard feelings among the older firms in the city which lost workers. However, it asserted that it wanted to cooperate wherever possible and wanted to become a part of the industrial community. J. A. Williams, General Manager of the Columbus plant, stated optimistically that "Curtiss-Wright is a definite part of Columbus. Already

CHART 1—Percentage Gain in Workers, Columbus, Ohio, 1940-1950

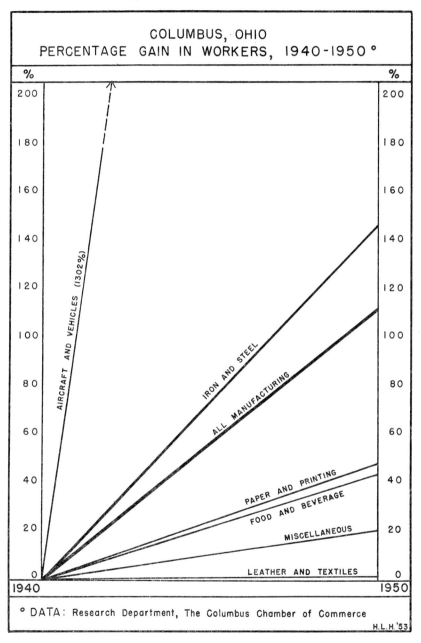

COLUMBUS, OHIO
PERCENTAGE GAIN IN WORKERS, 1940-1950°

° DATA: Research Department, The Columbus Chamber of Commerce

H.L.H.'53

we are rooted deeply in the soil and are definitely here to stay . . .
We hope to be one of the staid, old organizations of Columbus."[22]

In addition to the establishment of new plants, war-time contracts permitted plant expansions and conversions. Franklin County,
and Columbus, profited in all ways. More than a billion and a half
dollars was invested in Ohio's industry during the war—Franklin
County had a total investment of $53,023,000 or about 3 per cent
of the state's total. Of this, $44,633,000 was spent on new plants
(principally Curtiss-Wright), $6,268,000 in the expansion of old
plants, and $2,122,000 in the conversion of existing facilities.[23] Table
5 shows a comparison between Franklin County and the state in the
investment of these funds.

TABLE 5—The Value of Public-Financed Industrial Facilities in Ohio and
Franklin County During World War II, July 1940-May 1944

Products	Value (Dollars)	
	Ohio	Franklin County
Aircraft	$478,891,000	$31,313,000
Ships	33,030,000	27,000
Ordnance	232,662,000	1,544,000
Explosives	146,970,000	31,000
Iron and Steel	247,575,000	5,940,000
Non-Ferrous	107,186,000	41,000
Machinery	202,636,000	11,721,000
Chemicals-Petroleum	136,573,000	1,079,000
Food and Others	92,076,000	1,327,000

Source: The Geographic Distribution of Manufacturing Facilities Expansion, July 1940–
May 1944, Washington, June 1, 1945, Exhibit L, p. 63.

With the end of the war, Columbus had the labor, space, and
transportation facilities to attract new firms. It has been the movement of large, national firms to the city that has been the major
factor in changing the industrial structure of Columbus. Such a
movement was the construction of the Ternstedt Division plant
of General Motors which employed approximately 3,500 workers
in the manufacture of hardware products for Fisher Body. Its
planned location is in a nonindustrial suburban area west of the
city. The supply of semi-skilled labor, good transportation facilities,

[22] "Salute to Curtiss-Wright," The Columbus Sunday Dispatch, November 30, 1941, p. 3.
[23] The Geographic Distribution of Manufacturing Facilities Expansion, July 1940-May
1944 (Washington, D. C.: Government Printing Office, June 1, 1945), Exhibit N, p. 80.

The North American Aviation Plant on the East Side of the City

and freedom from competition with similar firms made this location attractive. Today, the plant is one of the stable firms that has added to the growing importance of Columbus as an automotive parts center and as an industrial community.

After Curtiss-Wright closed its operations, part of the huge plant was occupied by the Lustron Corporation, which was a government-financed private concern. With the closing of the financially unsound Lustron Corporation, the North American Aviation Corporation occupied the same building and began the production of jet aircraft for the military forces. (See the photograph on page 61. This shows clearly the extensive, one-story plants, the large areas devoted to parking space, and the available transportation facilities. In the background is Port Columbus). Today, this company, which came to Columbus to make use of the partially trained labor force available in southeastern Ohio, West Virginia, and Kentucky, employs about 17,000 workers. It has expanded plant space considerably.

The huge, new Westinghouse plant has been built west of the city near the site of the General Motors plant. It is an impressive addition to the city, and, as the major appliance manufacturing center for the entire Westinghouse organization, promises to be a stable, peace-time operation.

Summary

The great change in manufacturing brought about in Columbus since 1940 is the result, essentially, of one factor. When the Federal government chose to erect the Curtiss-Wright plant in Columbus, the economy of the city was destined to change. The manifold effects of the location of this plant upon the industrial community provided the basis for change. The new plant broke a "strangle-hold" on industry held by a few old-line firms. It brought a new concept of manufacturing to the city and, with it, high-wage, unionized labor policies not common to Columbus. It provided the city with a surplus of semi-skilled labor at the end of the war. This, in turn, was attractive to national organizations considering relocation. During the war, and since, the plant provided a huge market for local sub-contractors. The number of machine shops in Columbus increased five times, as a consequence. The nature of its manufacturing processes and of its products (as well as those of its successors) has resulted in a somewhat greater instability in the city's industrial base.

Thus, this one plant, established by the Federal Government, provided the incentive for the industrialization of Columbus, Ohio in the 1940's and was a turning point in the city's history. By reviewing the industrial activity of Columbus in 1953 and by considering all of the forces, historical and current, which have affected this activity, it will be possible to draw some conclusions about the future of the Columbus industrial community.

CHAPTER IV

LOCATION OF MANUFACTURING IN COLUMBUS, 1953

A review of the industrial evolution of Columbus and an analysis of the physical and economic forces which influenced it have been the principal concerns to this point. It now remains to study the present pattern of industrialization in Columbus and to ascertain the value of the forces, historical and contemporary, which have affected the localization of industry.

To obtain the necessary information, responsible representatives of 204 manufacturing establishments were interviewed.[1] This number included all manufacturing establishments employing more than 10 workers, excluding food and beverage, printing, converted paper, lumber, and nonmanufacturing businesses.[2] During the interviews, information was gathered relating to the nature of the plant's operation and the company official was asked to evaluate the various forces which influenced the location of the plant in the city. Consideration was given to factors relating to national position as well as to actual site within the city. Whenever possible, manufacturing operations were witnessed in order to obtain an understanding of processes and to gain an appreciation of any problems of site relating to or developing from process. Later the information was tabulated and evaluated; the plant locations were mapped and studied.

[1] The value of the interviews was enhanced greatly by the fact that responsible executives took part in them. Interviews were held with men in the following capacities:

Chairman of the Board	1	Plant Manager	45
President	74	Purchasing Agent	4
Vice-President	29	Director, Industrial Relations	5
Secretary	12	Director, Personnel	9
Treasurer	5	Office Secretary	8
Auditor	5	Position not Known	4
Engineer	3		

[2] Most of these are common to all cities with a population of 100,000 or more; their market is distinctly local, their product not unique to Columbus, nor do they differentiate the city in any way. For a complete listing of Columbus' manufacturers by company name, employee size, and by product, see the *Manufacturers Directory, Columbus, Ohio*, published annually by the Industrial Department, The Columbus Chamber of Commerce.

As a result of the field interviews and the mapping of the plants studied by their locations in the city, 6 industrial areas were established. For each the following information is discussed: plant distribution, age of plants by area, movement of plants within the city and the related stability of the industrial areas, patterns of industrial growth within various areas and employment by area and by plant. This information provides the basis for this chapter.

A second result of the interviews was the classification of all manufacturing establishments into 21 industry-groups based upon *product* and/or *function*. These industry-groups provide the framework about which the industry's history in Columbus is discussed. The forces which have been effective in the industry's growth are analyzed, and the prospects for the future of the industry in Columbus are considered.

Boundaries of Industrial Areas

The delineation of boundaries is frequently an arbitrary matter: this has proved to be so in establishing some of the boundaries for the 6 industrial areas of Columbus used in this study. No boundary was preconceived. Wherever a physical feature could satisfactorily serve, it was used. Other boundaries were based upon an analysis of plant sites, the processes involved, and the relationships established between plants within an area. The 6 industrial areas delineated for the purpose of this study are:

North Columbus	Downtown Columbus
South Columbus	West Columbus
Northwest Columbus	East Columbus

The boundaries of these areas are shown on Map 4 and described below.

No attempt was made to organize the industrial areas on the basis of the type of manufacturing dominant. This method would have been useful in a few instances but the diversity of local manufacturing and the absence of "type" areas precluded its use.

Downtown Columbus is perhaps the most difficult of the industrial areas to define. The Downtown area is the commercial-industrial center of the city. With the exception of the Scioto River on the west, its boundaries are not natural. In an effort clearly to

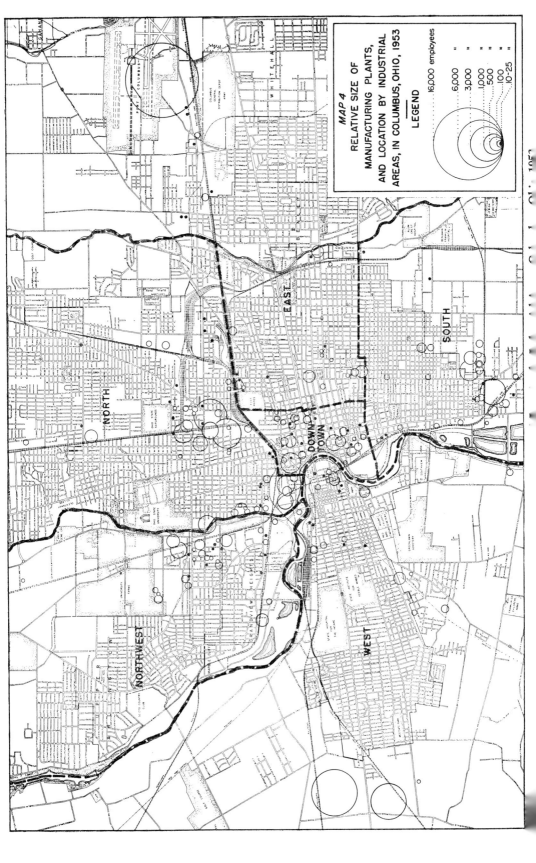

MAP 4

RELATIVE SIZE OF MANUFACTURING PLANTS, AND LOCATION BY INDUSTRIAL AREAS, IN COLUMBUS, OHIO, 1953

LEGEND

16,000 employees
6,000
3,000
1,000
500
100
10-25

delineate the Downtown area, certain common physical-economic features were observed and used as criteria: multiple-story manufacturing units, loft-type manufacturing operations, high proportion of female workers on the industrial payrolls, and close ties with the activities and services common to the commercial core of the city, were considered singularly and/or in combination.

As a result of these considerations, the northern boundary of the Downtown parallels the main east-west railroad yards of the city west to Union Station on High Street, thence to the Penitentiary, where it dips south to join the Scioto River. The eastern boundary corresponds with Grant and Cleveland Avenues; here a distinct break in the physical structure of the buildings occurs and the type of activity differs. To the south, Sycamore Street and Livingston Avenue are a joint boundary.

South Columbus is rather well-defined. Sycamore Street and Livingston Avenue and east to Alum Creek form the northern boundary of this area. Alum Creek, on the east, and the Scioto River and the quarry lands on the west, provide distinct physical boundaries for this industrial area.

East Columbus extends eastward from the Cleveland Avenue boundary of the Downtown area. To the north, the east-west railroad lines form the boundary, and to the south, Livingston Avenue as far east as Alum Creek. The entire suburban and rural area immediately to the east of Alum Creek is included within the East Columbus area.

North Columbus is the large tract between Alum Creek, on the east, and the Olentangy River, on the west, lying north of Downtown Columbus and the east-west railroad lines and extending to Granville Road.

West Columbus is that part of the city west of the Scioto River. Conceivably, that part of West Columbus just across the river from the Civic Center might be included in Downtown Columbus. It is separated by a physical barrier, however, and the nature of the industrial activity is of such an order as to differentiate the two areas.

Northwest Columbus is the area lying between the Olentangy and Scioto Rivers.

Distribution of Manufacturing Activity

Within the framework of the industrial *area,* there are a number of highly concentrated industrial *communities* in which most of the area's plants are located and most of the workers are employed. Manufacturing activity is rarely restricted to a single, clearly defined community. However, within the major industrial areas one or two individual communities may dominate. Beyond these, the secondary manufacturing operations function.

Thirty-five years ago, a sociologist at The Ohio State University[3] described the three significant industrial communities in Columbus as follows: (a) the group of plants lying along either side of the New York Central Railroad tracks north of the downtown business district and centered about the Jeffrey Manufacturing Company's buildings on North Fourth Street; (b) a group south of First Avenue bordering the Olentangy River and extending into the downtown area; and (c) the South Columbus community where the large steel and foundry operations of the city were then situated.

In the years since McKenzie made his study, the location of manufacturing activity in Columbus has undergone a pronounced change. The three areas McKenzie referred to are still important manufacturing communities but they have undergone changes and new communities have arisen to challenge them. Some of the changes which have occurred are discussed below.

Number of Manufacturing Plants, by Areas

Considering only the 204 plants which have provided the basis for this study, Table 6 shows the actual number and the percentage distribution of plants in 1953 by industrial area in Columbus.

When Table 6 is studied in conjunction with Map 4, showing the present sites of the manufacturing establishments it is seen that the industrial "communities" described by McKenzie persist. These centers of activity 35 years ago remain dominant. For example, over 80 per cent of the 53 plants in North Columbus are concentrated

[3] McKenzie, Roderick D., "The Neighborhood: A Study of Local Life in the City of Columbus, Ohio," *The American Journal of Sociology,* Vol. 27, No. 2, September 1921, p. 151.

TABLE 6—Number and Percentage Distribution of 204 Manufacturing Plants, by Industrial Areas, Columbus, Ohio, 1953

Area	Number	Per Cent
North	53	26.0
South	38	18.6
Northwest	33	16.2
Downtown	31	15.2
West	26	12.7
East	23	11.3
TOTAL	204	100.0

either in the major industrial agglomeration in the city—along the New York Central Railroad north of the Downtown area, or in the less heavily settled community along the east bank of the Olentangy River. The remainder of the plants in North Columbus are scattered. Few relationships are established among any of these plants: they are, for the most part, independent and "isolated" units.

The second largest number of manufacturing establishments, 38 or approximately 19 per cent of the total, is found in *South Columbus*. Reference to Map 4 shows that the significant industrial community in South Columbus lies just beyond the southern limits of the city in Marion Township, as described earlier by McKenzie. Here are the largest and oldest plants in the area. They form the heart of an industrial community that has tended to stabilize. New plants which have established in South Columbus have shied away from this older area—only one plant in 12 which located in South Columbus since 1946 has located in this older district outside the city limits—so that many small, new organizations are to be found scattered throughout South Columbus.

The 31 plants located in *Downtown Columbus* represent no major concentrations of industry types. With the exception of two shoe companies and one or two metal-processing plants, no large plants are present. For the most part, small firms occupy scattered plants or are to be found in loft-type quarters within the commercial center of the city. More than one company is operating in an abandoned brewery that has been redesigned for its use. With the exception of one shoe manufacturer, few companies in the Downtown area occupy buildings constructed for their specific needs.

Thirty-five years ago there was no concentration of industry in the East, West, or Northwest industrial areas. Today, each of these areas has considerable manufacturing activity as indicated by the fact that in 1953, 40 per cent of all manufacturing plants in Columbus were in these three areas. Branch plants of national organizations have played a prominent role in this development. Generally, they have instituted a trend to suburban locations. An outgrowth of this has been the erection of plants of modern design, attractively landscaped, and with adequate grounds available for parking and possible expansion. Usually, too, the companies have displayed some evidence of planning with respect to accessibility to national markets and raw materials.

In the *East Columbus* industrial area there has been no marked agglomeration of manufacturing plants although Port Columbus has been the focal point for a secondary industrial community. It is secondary only in number of plants (23 plants or 11.3 per cent of plants in 1953): in worker size and in importance to Columbus in dollar value, probably no other facility in Columbus exceeds the North American Aviation plant. The construction of the Curtiss-Wright aviation plant at this site in 1941 and the dominance of the aviation industry in the area since, has been a major factor in the growth of this section.

The most significant industrial growth in Columbus since World War II has occurred on the suburban fringe of the *West Columbus* industrial area. The growth here has materialized due largely to the construction of the General Motors plant in 1946, and the large Westinghouse refrigerator plant in 1953. While these are but two of the 26 plants in West Columbus, their influence upon the industrial pattern of the city has been exceptionally strong. Their suburban sites have provided what appears to be the nucleus for further industrial activity. Undoubtedly their effect upon the expanding housing program, with its related shopping units, which has taken place recently in the area, has been considerable. It would seem that once industry recognized the attractiveness of the community, residential and commercial interests became attentive. The bulk of the plants in West Columbus are widely scattered over the broad area with a minor concentration of small factories on the river flats just west of Downtown Columbus.

Unlike the East and West areas, *Northwest Columbus'* plants are fairly heavily concentrated near the Olentangy River from Goodale Street north to the university farms. This industrial community is bordered by residential housing and by the university. The organizations which have located here have developed modern and reasonably attractive plants and sites. Actually, the industrial operations do not interfere with the normal functions of the residential community.

Age of Manufacturing Establishments

The median age of the 204 manufacturing plants in Columbus, based upon their founding date in Columbus, is 29 years; this varies by industrial area, with a high of 38 years in North Columbus and a low of 16 years in West Columbus (Table 7). The 204 plants range in date of founding from 1850 to 1953.

TABLE 7—Median Age and Range in Age of Manufacturing Plants in Columbus, Ohio, by Industrial Areas

Area	Number of Plants	Range in Age	Median Age (In Years)
North	53	1850–1949	38
South	38	1850–1951	33
East	23	1859–1950	33
Downtown	31	1852–1952	28
Northwest	33	1895–1952	19
West	26	1874–1953	16
TOTAL	204	1850–1953	29

North and South Columbus are the sites for a large number of the older industrial firms; East Columbus also has many older firms. Only the Northwest and West areas display distinct signs of recent industrial development.

Perhaps more valid than the median age of plants in Columbus in considering the current geographic location of plants and in ascertaining the areas of decline and growth within the city is the median number of years that manufacturing plants have been located on their present sites (Table 8). By comparing the data in Tables 7 and 8 it becomes apparent that movement of industry within the areas and in the city has actively taken place. For example, there are plants in both the North and South Columbus areas which have been in Columbus since 1850, but in the North area no plant was on its present site before 1870, and in the South area, before 1892. In the North area, the median number of years in Columbus is 38; the median number of years on the present site, 26. In the North-western area of the city the median number of years in Columbus is 16, while the median number of years on the present site is 8. No plants were located in the Northwest area prior to 1920, but by 1953, 33 plants or 16 per cent of the total number of plants in the city had moved into or been established in this area.

TABLE 8—Median Number of Years that Manufacturing Plants Have
Been on Present Sites, by Area, Columbus, Ohio

Area	Number of Plants	Range in Years on Present Site	Median Number of Years on Present Site
North	53	1870–1951	26
South	38	1892–1952	26
Downtown	31	1852–1952	20
West	26	1906–1953	12
East	23	1894–1950	9
Northwest	33	1920–1952	8
TOTAL	204	1852–1953	18

The development of manufacturing in the East and West Columbus areas has been relatively recent although both areas have had some plants since the 1860's and 1870's. These two areas are the sites for a number of older Columbus firms which were once located in other industrial areas. In the East Columbus area, the median number of years in Columbus of the 23 plants in the area in 1953 was 33, while the median number of years on the present site was only 9. Although the West Columbus area had some manufacturing as early as 1874, the median number of years in Columbus of the 26 plants in this area in 1953 was 16, and the median number of years on the present site was 8.

Periods of Expansion in Manufacturing

Of the 204 plants studied in 1953, only 41 or 20 per cent of them were established in Columbus prior to 1900 (Table 9). During the period from 1900 to 1919 another 45 plants were added so that by the end of World War I, 42 per cent of the plants in the city in 1953

TABLE 9—Periods of Establishment in Columbus: Number and Percentage Distribution of Plants, by Period of Establishment, by Industrial Areas

Period	Industrial Area						Total
	North	South	Downtown	East	West	Northwest	
			Number				
1946–1953	5	4	2	3	7	8	29
1940–1945	5	3	4	5	3	5	25
1920–1939	13	13	11	6	9	12	64
1914–1919	6	2	2	2	1	3	16
1900–1913	11	7	2	3	3	3	29
Pre-1900	13	9	10	4	3	2	41
Total	53	38	31	23	26	33	204
			Per cent, by Periods, by Industrial Area[a]				
1946–1953	17.2	13.8	6.9	10.3	24.1	27.6	100.0
1940–1945	20.0	12.0	16.0	20.0	12.0	20.0	100.0
1920–1939	20.3	20.3	17.2	9.4	14.1	18.8	100.0
1914–1919	37.5	12.5	12.5	12.5	6.3	18.8	100.0
1900–1913	37.9	24.1	6.9	10.3	10.3	10.3	100.0
Pre-1900	31.7	22.0	24.4	9.8	7.3	4.9	100.0
Total	26.0	18.6	15.2	11.3	12.7	16.2	100.0
			Per Cent, by Industrial Area, by Periods[a]				
1946–1953	9.4	10.5	6.5	13.0	26.9	24.2	14.2
1940–1945	9.4	7.9	12.9	21.7	11.5	15.2	12.3
1920–1939	24.5	34.5	35.5	26.1	34.6	36.4	31.4
1914–1919	11.3	5.3	6.5	8.7	3.8	9.1	7.8
1900–1913	20.8	18.4	6.5	13.0	11.5	9.1	14.2
Pre-1900	24.5	23.7	32.3	17.4	11.5	6.1	20.1
Total	100.0	100.0	100.0	100.0	100.0	100.0	100.0

[a] Per cent may not always equal 100.0 due to rounding.
Source: Developed from Appendix Table 1.

had been located in Columbus. During the 20-year period 1920-1940, roughly the period between the two world wars, another 64 plants or 31 per cent of the total were added. The expansion in manufacturing in the whole economy attendant upon World War II was reflected in the growth in manufacturing in Columbus when 25 plants were added during the 5-year period 1940-1945. This accelerated rate of growth continued in the post-war period, and in the 7-year period, 1946-1953, 29 new plants located in Columbus. Thus, during the 13-year period, 1940-1953, 54 new plants or 26.5 per cent of the 204 plants were established.

Relative Growth in Industrial Areas

Older Industrial Areas—The North, South, and Downtown industrial areas continued through 1953 to be the areas of the greatest concentration of manufacturing plants with 122 or 60 per cent of the 204 plants being located in these three areas. Also, these three areas continued to have the largest concentration of the oldest plants in the city, with 24.5 per cent of the plants in the North area in 1953 having been established in Columbus before 1900; 23.7 per cent, in the South area, and 32.3 per cent, in the Downtown area (Table 9). Almost one-half of the plants in each of these three areas were established in Columbus prior to 1920—56.6 per cent in the North area, 47.4 per cent in the South, and 45.3 per cent in the Downtown area. During the period of expansion between 1920 and 1940, these three areas continued to offer attractive sites for new plants, and of the plants in these areas in 1953, 24.5 per cent in the North, 34.2 per cent in the South, and 35.5 per cent in the Downtown area were established in Columbus during this 20-year period. Since 1940, and particularly since 1946, these three areas have grown less rapidly than the more recently developed East, West and Northwest areas. Of all the plants in the three older areas in 1953, only 19.8 per cent in the North, 18.4 per cent in the South, and 19.4 per cent in the Downtown area have been established in Columbus since 1940; only 9.4 per cent in the North, 10.5 per cent in the South, and 6.5 per cent in the Downtown area have been established since 1946.

Newer Industrial Areas—The East, West and Northwest industrial areas have been developed both by the movement of plants from the older areas and by the location of relatively larger proportions of newly established plants in these areas. In the East area, of the 23 plants in 1953, only 1 plant or 4.3 per cent of the total was located on its present site prior to 1900 (Table 10), while 4 plants or 17.4 per cent of the plants now in the area were established in

TABLE 10—Period of Location on Present Site: Number and Percentage
Distribution of Plants, by Period of Location on Present Site,
by Industrial Areas, 1953

Period	Industrial Area						Total
	North	South	Downtown	East	West	Northwest	
			Number				
1946–1953	9	12	5	10	11	16	63
1940–1945	5	0	5	5	3	5	23
1920–1939	23	10	16	2	11	12	74
1914–1919	3	4	2	1	0	0	10
1900–1913	6	9	2	4	1	0	22
Pre-1900	7	3	1	1	0	0	12
Total	53	38	31	23	26	33	204
			Per Cent, by Periods, by Industrial Areas[a]				
1946–1953	14.3	19.0	7.9	15.9	17.5	25.4	100.0
1940–1945	21.7	0.0	21.7	21.7	13.0	21.7	100.0
1920–1939	31.1	13.5	21.6	2.7	14.9	16.2	100.0
1914–1919	30.0	40.0	20.0	10.0	0.0	0.0	100.0
1900–1913	27.3	40.9	9.1	18.2	4.5	0.0	100.0
Pre-1900	58.3	25.0	8.3	8.3	0.0	0.0	100.0
Total	26.0	18.6	15.2	11.3	12.7	16.2	100.0
			Per Cent, by Industrial Areas, by Periods[a]				
1946–1953	17.0	31.6	16.1	43.5	42.3	48.5	30.9
1940–1945	9.4	0.0	16.1	21.7	11.5	15.2	11.3
1920–1939	43.4	26.3	51.6	8.7	42.3	36.4	36.3
1914–1919	5.7	10.5	6.5	4.3	0.0	0.0	4.9
1900–1913	11.3	23.7	6.5	17.4	3.8	0.0	10.8
Pre-1900	13.2	7.9	3.2	4.3	0.0	0.0	5.9
Total	100.0	100.0	100.0	100.0	100.0	100.0	100.0

[a] Per cents may not always equal 100.0 due to rounding.
Source: Developed from Appendix Table 1.

Columbus prior to 1900 (Table 9). Of the 23 plants in the East
area in 1953, 8, or 33.7 per cent have been established in Columbus
since 1940, while 15 of the 23, or 64 per cent, of the plants in the
area were located on their present sites since 1940.

Of the 33 plants in the Northwest area in 1953, none was
located on its present site prior to 1920, yet 8, or 24 per cent of
these 33 plants were established in Columbus prior to 1920. Twenty-
one or 63.7 per cent of these plants were located on their present
sites during the 13-year period 1940-1953, but only 8, or 39.4
cent of them were established during this period. Sixteen plants
or 48.5 per cent of the total were located on their present sites in the

Northwest area during the 1946-1953 period, but only 8 plants or 24 per cent of the plants in the area were established during that period.

The development in the West area has been similar to that in the Northwest. Of the 26 plants in the area in 1953, only 1 plant was located on its present site prior to 1920, but 7 of the plants or 26.8 per cent of the plants in the area in 1953 were established in Columbus prior to 1920. Fourteen plants or 53.8 per cent of the number now in the area have been located on their present sites since 1940, but only 10 or 38.4 per cent of them were established in Columbus since 1940. During the 7-year period 1946-1953, 11 plants or 42.3 per cent of the total number in the area were located on their present sites, but only 7 of them or 26.9 per cent of the total were established during this period.

Movement of Industry in Columbus

Of the 204 plants, 68 or 33.3 per cent of them have moved from the areas in which they were originally established to other areas in the city (Table 11). Of the 68 plants which have moved out of

TABLE 11—Number of Plants, by Industrial Area, Remaining in the Area in Which Established, and the Number Having Moved Into or Out of the Area

Area	Number Now In Area	Number in Area from Beginning	Number Moved Into Area	Number Left the Area	Number Having Been in the Area (total)
North	53	39	14	14	67
South	38	20	18	3	41
Downtown	31	28	3	37	68
East	23	17	6	3	26
West	26	17	9	10	36
Northwest	3	15	18	1	34
Total	204	136	68	68	272

Source: Developed from Appendix Table 1.

the area in which they were originally established, 51 or 75 per cent moved from the Downtown and North Columbus areas. The Downtown area, in its role as a "cradle" for industry lost 37 plants and gained only 3. The loss of 14 plants in the North Columbus area, however, was balanced by an equal number moving into the

TABLE 12—Number of Plants Having Moved from Area in Which Originally
Established, by Areas into Which They Moved

Area	Plants Established in Area[a]	Plants Having Moved from the Area		Moved to Present Site In:					
				North	South	Down Town	East	West	North West
	Number	*Number*	*PerCent*			*Number*			
North	53	14	26.4	—	4	1	0	2	7
South	23	3	13.0	1	—	1	1	0	0
Downtown	65	37	56.9	10	8	—	3	6	10
East	20	3	15.0	1	1	0	—	1	0
West	27	10	37.0	2	4	1	2	—	1
Northwest	16	1	6.3	0	1	0	0	0	—
Total	204	68	33.3	14	18	3	6	9	18

[a] Number now in the area that have been there since their establishment plus the number
that have moved out into other areas.

Source: Developed from Appendix Table 1.

area, 10 of which moved in from the Downtown area (Table 12).
Only 3 of the plants originally established in South Columbus have
moved to other areas, (Table 11, 12) while 18 plants established in
other areas have moved into the area, 8 of them from Downtown
Columbus, 4 each from North Columbus and West Columbus, and
1 each from the East and Northwest areas (Table 12). Although
almost one-half of the plants that moved out of Downtown Columbus (18 of 37) moved into North or South Columbus, 19 moved into
the other three areas; 3, into East Columbus; 6, into West Columbus;
and 10, into Northwest Columbus.

In the Northwest area, only 16 of the 33 plants in the area in
1953 were originally established in the area, and only 1 of these

TABLE 13—Number of Plants Having Moved into Other Areas, by Area
into Which They Moved, and by Areas from Which They Moved

Area	Number of Plants Moved into Area	Original Area Sites					
		North	South	Downtown	East	West	Northwest
North	14	—	1	10	1	2	0
South	18	4	—	8	1	4	1
Downtown	3	1	1	—	0	1	0
East	6	0	1	3	—	2	0
West	9	2	0	6	1	—	0
Northwest	18	7	0	10	0	1	—
Total	68	14	3	37	3	10	1

Source: Developed from Appendix Table 1.

moved from the area (into South Columbus), while 18 plants moved into the area from other areas, primarily from the Downtown area (10 plants), and the North Columbus area (7 plants).

The gains and losses in the East and West Columbus areas have been less pronounced, although there has been more movement into and out of West Columbus than into and out of East Columbus. However, in East Columbus 3 more plants moved into the area than moved out of it, while in West Columbus 1 more plant moved out than moved in (Table 11). Both West and East Columbus drew plants from the Downtown area; West Columbus, 6, and East Columbus, 3.

Flight from Downtown

From the foregoing analysis it is apparent that the North Columbus area and the Downtown area have been the sites for the location and development of many *new* enterprises. In these two areas, 67 and 68 plants, respectively, have been located at some time (Table 11). In 1953, the number in North Columbus had dropped to 53; in Downtown Columbus, to 31. The lesser decline in numbers in North Columbus was due primarily to the movement of plants into the area from the Downtown area. Of the 65 plants which were originally established in the Downtown area at sometime 37 or 57 per cent have left the area, and since 1940 only 6 newly established plants have entered the area. Of the 37 plants that moved from the Downtown area, about one-half of them moved into the contiguous North and South Columbus areas—10 into North Columbus and 8, into South Columbus. Three plants moved into East Columbus; 6 into West Columbus; and 10 into the Northwest area.

Size of Plants, 1953

The 204 manufacturing plants employed a total of 62,404 workers in 1953. The number represented about 80 per cent of the entire manufacturing force in Columbus, based on comparisons made with the estimates formulated by The Econometric Institute of New York City in their study of the Columbus Metropolitan area.[4] The

---

[4] Reports of the findings of The Econometric Institute, which undertook its study for the Columbus Chamber of Commerce, appeared in *The Ohio State Journal*, May 15, 1953, p. 1.

distribution of workers throughout the city is not even, nor is it closely correlated with the number of plants in the individual areas. Rather, it is related to the size of plants as measured by the number of workers employed, and the relative proportions of large and small plants within each area.

The three older industrial areas, North, South and Downtown Columbus, together had 60 per cent of the plants but employed only 46 per cent of the workers (Table 14). East Columbus with only 11 per cent of the plants employed 30 per cent of the workers, due primarily to the location of one large plant in the area, the North American Aviation plant, which alone employs over 17,000 workers. Similarly, West Columbus with only 12.7 per cent of the plants

TABLE 14—Number and Per Cent of Plants and of Employees, by Areas, 1953

Area	Plants		Employees	
	Number	Per Cent	Number	Per Cent
North	53	26.0	15,624	25.0
South	38	18.6	8,099	13.0
Downtown	31	15.2	5,126	8.2
East	23	11.3	18,850	30.2
West	26	12.7	10,571	16.9
Northwest	33	16.2	4,134	6.6
Total	204	100.0	62,404	100.0

Source: Compiled from Appendix Table 1.

employed 17 per cent of the workers, due to the location of two plants in this area employing more than 3,000 workers each. Northwest Columbus, on the other hand, with 16.2 per cent of the plants employed only 6.6 per cent of the workers, although there are 3 plants in this area employing from 500 to 750 workers.

Although both small and large plants are found in every area, there is a larger concentration of the smaller plants in the three older industrial areas, North, South, and Downtown Columbus. These three areas combined had 63 per cent of the plants in the 10-24 worker class; 53 per cent in the 25-99 class; 64 per cent in the 100-249 class, and 67 per cent in the 250-499 class (Table 15). Of the 122 plants in these 3 areas combined, 108 or 88 per cent employed less than 500 workers; 77 or 63 per cent, less than 100; and 30 or 25 per cent, less than 25.

TABLE 15—Number and Percentage Distribution of Plants, by Areas, by Number of Workers Employed

Area	Number of Plants	Number of Employees							
		10–24	25–99	100–249	250–499	500–749	750–999	1,000–2,999	3,000 or more
		Number of Plants							
North	53	16	18	8	3	1	4	2	1
South	38	6	20	6	2	1		3	
Downtown	31	8	9	7	5		1	1	
East	23	7	10	3	2				1
West	26	7	11	4	2				2
Northwest	33	4	20	5	1	3			
Total	204	48	88	33	15	5	5	6	4
		Per Cent of Total, by Size							
North	26.0	33.3	20.5	24.2	20.0	20.0	80.0	33.3	25.0
South	18.6	12.5	22.7	18.2	13.3	20.0		50.0	
Downtown	15.2	16.7	10.2	21.2	33.3		20.0	16.7	
East	11.3	14.6	11.4	9.1	13.3				25.0
West	12.7	14.6	12.5	12.1	13.3				50.0
Northwest	16.2	8.3	22.7	15.2	6.7	60.0			
Total	100.0	100.0	100.0	100.0	100.0	100.0	100.0	100.0	100.0
		Per Cent of Total, by Area							
North	100.0	30.2	34.0	15.1	5.7	1.9	7.5	3.8	1.9
South	100.0	15.8	52.6	15.8	5.3	2.6		7.9	
Downtown	100.0	25.8	29.0	22.6	16.1		3.2	3.2	
East	100.0	30.4	43.5	13.0	8.7				4.3
West	100.0	26.9	42.3	15.4	7.7				7.7
Northwest	100.0	12.1	60.6	15.2	3.0	9.1			
Total	100.0	23.5	43.1	16.2	7.4	2.5	2.5	2.9	2.0

Source: Compiled from Appendix Table 1.

Within these 3 areas, the greatest concentration of smaller plants was in the North Columbus area, followed by Downtown Columbus and South Columbus. The relatively large proportion of smaller plants in these areas account largely for the 60-46 ratio between percentage of plants and percentage of employees since of the 20 plants employing 500 or more workers, 14 are located in these three areas. In the East Columbus area with 11 per cent of the plants in the city and 30 per cent of the workers, 17, or 74 per cent of its 23 plants employed less than 100 workers, the largest percentage of workers being accounted for by one large aviation plant. Similarly, of the 26 plants in West Columbus, 18 or 69 per cent employed less than 100 workers, but 2 plants employed more than 3,000 workers.

Employment of Women

Of the 62,404 workers employed by the 204 plants in 1953, 13,661 or 22 per cent were women. Of the women employees, 28 per cent and 20 per cent, respectively, were employed in plants in the East

TABLE 16—Number and Percentage Distribution of Employees, by Sex, by Areas, and Within Each Area

Area	Number Employed			Percentage Distribution by Areas			Percentage Distribution within Each Area		
	Male	Female	Total	Male	Female	Total	Male	Female	Total
North	12,956	2,668	15,624	26.6	19.5	25.0	82.9	17.1	100.0
South	6,655	1,444	8,099	13.7	10.6	13.0	82.2	17.8	100.0
Downtown	2,943	2,183	5,126	6.0	16.0	8.2	57.4	42.6	100.0
East	15,011	3,839	18,850	30.8	28.1	30.2	79.6	20.4	100.0
West	7,745	2,826	10,571	15.9	20.7	16.9	73.3	26.7	100.0
Northwest	3,433	701	4,134	7.0	5.1	6.6	83.0	17.0	100.0
Total	48,743	13,661	62,404	100.0	100.0	100.0	78.1	21.9	100.0

Source: Compiled from Appendix Table 1.

and West Columbus areas. The heavy concentration of women employees in these two areas reflect the presence of the one large plant in the East area and the 2 large plants in the West area. North Columbus ranked third with 19.5 per cent of the women employees, followed by Downtown Columbus with 16 per cent of the total. Downtown Columbus is the only area in which its percentage of female workers is greater than its percentage of total workers, having only 8.2 per cent of all workers but 16 per cent of all women workers. In the Downtown area, 42.6 per cent of all the workers employed in manufacturing are women. In West Columbus slightly more than one-fourth (26.7 per cent) of all workers are women, and in East Columbus, slightly more than one-fifth (20.4 per cent). In the North, South, and Northwest areas, women workers constitute only about 17 per cent of the total.

CHAPTER V

MAJOR TYPES OF INDUSTRY AND INDUSTRY GROUPS IN COLUMBUS, 1953

Any scheme for the classification of industries into types and groups is fraught with difficulties. Nevertheless, some scheme of classification is essential to an orderly discussion of growth and change. The basic scheme adapted for this study was a relatively simple one. After the interviews with industrial representatives were completed, each plant was assigned to an industry group based upon either the *product* manufactured, or the *function* performed. Plants classified on the basis of the product manufactured include such plants as shoe factories, textile plants, industrial machinery manufacturers, etc. Plants classified on the basis of a process or function performed include those in such industries as forging, foundries, stamping and extruding, etc.—plants producing a great variety of unrelated finished items, but items related by plant function.

With this classification scheme as a basis, the 204 manufacturing plants employing 10 or more workers in 1953 were classified into five major industry types with a miscellaneous category to accommodate four plants which did not fall easily into any types, 22 major industry groups, and 10 sub-groups.

Industry Types and Groups

The five major industry types are: Chemical Industry; Metal Industry—Fabricating; Metal Industry—Processing; Shoe and Textile Industry; Wood and Paper Products Industry. The 22 major industry groups and the 10 sub-groups are shown in the stub of Table 17. With few exceptions, although important exceptions, the general structure of the industrial pattern in Columbus emerged during the last half of the nineteenth century. By 1900, at least one plant had been established in 23 of the major industry groups or sub-groups, and by 1906 every group was represented except the rubber products

TABLE 17—Year of Establishment of the Oldest Active Plant in Each of the Major Types of Manufacturing Industry Groups and Sub-Groups in Columbus, Ohio, 1953

Type and Industry Group	Number of Plants 1953	Year or Establishment of Oldest Plant	Type and Industry Group	Number of Plants 1953	Year or Establishment of Oldest Plant
Chemical Industry	35	1883	Metal Products: Processing	64	1852
Ceramic Products	4	1896	Forging Industry	5	1852
Chemical Products:			Foundry Industry:		
Fertilizer	4	1894	Iron and Steel	8	1880
Pharmaceuticals	4	1886	Non-Ferrous Metals	7	1850
Paints	4	1884	Machine Shop Industry	26	1893
Miscellaneous Chemicals	4	1883	Stamping and Extruding	9	1865
Dental Products	3	1903	Structural Steel	6	1885
Glass Products	5	1900	Ornamental Iron	3	1905
Plastic Products	3	1902	Shoe and Textile Industry	23	1865
Rubber Products	3	1933	Shoe Industry	9	1865
			Textile Industry	14	1899
Metal Industry: Fabricating	58		Wood and Paper Products	20	1880
Electrical Equipment	9	1906	Casket Industry	5	1880
Heating & Cooling Equipment	13	1859	Paper and Paper Containers	7	1890
Industrial Machinery	16	1865[a]	Furniture and Fixtures	8	1882
Tool & Implement Industry	4	1850[a]	Miscellaneous Industries	4	1877
Transportation Equipment			Pumps	1	1877
Aircraft	1	1950	Sucker Rods	1	1900
Automobile Parts	8	1894	Glues and Adhesives	2	1900
Fire Engines, Truck Bodies	6	1898			
Railroad	1	1905			

[a] Nearest approximate date.

Source: Appendix Table 1.

CHART 2—Year of Establishment in Columbus of the Oldest Active Company
in Each Industry Group or Sub-Group

SOURCE: Table 17

industries and the aircraft industry, the first plant in the former group having been established in 1933, and in the latter, in 1950 (Table 17 and Chart 2).

During the first half of the twentieth century new plants were added in all of the major industry types and groups but the expansion was more pronounced in some groups than in others. The relative importance in 1953 of the major types of industry as measured by the number of plants and the number and per cent of workers employed is shown below.

Type of Industry	Number of Plants 1953	Number of Workers	Per Cent of Workers
Metal Industry: Fabricating			
Including Aviation	58	42,438	67.9
Excluding Aviation	57[a]	25,398[a]	40.6[a]
Metal Industry: Processing	64	8,484	13.6
Chemical Industry	35	5,027	8.0
Shoe Industry	9	2,348	3.8
Textile Industry	14	2,224	3.6
Wood and Paper Products	20	1,763	2.8
Miscellaneous	4	205	.3
Total	**204**	**62,489**	**100.0**

[a] Not included in total.

Source: Appendix Table 1.

By 1953, the metal fabricating and the metal processing industries dominated the industrial scene. The 58 plants in the metal fabricating industries including the one large plant in aviation, employed 42,438 workers or about 68 per cent of the total number of workers. Excluding the large aviation plant, the 57 metal fabricating industries still employed the largest block of workers, 25,398 or 40 per cent of the total. The 64 metal processing plants employed 8,484 workers or 13.6 per cent of the total number of workers. Thus the metal processing and the metal fabricating plants, together constituted 60 per cent of the manufacturing plants and employed 81 per cent of the workers. The chemical industries with 35 plants and 8 per cent of the workers is the third largest group. The long established shoe industry with its 9 plants employs only 3.8 per cent of the workers, and the 14 plants in the textile industry, only 3.6 per cent. Wood and paper products together, with 20 plants, employ 2.8 per cent of the workers.

Size of Industry Groups

When the industry groups are arrayed on the basis of the number of workers employed, the top five groups are metal processing or fabricating industries—transportation equipment, elec-

TABLE 18—Major Industry Groups Arrayed by Number of Workers
Employed, Columbus, Ohio, 1953

Industry Group	Number of Plants 1953	Number of Workers, 1953			Average Number of Workers Per Plant
		Male	Female	Total	
Transportation Equipment					
Including Aviation	16	20,833	5,624	26,457	1,653
Excluding Aviation	15[a]	7,113	2,304	9,417	627
Electrical Equipment	9	5,446	2,255	7,701	855
Industrial Machinery	16	4,292	479	4,771	298
Foundries	15	3,422	133	3,555	237
Heating and Cooling Equipment	13	2,678	333	3,011	231
Glass Products	3	1,763	868	2,631	877
Shoes	9	993	1,355	2,348	260
Textiles	14	1,478	746	2,224	158
Stamping and Extruding	9	1,121	382	1,503	167
Forging	5	1,154	241	1,395	279
Machine Shops	26	1,203	154	1,357	52
Chemical Products	16	1,042	248	1,290	80
Paper Products	7	600	245	845	120
Plastic Products	5	500	205	705	141
Steel and Ornamental Iron	9	637	37	674	75
Furniture and Fixtures	8	490	47	537	67
Tools and Implements	4	433	65	498	129
Caskets	5	282	99	381	76
Miscellaneous	4	191	14	205	51
Dental Products	4	119	83	202	50
Ceramic Products	4	100	53	153	38
Rubber Products	3	28	18	46	15
TOTAL	204	48,805	13,684	62,489	306

[a] Not included in the total.

Source: Appendix Table 1.

trical equipment, industrial machinery, foundries, and heating and cooling equipment. The 69 plants in these five industry groups together constitute 33 per cent of the plants and employ 45,495 or 72 per cent of all workers (Table 18). The next three ranking groups are glass products, shoes and textiles, followed by the stamping and extruding industries and forgings, with machine shops and chemical products following closely. These top 12 industry groups employ 58,243 workers in 151 plants—93 per cent of the workers and 74 per cent of the plants.

The 10 smaller industry groups have their share of important and distinctive firms, however. The city's reputation in showcases, caskets, dental products, ceramic products, and in tools and implements is well known. These groups have achieved national distinction through the efforts of singularly outstanding firms. As a group they are not large employers, the average number of workers employed in each group, with the exception of the tools and implements group, being less than 100 (Table 18). In the main, these small-scale industry groups are made up of locally originated and locally owned firms. They make specialty products that are locally consumed for the most part. The dental products industry is an example. Three of the 4 firms in this group make teeth according to prescriptions furnished them by local dentists.

The 10 largest plants in the city as shown below employ 38,908 workers or 62 per cent of the total working force.

Establishment	Number of Workers, 1953	Year of Establishment
North American Aviation, Inc.	17,040	1950
Westinghouse Electric Corporation	5,275	1953
Timken Roller Bearing Company	4,134	1919
Ternstedt Division, General Motors	3,217	1946
Jeffrey Manufacturing Company	2,556	1876
Buckeye Steel Castings Company	1,861	1886
Kimble Glass Company	1,568	1932
Columbus Bolt and Forging Company	1,131	1852
Columbus Coated Fabrics Company	1,073	1900
Federal Glass Company	1,053	1900
Total	38,908	

Five of these 10 largest firms are among the industrial pioneers in Columbus having been established before or by 1900. They originated in Columbus and are essentially locally controlled. The two largest firms are relative newcomers to Columbus having been established since 1950. Two of the remaining 3 were established in the period between the two World Wars and the other, since World War II. These 5 firms are controlled by outside interests and their presence in Columbus indicates the growing and widespread interest in Columbus as an industrial center. The significance to Columbus of this post-World War II interest of outsiders in Columbus as a city in which to establish new plants is indicated by the fact that while outside interests to date control less than 20 per cent of the 204 plants, almost one-half of the total working force is employed in these plants.

It can be expected that the influence of national organizations upon the industrial growth and welfare of Columbus will continue to be great. National patterns in unions, in wage agreements, in minimum working standards, and in other phases of management-worker relations are but one phase of this influence. It will be felt as well in other fields—in the suburban movement of plants and population, in the development of modern one-story operations, and in wider contacts with national and international markets.

CHAPTER VI

THE METAL PROCESSING INDUSTRY

Included in the metal processing industry are 5 industry groups which produce semi-finished or finished metal parts for assembly or fabricating industries. The 5 industry groups comprising this major type of industry are: (1) forging, (2) foundries—iron and steel and non-ferrous metals, (3) machine shops, (4) stamping and extruding industries, (5) structural steel and ornamental iron plants. These are the basic metal producing industries. The 64 plants in these 5 industry groups employed 8,484 or 13.6 per cent of all manufacturing workers in the 204 plants in 1953, ranking first among the major industry types in the number of plants, and second only to the metal fabricating industries in the number of workers.

Many of the plants in this industry are among the oldest in the city. As shown in Table 19, 15 plants or 23 per cent of the 64 plants were established before 1900, and 28 of them or 44 per cent, before 1920. All 5 of the forging plants were established before 1914, and 4 of them, before 1900. During the period between the two world wars, 15 plants were established, new plants appearing in each of

TABLE 19—Metal Processing Industry: Number of Plants and Number of Workers in 1953, by Industry Groups, by Period of Establishment of Plants in Columbus

Industry Group	Number of Workers	Number of Plants	Period of Establishment					
			1946– 1953	1940– 1945	1920– 1939	1914– 1919	1900– 1913	Pre- 1900
			Number of Plants					
Forging	1,395	5					1	4
Foundries:								
Iron and Steel	3,324	8			3		2	3
Non-Ferrous Metals	231	7		1	2		2	2
Machine Shops	1,357	26	8	9	2	2	2	3
Stamping and Extruding	1,503	9	1		3	1	2	2
Structural Steel	633	6		1	4			1
Ornamental Iron	41	3	1		1		1	
Total	**8,484**	**64**	**10**	**11**	**15**	**3**	**10**	**15**

Source: Appendix Table 1.

the industry-groups except forgings. Since 1940, roughly the World War II and post-war periods, 22 additional plants (34 per cent of the total) have been added, 17 of which were machine shops.

The Forging Industry

There are no industries in Columbus that are older nor more stable than the Forging Industry. In 1957, the 5 plants in this group ranged in age from 57 years to 105 years. In June 1952, the Columbus Bolt and Forging Company celebrated its 100th year of successful operations in Columbus. The fact that no new companies have come to Columbus since 1900, however, suggests that the forces encouraging the early establishment of these industries in Columbus are no longer sufficiently strong to attract new industries of this type. The year of establishment of the individual firms in Columbus and the year they located at their present site are shown below.

Companies in the Forging Industry

Company Name	Area Location	Year Located: In Columbus	Year Located: At Site	Number Employed 1953
Berry Brothers Iron Works	North	1881	1881	65
Columbus Forge and Iron Company	North	1898	1898	96
Brightman Manufacturing Company	South	1895	1895	54
Columbus Anvil and Forging Company	South	1900	1900	49
Columbus Bolt and Forging Company	Downtown	1852	1852	1,131

Source: Appendix Table 1.

Plant Sites—The present building sites are those occupied by each company at the outset of its operations. This suggests something of the stability of the firms and of this industry in Columbus.

Three of the plants are on the fringe of the Downtown Area and one is within that area. The fifth, the Brightman Manufacturing Company, is part of the industrial concentration found beyond the southern limits of the city. Thus, these plants are in the older industrial sections. Their physical appearance confirms their age if not their productive capacity. All but the Columbus Bolt and Forging Company occupy one-floor structures; these are frequently red brick buildings which have had numerous additions. They are built to the street's edge and the landscaping common to the newer sections of the city is missing.

The only firm which could expand its operations on its present site is the Brightman Manufacturing Company. This firm has space available for limited expansion at its South Columbus site. The Berry Brothers plant is virtually hemmed-in by the Jeffrey Company; the Columbus Bolt and Forging plant has used all of its available ground. This has led one company to expand into multiple-story structures which inevitably result in higher operating costs. Storage and parking space are requirements which cannot be met easily.

According to representatives of two of these plants, if plant expansion programs were undertaken the firms would, of necessity, seek building sites beyond the present limits of the city. The land that is available for industry within the city is high-priced and generally unsatisfactory for large manufacturing organizations.

Factors in Location—The oldest company, Columbus Bolt and Forging, attributes its start in Columbus to the initiative and foresight of New England bolt-makers who came here at a time when the agricultural implement and railroad equipment markets were growing. A fine supply of labor and the availability of capital in Columbus were factors which permitted the development of the company. No doubt important in the success was the dominating position of Springfield, Ohio—at that time a leading forge center in the nation.

The other four companies were established here because of the close ties their founders had with this area. In every instance, the capital backing and the initiative of the early industrialists were prime factors in the firms' growth. Largely because of the expanding market in Ohio and neighboring states, the firms continued to grow and prosper. Production shifted from forgings for agricultural implement manufacturers and the railroads, to the manufacture of bolts, nuts, and screws for the buggy trade. Since 1900, the greater share of the market has been with the automobile industry.

Bonds—The forging companies are in no way parts of larger national organizations nor are there any strong relationships between these firms and any others in the city. Only the Berry Brothers Iron Works has developed any real bonds with other local firms. Its location on East First Avenue probably was due to the growth of

the Jeffrey Manufacturing Company. Berry Brothers began operations four years after the Jeffrey Company and has always sold a
large proportion of its finished goods to that firm.

Products—At the present time, the bulk of the forged products
is for the automobile industry. Brake rods, throttle rods, bumper
bolts, machine bolts, lug bolts, nuts, screws, and various truck
forgings are representative. In addition, forgings are made for the
mining machinery and conveyer industry, for road machinery, for
the electrical industry, and for the machine tool industry. Columbus
Bolt and Forging produces wrenches, pliers, tin snips, and other
hand tools. The Columbus Forge and Iron Company remains as the
only producer of forge anvils in the United States. The Brightman
Manufacturing Company specializes in nuts and bolts for railroad
equipment and farm implements. The finished products are usually
sold directly to the consumer who may further machine the forged
items. These companies do not compete since each engages in the
manufacture of its own specialities. Outside the city, competition
stiffens, especially in connection with the auto trade.

Markets—The Forging Industry serves two principal markets.
One is local—three plants sell forgings for mining machinery to the
Jeffrey Manufacturing Company. This accounts for approximately
50 per cent of the Berry Brothers' market. In addition, sales are with
Columbus Auto Parts, Seagrave Corporation, and General Motors.

Most of the market lies beyond the immediate region. This has
been cited as one of the principal handicaps to the industry's continued location here. The market is limited locally by the diversification of industries. Add to this the freight disadvantage which
these companies assert is encountered in the shipment of goods to
the major markets in Detroit and other Michigan cities, and it is
evident that Columbus' position has not improved relative to the
potential market.

A similar situation exists with raw materials. Because of these
handicaps, three of the forge plants would locate elsewhere if such
a possibility presented itself, and if business conditions permitted.
Detroit, Cleveland, Chicago, or Pittsburgh would be better locations
market-wise, or from the standpoint of raw material supply.

While Detroit is the biggest single market outside of Columbus, sales also take place in Cincinnati, Cleveland, Springfield, and other Ohio cities; in St. Louis, Philadelphia, and as far south as Atlanta, Georgia. The Columbus Forge and Iron Company carries on overseas trade as well but it is limited to what has become a minor product—forge anvils. Widely used in many "backward" nations, they are exported through a New York representative. Requests for drop-forgings from northwestern European and South American nations are frequent but little has been exported because of legal and technical difficulties encountered.

Raw Materials—The basic raw material is common steel which is purchased in Pittsburgh, Cleveland, Chicago, and Youngstown.[1] Alloys are purchased in Canton and Massillon. Practically no steel is procured locally since neither the quantity nor the variety is available from local warehouse stocks.

Transportation—Each plant is well-served by the railroads. Nearly all imported raw materials are transported by rail. In fact, one company has no adequate facilities for handling incoming materials by any other means. The Brightman Company, however, employs truck service for all shipments. The importance of trucking is a direct outgrowth of shipping costs. Those companies using rail facilities do so because of the large quantities of steel shipped in carload lots. In this case, the railroads provide lower freight rates than the trucking firms.

Many of the out-going products are shipped by truck for speed and convenience. On shipments to Detroit, truck transit takes about 12 hours and rail shipment between two to three days.[2]

Labor—One of the effects of the expansion of manufacturing in Columbus upon the older concerns in this industry is an increase in competition for labor. The labor force—95 per cent of which is native-born—attracts industry today as it has for the past 50 years. The older industries have followed a pattern of training their workers for jobs and can ill-afford to lose them. Since few men are actually skilled, this industry competes with others in the city for common labor.

[1] Columbus is a stop-in-transit point for steel: Pittsburgh to Columbus to Detroit (raw materials to processing to finished goods).

[2] Many truck shipments are at the insistence of the auto and truck industry which is anxious to sell this type of transit to other industries.

There are approximately 1,395 workers in the industry with over 1,100 of them on the payroll of the Columbus Bolt and Forging Company. The other four companies employ fewer than 100 workers each. About 240 women and 15 Negroes are employed. At an earlier date, the contract prison labor of the Ohio Penitentiary provided companies in this industry with a very low-wage force. The Columbus Bolt Works used this force and it is possible that the choice of its site, bordering the prison on the east, may have been related to its labor supply within the Penitentiary.

Work in the industry is heavy and hard but it is compensated by a fairly high wage. The average shop wage is about $1.90 an hour but the skilled workers, such as die setters, may earn up to $3.50 an hour. Generally, if the worker remains on his job from three to six months he will stay with the company. The Brightman Company has an old labor force that has been with the firm for many years. It is comprised of many good workers from the older German community in South Columbus.

New Firms—The labor problem is not the only one created by new concerns. In exchange for increased business and an enlarged local market, disadvantages have occurred in parking and housing. Many representatives of this industry believe that Columbus has experienced a rapid growth in industry without corresponding social growth. Inadequate housing and parking facilities, unsatisfactory highways, and delayed development in the extension of public utilities, have been the results of this expansion.

Utilities are generally satisfactory but two plants, the Columbus Anvil and Forging and the Columbus Bolt Works, supplement the city water supply with their own wells. Water shortages were experienced in South Columbus until an 18-inch main, installed recently, relieved the situation.

Prestige—As in the case of the Foundry Industry, to be discussed later, there is little prestige for an industry of this type in Columbus. Steel-making cities, such as Pittsburgh and Cleveland, are the present-day forge centers. Only through the services rendered by the local firms to primarily local industries has Columbus continued to maintain some of its early reputation as a center for the forging industry.

The Foundry Industry

The Foundry Industry like the Forging Industry was among the industries to develop early in Columbus, 5 of the 15 plants having been established before 1900 (Table 19) and another 4 plants added by 1914. Unlike the forging industry, 5 plants were added between 1920 and 1930, and another, during World War II. This industry, too, is a local-market-oriented, locally-initiated industry. Of the 8 iron and steel foundries and 7 nonferrous foundries in Columbus, all but one were started by local interests in anticipation of a growing market. While this is a relatively important industry in Columbus (ranking fourth in number of workers employed in 1953), the city does not at present have a wide reputation nationally as a foundry center. More than 40 years ago, however, when the Columbus foundries served a number of stove and furnace plants in central Ohio, the city did have prestige in this area. It was considered the eastern apex of a "foundry triangle" which had Indianapolis and Cincinnati at its other points.

Iron and Steel Foundries

Although iron and steel foundries were established in Columbus more than a hundred years ago, the oldest of the firms now operating, the M. Hertenstein Company, was established in 1880. Two additional foundries were added before 1900. Five of the 8 foundries were in operation by 1905, but two of the other three were established as late as 1936 and 1938. The foundries vary in size from 25 to 1,861 workers, with only 3 of the 8 plants employing 500 or more workers.

Plant Sites—Having been among the earliest of the industries established in Columbus, the plants, for the most part, are located in the older industrial areas of the city. Only 3 of them have moved from the original sites at which they were established. Two of these moved from the Downtown area; one, into South Columbus, and one, into the Northwest area. The third plant to change sites, the Buckeye Steel Castings Company, moved into South Columbus from its original site in North Columbus.

Four of the plants are in the heavy industrial South Columbus area. Bonney-Floyd began operations on Marion Road in 1904 when farm land was available there in large tracts at low cost. These

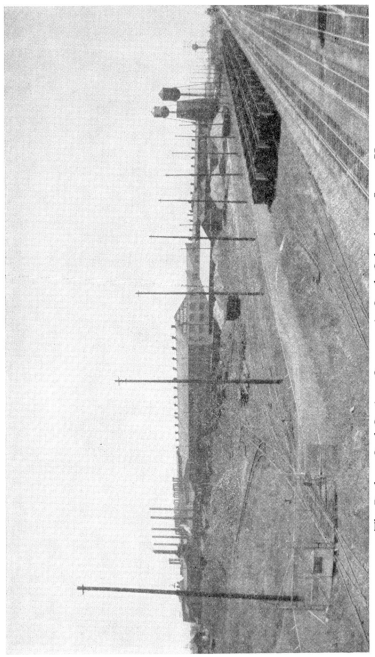

The Buckeye Steel Castings Company in South Columbus: a Large, Heavy Industry in an Old Industrial Area

Iron and Steel Foundries

Company Name	Area Location	Year Located: In Columbus	Year Located: At Site	Number Employed 1953
Ohio Malleable Iron Company	North	1902	1905	540
Columbus Co-op Foundry	North	1938	1938	12
M. Hertenstein Company	South	1880	1892	68
Buckeye Steel Castings Company	South	1886	1902	1,861
Chase Foundry	South	1896	1896	45
Bonney-Floyd Company	South	1904	1904	526
Columbus Malleable Iron Company	East	1936	1936	247
Poulton Foundry Company	Northwest	1921	1921	25

Source: Appendix Table 1.

advantages are now gone and cramped working conditions are common, but the site remains satisfactory. The Hertenstein Foundry is on family-owned land in South Columbus lying between South High Street and the Scioto River. Even though topography has dictated two levels of plant operation, the site has been satisfactory.

The Ohio Malleable Company moved to Fields Avenue in North Columbus in 1905 to expand its operations in what was then a non-residential area. Good railroad connections were available at this site within a few blocks of the Jeffrey Manufacturing Company. The small plants usually occupy older, one-story buildings. By the nature of the work—dirty, dusty, and smoky—the sites are not particularly attractive.

Factors in Location—Seven of the foundries were started through the initiative of local individuals. The growing stove, wagon, and machinery markets afforded potential trade. Local ties established at an early date were responsible for the success of some plants. The Ohio Malleable Iron Company sold foundry products to the Jeffrey Manufacturing and Kilbourne and Jacobs companies from 1900 on. Jeffrey purchased the foundry in 1905 to assure its supply of malleable iron chains and castings. About 30 per cent of all production in 1953 went to the Jeffrey organization.[3]

The Columbus Malleable Iron Company was organized by Cleveland interests. It is the only firm not controlled by Columbus interests. This plant, on Curtis Avenue, is an independent part of

[3] Late in 1953 the Ohio Malleable Iron Company was sold by the Jeffrey organization to the Dayton Malleable Iron Company.

the Lake City Malleable company which has other plants in Cleveland and Ashtabula. The Columbus plant was purchased in 1936 when an old foundry site was available for sale at a low price. With this purchase, the Lake City organization reduced competition in its field and strengthened its own structure.

There are no other strong industrial bonds but many of the smaller foundries serve the important local market. For years, the Poulton Foundry has done practically all of the cast iron work for the Weinman Pump Company. There have been ties with other pump manufacturers in the past.

Products—A variety of cast products is typical of the industry. Four of the firms produce gray-iron castings—the Hertenstein, Poulton, Chase, and Columbus Co-op plants; the Columbus Malleable and Ohio Malleable firms produce malleable iron castings; and the Buckeye Steel Castings and Bonney-Floyd companies make a variety of steel castings.

Castings for the railroad, automobile, mining machinery, and agricultural equipment industries dominate the production, but pumps, valves, chains, gears, die and tool parts, truck parts, tank car parts, and parts for the heating and cooling equipment industry, are also made. The bulk of these products is shipped directly either to a consumer who uses the casting as it is (the railroad industry, for instance), or to a processor who machines it for use in a finished product (the automobile industry).

Markets—The large foundries reach national and international markets. However, for the most part, shipments abroad are only "token" shipments except in the case of Buckeye Steel Castings Company which supplies car couplings to railroads in Europe, South America, and South Africa. The Columbus Malleable Iron Company has sold pipe-line joint castings to Middle Eastern nations for use in their oil fields and has recently shipped railroad castings to Venezuela for use on the U. S. Steel's railroads there.

Nationally, the Buckeye Steel Castings Company sells in a competitive market to any railroad building or repair shop. The Hertenstein Foundry supplies a number of stove manufacturers in Ohio and West Virginia with grey-iron castings. The Chase Foundry and Ohio Malleable Iron concentrate their sales in the truck and automotive fields. The former sells special castings to the manufacturers of special duty heavy trucks while 70 per cent of the latter firm's output goes to the auto industry. The Bonney-Floyd Company ships goods to agricultural equipment makers and to power shovel companies in a few large mid-western centers.

Competition—Competition exists among the small foundries but it is limited: each shop, for the most part, makes its own specialty items. When work is short, competition increases but it is "friendly." Each of the small shops has regular customers within an area not more than 50 miles from the foundry. These market-oriented firms, producing high-bulk, low-value products, are limited by unfavorable freight rates.

Competition among the larger firms is at the national level. The American Steel Foundry at Alliance, the Ohio Steel Foundry at Springfield, and Commercial Steel Castings and Alloy Steel Castings in Marion, are Ohio firms that offer direct competition in the larger domestic markets.

Raw Materials—Pig iron is supplied by Cleveland, Toledo, Pittsburgh, and Buffalo furnaces with secondary sources in Portsmouth, Middletown, Erie, Birmingham, and Daingerfield, Texas. The Hertenstein Company brought pig into the city from Germany, Scotland, Chile, and France; the Columbus Malleable firm brought it primarily from Germany during periods of shortages.

Some scrap steel is used in the open hearths of the Buckeye Steel plant and in the electric furnaces at Bonney-Floyd. This is usually obtained locally.

Coal and coke are brought in from western Pennsylvania and West Virginia. Sand, for use in forming molds, may be fine- or coarse-grained. Fine sands come from Galion, Sandusky, and Conneaut, Ohio, while the latter are obtained either locally or in New York. Some manganese comes here from Mansfield and one plant gets limestone from Missouri.

Transportation—The small firms transport their materials by truck. The larger companies use the railroads due to the greater quantity of bulk goods handled. The Buckeye Steel Castings Com-

pany ships practically everything by rail and it specifies rail shipments on incoming materials since the railroads are Buckeye's biggest
customer.

Labor—The 8 plants in this industry employ 3,324 workers.
Few women are employed. Negroes find ready employment, espe-
cially in the malleable and steel foundries, where work is heavy.
Almost 50 per cent of the workers in these foundries are Negroes.

Skilled foundrymen are scarce. Common laborers, ". . . such
as they are . . ." are available but they lack training. "Floaters," who
are unreliable and who create instability, are present. These men
shift from job to job, from plant to plant. The small plants do not
lose their best men, however, since loyalties to company and trade
are strong, generally. New industries moving into the city have not
taken the skilled foundrymen but they have absorbed much of the
untrained force.

Increased wage rates in the city have been the major effect of
the location of new firms. This is true not because of a scarcity
of workers but because certain plants heavily engaged in defense
work were permitted to raise their wages above the city's average
during the period of wage controls. The older, smaller companies
found it difficult to hold their workers under these conditions.
While the city has never been a strong union center, increased
industrialization has resulted in growing union strength. A final
consequence of recent industrialization has been a continuing decline
in the number of white foundry workers and the reduction of the
pool of partially trained workers.

Handicaps—Some apparent physical handicaps plague this
industry. Foundries in South Columbus have crowded sites and
suffer occasionally from a lack of sufficient water. Other plants
lack space for expansion or are housed in inadequate buildings.
More significant, however, is the relatively declining market in
Columbus for foundry products. Although some of the new companies entering the city have afforded some new markets, they have
not compensated for the decline in other areas. The absence of
manufacturers who utilize foundry products has handicapped continued growth of the industry.

Firms coming to the city within the last 15 years have influenced the expansion of supply and warehouse facilities in the city, however. Increased supplies are a benefit to the entire industrial community.

Utilities—Public utilities are normally satisfactory. Electricity is satisfactory although two companies supplement purchased power with their own. The Bonney-Floyd plant, said to be the biggest electric consumer in the city, receives very good service. A gas shortage during the winter months is a minor handicap that is being overcome slowly.

Nonferrous Metals Foundries

Of the 7 nonferrous metals foundries, 2 were established before 1900; the oldest, the Triumph Brass Company, as early as 1850. Two more plants were established in 1907, and after 18 years, a fifth, in 1925, followed by a sixth plant 11 years later in 1936. The seventh plant, the Industrial Aluminum Company, was established in 1945. In general, the plants in this industry are small. The largest, the Atlas Brass Foundry Company, employs around 90 workers, with the number of workers employed in the other 6 plants ranging between 10 and 40.

Plant Sites—With the exception of the Columbus Brass Manufacturing Company which moved from the North Columbus area into the Northwest area in 1952, the plants are located in the older industrial areas of the city, 3 of them in South Columbus, 2 in North Columbus, and one in East Columbus.

Nonferrous Metal Foundries

Company Name	Area Location	Year Located: In Columbus	At Site	Number Employed 1953
Simplex Foundry Company	North	1907	1925	10
Franklin Brass Company	North	1925	1927	31
Triumph Brass Company	South	1850	1919	23
Buckeye Pump and Manufacturing Company	South	1897	1913	40
Atlas Brass Foundry Company	South	1907	1907	91
Industrial Aluminum Company	East	1945	1945	15
Columbus Brass Manufacturing Company	Northwest	1936	1952	21

Source: Appendix Table 1.

The Atlas Brass Foundry Company and the Buckeye Pump and Manufacturing Company are in residential sections of South Columbus. They occupy residential dwellings which have been converted into plant and office space. The Triumph Brass Company, also in South Columbus, is relatively close to the Downtown area. The Franklin Brass Foundry in North Columbus and the Industrial Aluminum Company in East Columbus are both adjacent to the Pennsylvania Railroad yards east of Cleveland Avenue. Although the sites are not attractive the adequacy of the buildings compensates for the smoke, dirt, and noise. The Simplex Foundry in the North area is located on a small lot on Michigan Avenue in a one-story building. Being small-scale operations, many of these plants occupy buildings formerly housing nonindustrial businesses. The Industrial Aluminum Foundry is in a building originally used as a restaurant. The Columbus Brass Manufacturing Company occupies the former show rooms of the Lehman Lumber Company in Northwest Columbus. This company, the only plant to relocate recently, has a modern building and large lot, in sharp contrast to the small crowded facilities now occupied by the other plants—the Franklin Brass Foundry has a 30 foot square garage, and the Simplex Foundry Company, also, is housed in a crowded garage.

All but two of the plants, Industrial Aluminum and Atlas Brass, have had previous locations. Triumph Brass, the oldest company, first began operations in old Franklinton. The convict labor of the penitentiary, used to produce cast kitchen utensils, was a factor in its relocation near the penitentiary at one time. A number of moves to other sites were made before the present one on Wager Street was chosen in 1919.

While these companies are handicapped by crowding and poor physical facilities, the advantages of their locations with respect to markets, raw materials supply, and transportation services offer some compensation.

Products—Brass foundries dominate the group: 6 of the 7 firms produce brass castings. Four firms also produce aluminum castings, and one makes bronze and iron casts as well. The aircraft industry and the building-trades industry afford the major markets; castings for automobile and electronic equipment manufacturers are of lesser importance. In some cases, the rough castings go to machine shops before they reach the consumer. For the plumbing and contracting industry, wholesalers and distributors receive the castings directly.

Local Ties—All of the nonferrous foundries were promoted by the initiative and inventiveness of residents of Columbus. None has ties beyond the city. Five are entirely independent. The Industrial Aluminum Company, on the other hand, was purchased recently by the Columbus Dental Manufacturing Company, and the Triumph Brass Foundry was taken over by the Ebco Manufacturing Company a few years ago. Whereas Triumph makes practically nothing that is used by Ebco, the Industrial Aluminum Foundry makes a few products for the dental firm. No other ties exist currently although the Simplex Foundry had ties with the old Raney Company, making aluminum heads for the Raney carpet sweeper until 1922.

These firms would relocate here under present conditions. The strongest tie is the market. Curtiss-Wright was a major market during the war and Ranco, Incorporated and Exact Weight Scales remain important. North American Aviation offers the most important single market to the industry today. Competition is insignificant. Most shops have their own customers—machine shops which engage in sub-contract work for the aircraft and automotive parts concerns.

Markets—The majority of the plants reach a market throughout the central lake states although sales are concentrated largely within the Columbus area. Freight rates are a limiting factor in the extension of the sales territory—so much so that only one plant ships west of the Mississippi River or south of the Ohio River. Plumbing products are marketed in New York, Chicago, Louisville, and locally. Detroit, Pittsburgh, Toledo, Cleveland, Mount Vernon, Muskingum, and other cities within a 200-mile radius form the core of the market.

Raw Materials—Few raw materials are acquired in central Ohio. Brass ingot, rod, and sheet, are purchased in Chicago and Cleveland, and from outlets in Cincinnati, Detroit, Pittsburgh, Buffalo, and Waterbury. Aluminum ingot is purchased from the major aluminum producers in Chicago, Newark, Cleveland, and Cincinnati. Lead and zinc are brought here from Chicago and St. Louis whereas copper alloys are purchased in neighboring communities. Core and mold sands may be obtained locally or in Galion, Zanesville, or New York State. Pig iron and steel come from Pittsburgh.

Transportation—Generally, 90 per cent of the outgoing shipments are by truck but railroads are important for incoming shipments. Truck service is quicker and more efficient for the small company, and for local deliveries. Four companies have railroad spurs but they are rarely used and then only to handle sand or other bulk goods.

Public Utilities—All plants use city water but a few supplement this with their own wells which supply needed pressure for testing operations. The electric supply is generally adequate although two firms have had costly shutdowns due to power failures.

The fluctuating gas supply during winter months is another major complaint. Companies requiring gas for industrial operations or for heating are affected.

Public transit facilities and parking facilities are adequate for the small firms. A major handicap is the lack of properly zoned building space. Land is high-priced and good sites are scarce. None of the crowded firms can expand economically at its present site.

The Stamping and Extruding Industry

The stamping and extruding industry, like the forging and foundry industries, emerged in the post Civil War period, the oldest firm currently operating, the D. L. Auld Company, having been established in 1868. The next oldest firm now operating, the Buckeye Stamping Company, was established 34 years later, in 1902. The other 6 firms in this group were established at varying intervals between 1906 and 1946.

Plant Sites—The plants are located primarily in the older industrial areas of the city, with 3 in the Downtown area, 2 each in the South and West Columbus areas, and one each in the North and Northwest areas.

All but the most recently established plant, the Columbus Stamping and Manufacturing Company, established in 1946, have moved at some time from the sites originally occupied. Six of the 9 plants were originally located in the Downtown area. Two of

Stamping and Extruding Companies

Company Name	Area Location	Year Located: In Columbus	Year Located: At Site	Number Employed 1953
D. L. Auld Company	North	1868	1920	447
Buckeye Stamping Company	South	1902	1910	55
National Aluminum Company	South	1939	1948	49
Lilley-Ames Company[a]	Downtown	1865	1950	160
United Seal Company	Downtown	1906	1915	19
Capital Manufacturing and Supply Company	Downtown	1925	1937	250
B and T Metals Company	West	1938	1940	426
Columbus Stamping and Manufacturing Company	West	1946	1946	45
Banner Die, Tool and Stamping Company	Northwest	1918	1933	52

[a] Company ceased operations in Columbus after this study was completed.
Source: Appendix Table 1.

these have remained in the Downtown area, although they have changed sites within the area, and one plant moved into Downtown from South Columbus. Of the 4 plants moving from the Downtown area, one each went into the South, North, West, and Northwest areas (Appendix Table 1). Thus, the plants are scattered throughout the city, and have few important functional ties within the community. The Buckeye Stamping Company, however, responded to a Columbus market in 1910 when it relocated in expanded quarters in South Columbus to be near the Federal Glass Company. The Columbus Stamping and Manufacturing Company, originally a Chicago firm, located here in 1946 to be near its principal market, the Columbus Bolt and Forging Company. The B and T Metals Company has an interesting history. It began operations in the basement of the B and T Carpet and Linoleum Company on South High Street. The manufacture of metal stripping—used to hold linoleum in place—was a sideline to the flooring business. Gradually, this phase of the business increased to the point where competitors speak of the B and T organization as one of the most important extruders of aluminum in this country. The firm currently occupies expanded quarters in West Columbus.

The Lilley-Ames Company, once the largest manufacturer of fraternal regalia in the world, is now owned by the U. S. Chromite Company; it produces metal stampings for the military forces. Its location here 85 years ago was a result of an individual's choice. Lilley-Ames declined in importance as a manufacturer during the depression and abandoned its large, multiple-story buildings on East Long Street. Operations at the time this study was made were centered in a second floor on East Broad Street with scattered holdings in other sections of the city.[4]

The changes in the plant sites of other firms have occurred for expansion and modernization purposes. The D. L. Auld Company moved to its present site in 1920 when it doubled productive capacity in a change from the manufacture of jewelry to automobile and appliance name plates. The Banner Die, Tool and Stamping Company moved from the Downtown in 1933 to Northwest Columbus to gain more space in a less congested industrial area. And in the case of The National Aluminum Company, which occupies a large, single-story cement block building on Alum Creek Drive just a few feet beyond the city's limits, space for expansion and a lower tax rate undoubtedly played a role in location.

In contrast, the Capitol Manufacturing and Supply Company operates in an older, three-story building in the heart of the crowded industrial Downtown, and the United Seal Company uses upper floors of an old building in this area. In both cases, the availability of building space was a factor in location.

While relocations of plants within the city have been numerous, only one concern would consider leaving Columbus. Pittsburgh would be a better location for this firm since its raw materials are there and its major market is found in western Pennsylvania. On the other hand, most companies would not leave central Ohio but they might consider relocating their plants on the fringe of the city if only because adequate space within the city is missing.

Handicaps—Whatever handicaps exist are local. Most of these are outweighed by advantages of a national order. The Buckeye Stamping Company, in South Columbus, and the Banner firm, in the newly developed Northwest, both have inadequate transit service since they lie beyond the political city. With narrow streets and the absence of through-routes, auto and truck accessibility is hindered. Other public utilities are satisfactory, however.

[4] Since this study was completed, this company has ceased to operate in Columbus.

Advantages—The distinct advantage of Columbus is its access to national markets. Four firms sell to the automobile industry; Columbus is in an excellent position for them to reach this market. Two firms are ideally situated to meet the growing market in building and construction. Markets in appliances and other electrical equipment fields are within a few hundred miles. The relatively close source of steel, steel products, aluminum, and other raw materials is an added advantage. Fairly cheap, nonunion, and stable labor is present here, in comparison with many other Ohio communities. Labor is an increasingly important factor in the location of industry.

Markets—Competition for markets is not great locally but a number of competitors are within 100 miles of Columbus. The variety of products includes automobile stampings, name plates, tin cans, pipe fittings, rollers, various types of aluminum extrusions, metal seals, and miscellaneous products for the automotive, electrical equipment, and construction industries.[5] The markets vary—the Columbus Stamping and Manufacturing Company has nearly 60 per cent of its market here, but Buckeye Stamping, Capitol Manufacturing and Supply, United Seal, and B and T Metals companies concentrate their sales in the national market. Foreign markets are tapped, too, but they are not currently important. The D. L. Auld Company has a wide range of sales from the auto centers in Detroit, South Bend, and Toledo, and to the appliance manufacturers in the Miami Valley. Recently, the firm began the manufacture of aircraft parts for national distribution. The Banner Die, Tool and Stamping Company sells to the automotive market in the above named areas as well as in Cleveland, Pittsburgh, and Fort Wayne. Appliance sales are to producers in Dayton. Local sales now average 40 per cent of this firm's total compared to 75 per cent in 1942.

About 90 per cent of the shipments of goods is by quick and efficient truck service for the less-than-carload shipments which occur in this industry. Trucking is cheaper than railroad service for

[5] B and T Metals and The National Aluminum Company have engaged in the extrusion of plastics. At the present time, the production of plastic materials is said to be relatively insignificant.

this type product; the latter is rarely used. Representatives of the industry stated that railroad service was generally unreliable and time consuming.

Raw Materials—Raw materials are transported by truck in almost every instance. Steel products from Cleveland, Youngstown, Middletown, Sharon, Pittsburgh, Weirton, and Wheeling; brass from Detroit and New Jersey; and aluminum ingot and bar obtained from Kaiser in Newark as well as from national plants, are the basic raw materials. Plastics, obtained from chemical companies in the mid-west and east, are now being used to replace costly and scarce metals.

Labor—The industry employs about 1,500 workers with one-fourth women. Women can perform the simple stamping operations and thus replace males who have turned to other, higher-paying industries. One-third of the working force is Negro. This very high relative figure can be attributed to the hiring policy of one firm—B and T Metals. This firm, originally owned and operated by a white man, is now owned by Negroes many of whom were former employees.[6] Consequently, approximately 90 per cent of its working force is Negro. The other firms, combined, employ only 75 Negroes. Labor unions do not dominate this industry although bitter disputes have occurred in the past. The large unions have not gained control of the plants. It would seem, however, that a more intensive unionization will occur in the future since these firms are tied closely to the heavily unionized automotive and electrical equipment industries.

Many semi-skilled or trained workers have been lost to these industries through the lure of higher wages and attractive incentive programs. Increased operating costs and tighter competition for services have resulted.

The Structural Steel and Ornamental Iron Industry

The plants in this industry group produce no iron or steel but purchase these products from steel centers and fabricate them into

[6] Competitors in other parts of Ohio have many fine things to say about B and T. The present management has raised this company to a position of leadership in the aluminum extrusion industry.

structural steel shapes and ornamental pieces for a variety of uses.[7] The market for their products is predominantly local—Columbus and Central Ohio. Six of the 9 plants in this group produce structural steel parts, and 3 are ornamental iron shops. With the exception of one company, the Dresser-Ideco Company which employed around 400 workers in 1953, the plants are all small. They are all located in the older industrial areas of the city, and only 4 of them have moved from the sites on which they were originally established.

Structural Steel and Ornamental Iron Companies

Company Name	Area Location	Year Located: In Columbus	Year Located: At Site	Number Employed 1953
Structural Steel				
Columbus Steel Industries, Inc.	North	1920	1920	10
Dresser-Ideco Company	North	1921	1921	408
Porcelain Steel Building Company	North	1934	1934	51
C. E. Morris Steel Company	East	1885	1905	48
Federal Steel Fabricating Company	East	1942	1942	31
J. T. Edwards Company	West	1932	1942	85
Ornamental Iron				
Artcraft Ornamental Iron Company	North	1937	1945	13
Buckeye Wire and Iron Company	West	1905	1935	13
Columbus Metal Craft Company	West	1946	1946	15

Source: Appendix Table 1.

The Structural Steel Companies

The oldest company, The C. E. Morris Steel Company, has been in Columbus since 1885; the two most recently established, the J. T. Edwards Company and Federal Steel Fabricators, Incorporated, since 1942. The Dresser-Ideco Company is the largest in the group. It also reaches the widest market and produces the greatest variety of products. Originally producing oil derrick equipment, the company has concentrated heavily upon satisfying the growing needs of the television, radio, and aircraft industries for aerials, towers, beacons, and hangars. Whereas the majority of the smaller

[7] Although Ohio ranks second in the nation in the production of steel, Columbus has not had a primary iron and steel industry since 1927 when the American Rolling Mill Company (Armco) moved its facilities from the city to Hamilton, Ohio. Even in 1927, Columbus offered no market for the blast furnace products. The furnaces moved to Hamilton for integration with the Middletown mills.

firms are limited to an Ohio market, Dresser-Ideco sells its products throughout the world through this local plant as well as through branches in other parts of the country.

Two other plants reach a national market; they serve those parts of the nation in which their parent company operates. The Porcelain Steel Buildings Company, a subsidiary of the White Castle System, and the Federal Steel Fabricating plant, a subsidiary of the Universal Concrete Pipe Company, are not of local origin. The White Castle System has small restaurants in eastern and mid-western cities. In 1927, it undertook to build a porcelain steel building to house the restaurants. With the success of this experiment, the Porcelain Steel Buildings Company came into existence. The organization moved to Columbus in 1934 since Columbus was centrally located for the entire system. The availability of raw material and a reasonably low-wage labor force were added incentives.

The Federal Steel Fabricating plant in East Columbus makes reinforced concrete frames. The plant was located here as part of the company's expansion of a local machine shop. Operations are tied to the functions of the parent firm.

The C. E. Morris Steel Company, the J. T. Edwards Company, and Columbus Steel Industries, Incorporated, are local concerns that fabricate and cut steel for bridges, buildings, and other construction. Competition is heavy since markets are limited to an area within 100 miles.

Raw Materials—Pittsburgh is the principal source of structural, bar, and sheet steel. A few of the smaller concerns purchase steel from local warehouses with Chicago, Cleveland, and Dayton, secondary sources. During a critical shortage, steel was brought here from Japan.

Most companies transport by truck but Dresser-Ideco relies upon rail shipment. Generally, truck service is cheaper, quicker, and more convenient for the small organizations which are not able to handle carload lots.

Labor—Six hundred and thirty-three workers are employed by the structural steel firms (about 400 of them by Dresser-Ideco, which is also the only firm with a union). Few skills are required of any worker since physical labor is the prime requisite. Workers are easily trained to cut steel beams and to weld or rivet parts and sections. Labor is readily available but many plant supervisors said that the average worker is a "floater"—consequently, labor turnover and absenteeism are high. This situation is due, in large part, to the low wages.

Effects of New Plants—Such new firms as North American Aviation and General Motors have had a beneficial effect upon this industry. The demand for supplies of raw materials has caused increased warehousing and stockpiling in the city. This has benefited the smaller firms which were unable to demand this service in the past.

Utilities—Utilities are fairly satisfactory. The Morris Steel Company, on Curtis Avenue, has suffered numerous power failures, however. These have been particularly serious in this part of the city: other Curtis Avenue firms report similar trouble with electric power. Inadequate public transit service and poor parking facilities create difficulties at the Dresser-Ideco and Morris plants. Both are in old industrial areas.

The Ornamental Iron Companies

These 3 small, locally-owned shops have a market that is distinctively local. Two of the shops are in West Columbus and one in the North Columbus area. Each produces finished ornamental iron work either of standard stock or for the custom trade. Competition is strong but Columbus is a good location because of the growing market which has accompanied new home construction.

With the exception of inadequate gas service to the Artcraft Ornamental Iron Company in North Columbus, utilities are good. The two West Columbus firms, Buckeye Wire and Iron and the Columbus Metalcraft Company, are in old residential areas where space is cramped. The Artcraft firm has a modern building, attractively landscaped and decorated with ornamental iron.

Summary

The Structural Steel and Ornamental Iron Industry has no strong ties in Columbus. Only the Dresser-Ideco, Federal Steel, and Porcelain Steel Buildings companies have outside interests. Their positions here have resulted from policies dictated by their parent firms. The location of Columbus with respect to markets and raw materials is the principal factor which explains their success.

The Machine Shop Industry

The machine shop industry represents the ultimate stage in the metal processing industry. The primary function of the machine shop is that of further refining or machining metal parts produced by the forging, foundry, or stamping plants. The early establishment of machine shops in Columbus accompanied the establishment of forges and foundries. Three of the 26 active machine shops were established before 1900, and 4 others were added by 1920. Seventeen or 65 per cent of the 26 shops have been established since 1940, 9 of them during the war period, and 8 in the postwar period (Table 19). This rapid increase in the number of machine shops since 1940 reflects the war-time expansion in the operations of Columbus industries, the postwar location of large branch plants in the city, and, particularly, the opening of the North American Aviation plant in 1950.

Plant Sites—The 6 oldest shops, those established before World War I, were all established in the 3 older industrial areas, North, South, and Downtown Columbus, and although each has at some time moved from its original site, none has moved out of the area in which it was originally established. Of the 2 shops in the Downtown area, one was established in 1911; the other, in 1917. From the earliest days, the greatest concentration of shops has been in the North Columbus area. Of the 3 shops established before 1900, 2 were in this area (the other, in South Columbus), and currently, 9 of the 26 shops are here, 5 of them having been established since 1940. These shops, on East Fifth Avenue, are relatively near the North American plant. The next two areas of greatest concentration with 5 shops each are South Columbus and Northwest Columbus. All of the shops in the Northwest area have been established since 1940, and 3 of the 5 in South Columbus. Of the 4 shops in West Columbus, 3 have been established since 1940. Of the 17 shops established since 1940, 12 of them have moved from their original sites but most of them have remained in the same area. Most of the shops are in one-story cement block buildings on small lots, and the need for larger quarters has been a factor in the frequency with which sites have been changed.

Origin of the Shops—Most of the shops are locally originated and locally owned. Many of the owners have other businesses which

Machine Shops

Company Name	Area Location	Year Located: In Columbus	Year Located: At Site	Number Employed 1953
Hearn Die, Tool and Machine Company	North	1893	1893	22
Capital Die, Tool and Machine Company	North	1897	1928	21
Columbus Die, Tool and Machine Company	North	1906	1914	104
Modern Tool, Die and Machinery Company	North	1915	1950	41
Advance Tool, Stamping and Die Corporation	North	1940	1942	24
Ohio Machine Products, Incorporated	North	1943	1948	55
Central Automatic Company	North	1944	1948	10
H. L. Klein and Company	North	1946	1951	37
Stanwood Industries	North	1949	1949	16
Leukhart Machine Company, Incorporated	South	1896	1948	148
Superior Die, Tool and Machine Company	South	1928	1952	67
H. and E. Machine Company	South	1944	1949	11
Art-Mil Machine and Manufacturing, Incorporated	South	1949	1949	57
Metalcrafters, Incorporated	South	1950	1952	83
Central Ohio Welding Company	Downtown	1911	1930	20
Thurman Machine Company	Downtown	1917	1942	96
Wright and Company	East	1941	1944	10
Columbus Engineering Company	West	1938	1940	130
Buckeye Engineering and Manufacturing Company	West	1943	1949	15
General Machine Products Company	West	1951	1951	29
Mid-West Machine Company	West	1951	1951	131
Accurate Manufacturing Company	Northwest	1942	1945	27
Capital Machine Company	Northwest	1942	1948	90
Hatco Corporation	Northwest	1942	1946	41
Thompson Metal Fabricating Company	Northwest	1951	1952	42
Capital City Manufacturing Company	Northwest	1952	1952	30

Source: Appendix Table 1.

represent their permanent investments; the machine shops are "sidelines," or temporary but profitable business ventures to be engaged in so long as the market lasts. Quite a few of the owners have at some time been employed at either the Jeffrey Manufacturing Company or at the Timken Roller Bearing Company in Columbus. They had saved money during the war years, and this, coupled with their own initiative and ingenuity, started them on their way. Only one firm was organized in another community. It moved here from Dayton because an important new market was recognized and labor relations were more favorable.

Products and Markets—The important products of these shops are parts for the local aircraft industry. Drilling, grinding, shaping, or cutting operations are performed on parts supplied to the shops by the aviation company. The machine shop is commonly a part of a sequence of operations as it machines foundry or forge products. Often the part is not finished when it leaves the machine shop. Some finishing and final assembly work may take place at the North American plant. Automobile parts—including roller pins, bearings, nuts, screws, and special tools and machines—are of secondary importance. Some sub-contracting work takes place for General Motors, usually involving tank parts for the Cadillac tank plant. A firm such as the Thurman Machine Company, an old Columbus machine shop, may also manufacture its own line of products, in this case industrial scales and precision instruments. Six of the firms are tool and die specialists but emphasis is currently on products for the aircraft and automobile industries.[8]

Raw Materials and Transportation—Machine shops operate on direct contracts from manufacturers. The companies handling sub-contracts under government orders have no choice in the materials they work with nor do they transport these goods. In dealing with North American Aviation Company under government contracts, a company truck delivers the raw materials to the shop and picks up the finished, machined parts when the order is ready. Absolutely no substitution of materials is permitted and samples for inspection must be prepared with each batch. While such supervision is difficult, it relieves the small shop of many responsibilities; it need not purchase nor transport goods.

Advantages and Disadvantages—The only advantages not enjoyed by these firms are on the local level. They operate in crowded buildings, have limited access to railroad facilities, and are victims

[8] Included are: Modern, Tool, Die and Machinery Company (1915), Capital Die, Tool and Machine Company (1900), Columbus Die, Tool, and Machine Company (1906), Superior Die, Tool and Machine Company (1928), Advance Tool, Stamping and Die Corporation (1940), and Thompson Metal Fabricating Company (1951).

of crowded streets. This latter fact applies especially to the firms on East Fifth Avenue. Access to market is an advantage and the availability of raw materials within 200 miles of the city by excellent rail and highway transportation is an important consideration. The labor picture is not so favorable, however.

Labor—About 1,200 men and 150 women work in the machine shops. Two plants employ only 10 workers whereas the largest shop has 148 employees. The skilled machinist is hard to find. Such a worker may be required to set up and operate a screw machine which may perform five to seven different timed operations upon one part. Work at lathes and milling machines may be carried on by semi-skilled workmen but a high degree of accuracy is required on aircraft and automobile parts so that partially trained workers are often handicaps. In addition to the screw machines and lathes, drill presses, milling machines, planes, and borers are used. The skills are required in setting-up the job, adjusting the tools, and checking the over-all operation.

Women are used at light tasks and those requiring patience. Most companies prefer not to use women but the shortage of qualified males makes their employment necessary. The competition of new firms and new industries has caused many skilled men to leave these small machine shop companies.

Specific Markets—The importance of North American Aviation as a market has been emphasized although General Motors, Surface Combustion, Ranco, Denison Engineering, Armstrong Furnace, American Blower, and others, also use the machine shops for sub-contract work. While there is little contact with the national market, some work may be done for companies in the immediate central Ohio area.

Raw Materials—Local warehouses are sources for steel, brass, and aluminum since the needs of this industry are for sizes and shapes commonly stocked. Steel requirements are further met in Cleveland, Dayton, Pittsburgh, Youngstown, and Chicago. Iron, brass, and aluminum castings are made locally. Practically all shipments, incoming and outgoing, are by truck. Less than 5 per cent of the commodities move by rail. This indicates the nature of the products: high-value, low-bulk items that are shipped short distances and meet deadlines. It also attests to the convenience of easier handling and lower costs.

Bonds—No bonds exist beyond Columbus and there are few ties within the city. The Machine Shop Industry is, in a sense, a service industry and its expanding operations, perhaps temporary in part, have developed to meet the growing industrial demands of Columbus.

CHAPTER VII

THE METAL FABRICATING INDUSTRY

Included in the metal fabricating industry are 5 industry groups which produce a variety of finished products, primarily from metals. The industry groups are (1) electrical equipment, (2) heating and cooling equipment, (3) industrial machinery, (4) tools and equipment, and (5) transportation equipment. These 5 industry groups in the metal fabricating industry dominate the manufacturing picture in Columbus, the 58 plants in the industry employing 43,438 workers in 1953, or 68 per cent of all workers in the 204 plants employing 10 or more workers. Within the industry, transportation equipment including North American Aviation employing 17,040 workers, is the dominant group with the 16 plants in the group employing 26,457 workers, or 60 per cent of all workers in the metal fabricating industry. The electrical equipment group ranks second within the industry with 7,700 employees, and industrial machinery, third with 4,770 employees.

A larger percentage of the individual plants within this industry is controlled by outside capital than in any other group since many of the more recently established plants are branches of larger corporations. This industry, more than any other perhaps, has given Columbus a place of prominence in the national industrial picture, and has contributed largely to industrial growth on a broad front. The Jeffrey Manufacturing Company and the Jaeger Machine Company, two of the oldest companies in the group, are known throughout the world, while many of the other firms have gained national reputations. The variety of products manufactured—no two plants make the same product—has kept Columbus from becoming a one-industry city, and this diversification has tended to enhance the industrial stability of the city.

Growth of the Industry

By the turn of the century, 9 of the plants still operating had been established and all of the 5 groups except electrical equipment

TABLE 20—Metal Fabricating Industry: Number of Plants and Number of Workers in 1953, by Industry Groups, by Period of Establishment of Plants in Columbus

Industry Group	Number of Workers	Number of Plants	Period of Establishment					
			1946–1953	1940–1945	1920–1939	1914–1919	1900–1913	Pre-1900
			Number of Plants					
Electrical Equipment	7,701	9	2	2	3		2	
Heating and Cooling Equipment	3,011	13		3	6		1	3
Industrial Machinery	4,771	16	3		6	4	1	2
Tools and Implements	498	4	2		1			1
Transportation Equipment (Total)	26,457	16	3	1	3	2	4	3
Total	43,438	58	10	6	19	6	8	9

Source: Appendix Table 1.

were represented by at least one plant (Table 20). By the close of 1913 or roughly before the outbreak of World War 1, 8 additional plants were established including 2 in the electrical equipment field, 4 in transportation equipment, and one each in industrial machinery and heating and cooling equipment. During the five years 1914-1919, 6 more plants were established, 4 in industrial machinery and 2 in transportation equipment. In the period between the two World Wars (1920–1939), 19 plants were added, 6 plants each in industrial machinery and heating and cooling equipment, 3 plants each in electrical equipment and transportation equipment, and one in tools and implements. Since 1940, roughly the World War II and post-war periods, 16 plants or 27 per cent of the 58 plants in the industry have been established or located in Columbus, the 3 largest since the end of the war—the Ternstedt Division of General Motors in 1946; North American Aviation in 1950; and Westinghouse Manufacturing Company in 1953.

The Tool and Implement Industry

Because this is an old and locally established industry that has only recently come under the influence of a national organization, it is discussed first. It is one of the few prestige industries in the city and, as such, was one of the first to give the city a national reputation.

Background of the Industry in Columbus—There is, in a sense, an old world quality to the growth of the Tool Industry.[1] The factors which usually explain the expansion of an industry do not apply to this one in Columbus. The Tool Industry requires relatively long apprenticeship before the worker becomes a skilled craftsman. A parent company, such as was the Ohlen-Bishop Company, the earliest tool maker in Columbus, frequently serves as a training school for skilled craftsmen. Thus, where there is an increased demand for tools, a "splintering" of the parent company may occur from time to time and a few craftsmen, with initiative and capital at their command, may organize their own companies. In turn, when the demand for the tool product expands further, the new company may experience the same "splintering" effect as some of its trained workers break away to establish their own businesses with a limited line of products.

The Tool Industry, a small one but with roots established in Columbus before the Civil War, has experienced just such a growth. The Ohlen-Bishop Company, which began operations in 1852 underwent many such "splinterings" (Chart 3). The three firms which now manufacture saws trace their location in Columbus to the presence of the older firm. The fourth company in this industry, the Union Fork and Hoe Company, has not been so related in its production of hand garden and farm tools.

The Ohlen Company began as a small family organization. A number of partnerships were formed before the Ohlen-Bishop name became familiar and the company's progress fluctuated. At

Tool and Implement Companies

Company Name	Area Location	Year Located: In Columbus	At Site	Number Employed 1953
Union Fork and Hoe Company	North	1860[b]	1907	233
Peerless Saw Company	South	1931	1931	24
Rockwell Tools, Incorporated[a]	Northwest	1951	1951	217
Blade Saw Company	Northwest	1946	1946	24

[a] A subsidiary of the Rockwell Manufacturing Company of Pittsburgh. It was purchased from the Ohlen-Bishop Company in 1951 (see also footnote 2).
[b] Nearest approximate date available.

Source: Appendix Table 1.

[1] The Tool Industry, as defined here, is restricted to those firms which manufacture saws and hand garden and farm implements. The Machine Tool Industry is separately discussed in the section on the Machine Shop Industry.

CHART 3—The Saw Industry: An Example of Splintering in an Industry

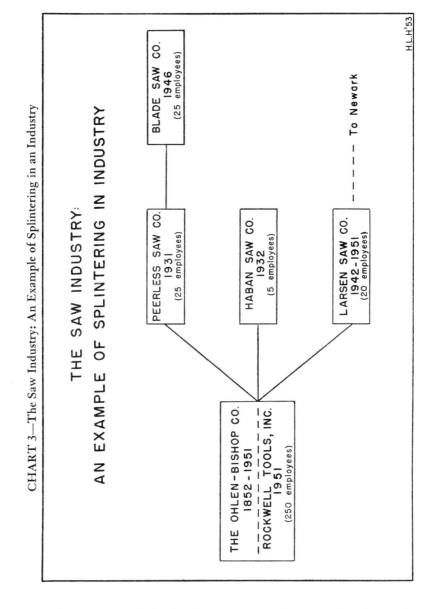

THE SAW INDUSTRY:

AN EXAMPLE OF SPLINTERING IN INDUSTRY

BLADE SAW CO.
1946
(25 employees)

PEERLESS SAW CO.
1931
(25 employees)

HABAN SAW CO.
1932
(5 employees)

LARSEN SAW CO.
1942-1951
(20 employees)

– – – – – To Newark

THE OHLEN-BISHOP CO.
1852-1951
– – – – – – –
ROCKWELL TOOLS, INC.
1951
(250 employees)

H.L.H.'53

times, it was one of the leading saw manufacturers in the nation but there were other periods of near failure. The firm built a modern plant, scientifically designed by Battelle Memorial Institute, on

Kinnear Road in Northwest Columbus in the post-war period, but in 1951 the business was sold to Rockwell Tools, Incorporated, a branch of the Rockwell Manufacturing Company of Pittsburgh.[2]

The other two saw companies located in Columbus have stemmed from the Ohlen-Bishop firm. The Peerless Saw Company, established in 1931, was started by five former employees of the Ohlen-Bishop Company. They located here because it was their home town and their restricted finances limited a further move. The company now specializes in high-quality saws for wood, non-ferrous metals, and plastics. Whereas the original market was local, sales are now national.

A "splintering" of Peerless Saw Company by some of its original owners gave rise to the Blade Saw Company in 1946. The firm located in Northwest Columbus in an available building on West Third Avenue. The local market is now of little consequence for this firm. Two other splinterings also have occurred: the Larsen Saw Company of Newark was originally started in Columbus and the Haben Saw Company was organized and continues here, employing less than 10 workers.

The Union Fork and Hoe Company has had no connection with the Ohlen-Bishop organization but its early history is connected with the early industrial operations of the Ohio Penitentiary. The company is one of many local firms that used cheap contract prison labor prior to 1900. Since 1907, the firm has been incorporated and has occupied a site on Dublin Avenue in the heart of an old industrial community in North Columbus. It suffers from many of the handicaps that other firms face in the older areas—parking space and expansion space are at a minimum. The 1907 incorporation resulted from the consolidation of the local plant with a New York firm. Columbus was chosen for the center because its location for marketing finished products and for buying ash timber and steel was ideal.

Advantages of the Location—Accessibility to raw materials and markets is an advantage enjoyed by all of these firms but this is permissive as a force: the impelling force in their locations was the influence of the established firms in the city. Since local sales

[2] Rockwell subsequently closed this plant and sold the property to The Ohio State University in 1955.

are minor, a national market is reached through jobbers or whole-sale hardware outlets. The Blade Saw Company produces saws for tool kits which are assembled by national distributors under various trade names. Rockwell Tools sent a large share of its production to its Delta Manufacturing Division for inclusion in similar kits. Competition among the firms exists locally and on a national level.

The Union Fork and Hoe Company has a market concentrated in central United States. Competition with the True-Temper organization of Conneaut, Ashtabula, and Geneva, Ohio, is keen. A sister plant, in New York state, markets tools and implements in the New England and Middle Atlantic states and a third plant, in Jackson, Mississippi, serves the south and southwest.

Raw Materials—Various steels used by Rockwell Tools and the Blade Saw Company are obtained from Pittsburgh and Ohio mills. Peerless Saw buys most of its steel from the Jessop Steel Company of Washington, Pennsylvania. For high-quality band saws, however, Swedish steel is purchased. The lumber for saw handles comes from Indiana, generally.

The Union Fork and Hoe Company buys steel in Pittsburgh and Ohio. The availability of ash wood was a principal factor in the firm's location and is still a major raw material.

Labor—Sufficient skilled labor is not now present. This situation is recent and has been aggravated by the arrival of new manufacturing concerns in Columbus. The saw companies cannot attract apprentices since their future is uncertain and the four to six years training does not seem worthwhile. At one time, labor was a principal advantage since Ohlen-Bishop trained large numbers in their trade. There are about 500 workers in the Tool and Implement Industry with nearly one-half employed by the Union Fork and Hoe Company. This firm's demand for labor is seasonal, with the low period in the summer. The Peerless Saw and Blade Saw companies each employ about 25 steady workers.

Bonds—The Tool Industry, with 100 years of successful operations, is highly specialized and for many years was a very stable industry. Local bonds are weak today yet the present stature of the saw companies can be traced to the influence of the Ohlen-Bishop organization upon plant location. In an industry-group where the influence of outside capital has been a dominant characteristic, the Tool Industry has been largely a Columbus-oriented industry.

The Industrial Machinery Industry

Whereas the Tool Industry can trace its development to its close orientation to Columbus, probably no other industry owes so much to the early inventive genius of its pioneers as does the Industrial Machinery Industry. Of the 16 firms, 13 have evolved from local inventions and entrepreneurship.

It is doubtful whether these inventions would have been made or that the industry would have succeeded were it not for the geographical position of Columbus in the heart of a state where minerals, agriculture, and manufacturing were so amply developed. The coal mines of Ohio inspired the ideas that resulted in coal-mining machines and conveying equipment, such as that made by the Jeffrey Manufacturing Company. The need for roadways and construction equipment resulted in the inventions of earth-moving equipment and cement mixers, such as produced by the Jaeger Company. The ever-present desire to produce more economically, moved men to invent. A sterile state does not inspire creative minds. Ohio challenged thinking; Columbus and other cities profited. In addition to the fertile mind and creative hand, geographic and economic factors in Columbus were favorable for the initial development and growth of this industry.

Age and Plant Sites—The oldest of the firms in this group, the Kilbourne and Jacobs Company, was established in 1865; the newest, Industrial Nucleonics Company, in 1950. The Jeffrey Manufacturing Company, the second oldest firm in the group was established in 1876. It was 27 years before the establishment of the Jaeger Machine Company in 1903 gave Columbus a third establishment in this field. The Exact Weight Scales Company was established 13 years later in 1916, and the other 12 companies, at more frequent intervals throughout the period since 1916.

All of the older plants have moved within the city to improve their sites, in fact only 5 of the 16 companies occupy their original sites and 4 of these have been established since 1935. A number

Industrial Machinery Companies

Company Name	Area Location	Year Located: In Columbus	Year Located: At Site	Number Employed 1953
Cream Cone Machine Company	North	1948	1948	40
Eldred Company	North	1946	1946	15
Jaeger Machine Company	North	1903	1910	943
Jeffrey Manufacturing Company	North	1876	1888	2,556
Kilbourne and Jacobs Company	North	1865	1870	151
Krouse and Jacobs Company	North	1937	1941	26
Bonded Scale and Machinery Company	South	1932	1936	42
American Solvent Recovery Corporation	East	1919	1919	82
Capital Elevator and Manufacturing Company	West	1918	1923	42
Miller Glass Engineering Company	West	1935	1935	62
Columbus Conveyor Company	Northwest	1919	1920	27
Denison Engineering Company	Northwest	1935	1942	439
Exact Weight Scales Company	Northwest	1916	1930	113
Industrial Nucleonics Company	Northwest	1950	1950	113
Pfening Bakery Machinery Company	Northwest	1927	1937	35
Scott Viner Company	Northwest	1926	1951	85

Source: Appendix Table 1.

remain relatively close to the crowded industrial Downtown area but a few have pioneered the movement to suburban districts of light manufacturing. The Exact Weight Scales Company was the first plant to make this move. It moved in 1930 into a one-story, brick structure set back from the street and with a well-landscaped lawn in the Northwest industrial area, leading the way to other industrial buildings of this type in the area. The spacious, one-story Denison Engineering plant erected in 1942 on Dublin Road is another example, as are the new plants of the Industrial Nucleonics and the Scott Viner companies erected in 1950 and 1951, respectively, also in the Northwest area. The plants are located primarily in the North and Northwest industrial areas, 6 in each area, with 2 plants in the West area, and one each in the South and East areas.

Products—A variety of machines is assembled here. Portable industrial machinery—wheelbarrows, conveyors, concrete mixing equipment, harvestors, and elevators—are manufactured by six firms. Stationary machinery and equipment—scales, air purification systems, bakery machinery, hydraulic oil presses, nut and screw machines, various testing devices, and even ice cream cone-making machines—are made by ten firms.

The Exact Weight Scales Company, a Pioneer Manufacturing Plant in Northwest Columbus

Portable Machinery Producers—The oldest firm, the Kilbourne and Jacobs Company was founded in 1865 to manufacture wheelbarrows for the farm trade. A complete line of industrial hand trucks was developed as the company expanded; it emerged as one of the largest manufacturers of these items in the world. Competition was strong: 17 firms now manufacture hand trucks and 12 others produce wheelbarrows. New York City has been the major national market for hand trucks (40 per cent of the sales) with Ohio an important local market. This firm was closed in 1953; its plants and facilities were integrated into the Jeffrey Manufacturing Company. This gave the latter firm increased plant space south of its main plant and the right to patents and designs that had been exclusively Kilbourne and Jacobs'.

The Jeffrey Company was organized in 1876, an outgrowth of the inventive genius of F. J. Lechner, who invented a coal-mining machine, and the organizing ability of Joseph Jeffrey, who supplied the capital for the successful development of the machine. It is the largest manufacturer of coal-mining machinery in the world. The unplanned location in Columbus has proved remarkably successful since the mining markets of the east and west are economically reached. In addition to mining machinery, chains, conveyors, industrial machines, hand trucks, and other mining equipment are produced. The Jeffrey Company is the best example of integration in Columbus. To assure its supply of malleable castings and chain, the Ohio Malleable Iron Company, north of the Jeffrey plant, was purchased about 50 years ago.[3] The Galion Iron Works, in Galion, Ohio, was absorbed by Jeffrey to gain a manufacturing outlet for road-building machinery and to eliminate competition in the manufacture of conveying equipment. Direct linkage appears between Jeffrey and the Berry Brothers Iron Works. The latter firm, while independent, is surrounded by the Jeffrey plant and sends approximately 50 per cent of its production to the larger firm. Integration at the market has taken place with the expansion of Jeffrey's marketing facilities in Great Britain and South Africa. This extensive integration program has given Jeffrey stability in production and marketing.

[3] This operation has been sold recently to the Dayton Malleable Iron Co.

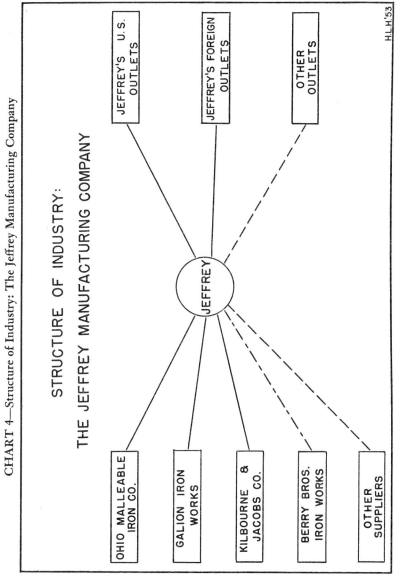

CHART 4—Structure of Industry: The Jeffrey Manufacturing Company

STRUCTURE OF INDUSTRY:
THE JEFFREY MANUFACTURING COMPANY

JEFFREY'S U.S. OUTLETS

JEFFREY'S FOREIGN OUTLETS

OTHER OUTLETS

JEFFREY

OHIO MALLEABLE IRON CO.

GALION IRON WORKS

KILBOURNE & JACOBS CO.

BERRY BROS. IRON WORKS

OTHER SUPPLIERS

H.L.H.'53

Two other firms started by natives who foresaw a growing market, manufacture conveyor equipment. The Columbus Conveyor Company was organized in 1919 to build custom-designed conveying equipment to move bulk materials. Many of its products mirror the inventive genius of its founder. The Bonded Scale and Machinery Company organized in 1932, has a diversified line including industrial scales, conveyors, vibrators, and crushers. Limited competition exists between these companies and Jeffrey. Nationally, the Joy Company of Franklin, Pennsylvania, competes with all of them in mining machinery. (Joy is a former employee of the Jeffrey Company.) The Columbus Conveyor Company restricts its sales to eastern United States but the Bonded Scale Company sells to a national and international market.

The Jaeger Machine Company began in 1903 to manufacture a cement-mixing machine—a tilting drum type of portable mixer—which was invented by the owner. With the support of local capital, the firm grew and prospered. Cement mixers, pneumatic drills, concrete spreaders, and other road-building equipment are produced for a world-wide market. Competition exists in Ohio with such firms as the Davey Compressor Company in Kent, and the Barrance Company and the Gorman-Rupp firms in Mansfield, but the major competitors are in New Jersey, Wisconsin, and Iowa. The Jaeger firm purchased control of a Cleveland competitor a few years ago and has moved that company's operations to Columbus.

The Capital Elevator Company and the Scott Viner Company also manufacture portable machinery. The first was founded in 1913 by a man who had earlier worked for an older local company that made elevators. He put his skills and money together and founded this business. With its dependence upon Columbus capital, the firm remained in the city and developed a market within an area of 300 miles. As a branch of the construction industry, it manufactures and installs industrial and passenger elevators and dumb waiters.

The Scott Viner Company, a manufacturer of agricultural implements, was started in Cadiz, Ohio, and later moved to Columbus, Wisconsin. A local plant was built in 1926; the present modern building was erected in Northwest Columbus in 1951. This was one of the first firms to make a pea viner and a sugar beet harvester; these are still important lines. Competition is stiff nationally with the International Harvester Company and the King-Wise firm the major competitors. The company also manufactures canning machinery for the processing of foods, sales of which are limited to the urban centers in the east and mid-west.

Stationary Machinery Manufacturers—Of the companies producing stationary machinery, the Exact Weight Scales Company founded in 1916, is the oldest. It was organized by a native of central Ohio who invented the over-and-under scale for use in repetitive weighing in food processing and most packing plants and in the chemical industries. A national market is reached with limited competition coming from Toledo Scales in Toledo.

The American Solvent Recovery Corporation, manufactures air purification equipment for the food processing industry and others. It was founded by natives who were backed by local capital. Located in East Columbus, the factory serves an area including Ohio, Michigan, and Pennsylvania.

Three small concerns, which have located here since 1935, can also trace their origin to the inventiveness of their owners. The Krouse Testing Machine Company produces machines to test the strengths of metals. They are used in testing laboratories in universities and in the automobile, aircraft, and steel industries. While the company did not start here, it moved to Columbus in 1937 when opportunities for increased financing and suitable space were made apparent.

The Eldred Manufacturing Company is a small plant that makes a large machine which bevels or glazes the edges of glassware. Mr. Eldred developed this idea while employed at the Federal Glass plant in South Columbus. His own company was formed in 1946. The machines, which take months to build, are sold throughout the world—they are found in operation in Brazil, Colombia, Mexico, Germany, Greece, and other nations. Carefully built, checked, and assembled before shipping, the finished machine is usually accompanied by Mr. Eldred who aids in its installation and in the training of operators.

One of the newest companies, and one which has created much interest locally and nationally, is the Industrial Nucleonics Corporation. It was organized in 1951 by two Ohio State University graduate engineers who found a way to use Beta rays (given off by an atomic pile) for testing the quality of continuously-produced steel, rubber, or paper. The company has grown rapidly with an expanding market. Its location in Columbus was based upon three factors: (a) the men are natives of the city and graduates of the university, (b) the plant is well-situated to serve the rubber markets of Akron, the steel markets of Ohio and Pennsylvania, and the paper markets of the Miami and Scioto valleys, and (c) the research facilities of the Battelle Memorial Institute and The Ohio State University are close at hand.

Another example of local inventiveness, initiative, and capital combining to succeed is the Denison Engineering Company. Organized in Delaware, Ohio, in 1931 where its pioneer work with hydraulic oil presses attracted wide attention, the company moved to Columbus when fire swept the original factory. The Budd-Ranney plant in Columbus, which had done machine work for Denison, was purchased at this time. Today, the firm occupies a modern and extensive factory on Dublin Road in Northwest Columbus. It experiences no local competition although similar presses are manufactured nationally. It has expanded sales and operations in this country and northwestern Europe.[4]

The three remaining firms, while utilizing local initiative and capital, have not developed from inventions in this area. The Pfening Bakery Machinery Company is an outgrowth of a salesman's knowledge of the machinery he sold and of the market potential. The company started here in 1930 as the owner knew the community and was able to raise money here. It is one of two such concerns in the nation; the other firm, in Albion, Michigan, is the largest. The market is scattered and it varies in size, but 3,000 bakeries across the nation are potential customers. About 20 per cent of the total sales are with Canadian firms, no similar machines being made there.

The Miller Glass Engineering Company, once a principal fabricator of glass-making machinery, now produces automatic nut machines. The machine was developed by the Budd-Ranney Company

---

[4] In June 1955, Denison Engineering Company was purchased by The American Brake Shoe Company as part of its diversification program.

and its basic ideas are employed in current models. Specialized nut machines are made to order. For example, the Ford Motor Company wanted a machine to make the nut which is used to hold Ford's spare tire in place. The Miller Company made this machine—the only one of its kind. The company's sales are national although centered in the manufacturing belt stretching from New York to Chicago.

A unique firm in the city is the Cream Cone Machinery Company which came here in 1946. A Cleveland firm founded in 1908, it manufactures machines for making ice cream cones in conjunction with its production of cones. Its market is very restrictive. Columbus was chosen for the plant site because a building was available in an area where labor was cheap and raw materials handy.

Handicaps—There are no common handicaps of location in this industry although individual firms may experience some special handicap. Public transit service is not adequate for a plant beyond the city limits (Scott Viner, Denison Engineering), nor is sufficient space for expansion by a firm in an older industrial area (Jeffrey Manufacturing Company), but the handicaps do not apply to the entire group.

Advantages—In contrast, the situation of Columbus in the nation affords many advantages. These companies enjoy a favorable freight rate in shipping their high-value, high-bulk products from this point. The proximity to major markets and accessibility to raw materials are two more reasons why the area has attracted new plants.

The research facilities of Battelle Memorial Institute and The Ohio State University are distinct advantages for plants which do not have the capital to support their own laboratories. These research organizations have become increasingly important factors in the location of industry. Although they are rarely impelling forces, they do influence development. As research needs increase with the future, the full value of such organizations will be realized by many other small Columbus firms. No doubt the research facilities of the university and the Battelle Memorial Institute will provide incentives to national industries as well. A last advantage, and one that will become intensified as industry expands and diversifies, is the growing market in the immediate central Ohio region. It is a market still not served economically by other manufacturing areas.

Raw Materials—Raw materials are varied but less than 10 per cent are purchased in the city. Steel is most important. Columbus warehouses supply 8 companies, with Pittsburgh, Cleveland, Middletown, Chicago-Gary, and Youngstown the important supply centers for the others. Most iron castings are purchased in the city; some come from Marion. The Jeffrey Company has its own brass foundry and its former subsidiary, the Ohio Malleable Iron Company, produces iron castings. Less important are aluminum and brass castings which are supplied locally.

Most of the machines are power-operated: motors come from Westinghouse, General Electric, and Master Motors distributors. Electric controls made by General Electric, Westinghouse, and Minneapolis-Honeywell are used widely. Power plants and diesel units are purchased from Chrysler, Continental, Hercules, and General Motors. Some local firms produce their own motors, however, because other manufacturers cannot meet their specific and changing needs. Rubber products, such as belting and tubing, come from Akron or from local warehouses. Lumber has decreased in importance with changes in the industry but it is supplied from sources in the Appalachians or on the west coast.

Transportation—Approximately 75 per cent of the shipping is by truck but the three largest companies prefer rail service. Commonly, where carload shipments are required, rail service is more economical. Railroads maintain a strong position in this industry with its nation-wide and export markets. The long hauls are more economical by rail.

For the smaller firms, trucks are most satisfactory. They are more convenient, require less dock space, can be easily loaded, and are ideal when speed is a requisite. A few firms whose finished product requires special handling have their own trucks.

Labor—Only three concerns regard the labor supply as adequate. Even though a major part of the work is assembling, there must be skilled machinists available to make the specialized and intricate products which will become integral parts of a working machine.

The small shops require a great amount of individual initiative which is not found in the average worker nor in the labor pool which is currently available. The large shop, while not requiring as much initiative, seeks the skilled worker because he is a more economical worker in the long run.

The industry as a whole employs about 4,700 workers with over half of them at the Jeffrey plant. Other large companies include the Jaeger Machine Company (943), Denison Engineering (439), Kilbourne & Jacobs (151), Exact Weight Scales (113), and Industrial Nucleonics (113).

Unions—Unions are not prevalent although they are active in three of the four largest plants. The increase in the number of new firms locating in Columbus has tended to tighten the labor market and tended to increase union activity.

Functional Bonds—Nine companies operate as the only unit in their organization, but 7 have immediate bonds, or are branch plants. No other company has the extensive ties of the Jeffrey Company, but the Jaeger Machine Company, until recently, operated branches in European countries. Most of these have been consolidated or lost due to the war. Exact Weigh Scales has a small branch in Toronto, Canada. The American Solvent Recovery plant is closely associated with the Barneby-Cheney Company of this city.

The Heating and Cooling Equipment Industry

Like the Industrial Machinery Industry, this industry owes much to the initiative and inventiveness of natives of Columbus. Unlike the Industrial Machinery Industry, however, the number of large branch plants which are members of this industry is high. With 5 national firms and 8 local concerns, the Heating and Cooling Equipment Industry is a mixture of local and national firms combining to give the city an established reputation.

The state of Ohio is the leading manufacturer of heating and cooling equipment in the nation. Columbus is a leading center of production with 5 of the 25 larger firms in the state located in the city. Smaller concerns are also present; they help to give character to the industry.

Age and Plant Sites—Three plants in this group were established before 1900; the oldest of these, Borger Brothers Boiler Works, in 1859, was followed by Columbus Heating and Ventilating Company in 1874, and F. O. Schoedinger Company in 1890. No plants have been added to this group since 1945 when Buckeye Furnace Pipe Company was established in the North industrial area, and Norman Products Company, in the Northwest.

Heating and Cooling Equipment Companies

Company Name	Area Location	Year Located: In Columbus	Year Located: At Site	Number Employed 1953
Quad Stove Company	North	1904	1904	22
Surface Combustion Company	North	1931	1931	840
Columbus Stove Company	North	1939	1939	75
Buckeye Furnace Pipe Company	North	1945	1945	68
Lattimer-Stevens Company	South	1920	1927	90
Oran Company	South	1937	1937	74
American Blower Company	South	1938	1938	471
F. O. Schoedinger Company	Downtown	1890	1921	93
Borger Brothers Boiler Works	East	1859	1946	20
Columbus Heating and Ventilating Co.	West	1874	1937	69
Armstrong Furnace Company	Northwest	1928	1947	502
Lennox Furnace Company	Northwest	1940	1940	559
Norman Products Company	Northwest	1945	1945	128

Source: Appendix Table 1.

Eight of the 13 companies in the group remain at their original sites. The 3 oldest companies have moved from their original sites but only one of them, Borger Brothers Boiler Works, moved out of the industrial area in which it was established.

One concentration of plants occurs in Northwest Columbus where the Lennox Furnace, Armstrong Furnace, and Norman Products companies are located. This is the new industrial development lying between the University and the Arlington residential district. The 3 plants are modern and spacious one-floor plants, set back from the street. Through attractive landscaping which enhances the appearance of their brick buildings, they have helped to form the nucleus of an important industrial community lacking the unfavorable appearance of many of the older industrial sections.

A minor concentration of plants is found in South Columbus where the Lattimer-Stevens, Oran, and American Blower companies are located within a few blocks of one another. The latter two plants

have been in the area only since 1937 and 1938, respectively; Lattimer-Stevens located on Marion Road in 1927. The buildings are
fairly modern and large but their attractiveness is diminished by
their surroundings in this old, crowded, and dirty industrial area.
Four companies remain on their original scattered sites in the North
Columbus area—Surface Combustion, Buckeye Furnace Pipe, Quad
Stove, and Columbus Stove, and the F. O. Schoedinger Company
remains in the Downtown area where it was established in 1927.
These 5 companies as presently located do not have space for future
expansion. They are in older buildings, commonly more than one
story in height and uneconomical to operate. The scarcity of parking space presents a problem also.

Products—Among the important products produced are domestic coal, gas and oil heating equipment. Various space and aircraft
heaters, conversion burners, gas ranges, automatic and barometric
draft controls, boilers, pipe fittings, and complete ventilating systems
are also made. Refrigeration and air conditioning equipment is
manufactured by the American Blower Company, which also makes
dust collectors and drives for refrigerator units.

Markets—The finished products are sold to a consumer market
by dealers and jobbers. No company enters the retail trade, but sales
are made to other manufacturers, to mail-order houses (such as
Montgomery-Ward), and to contractors.[5] The sales territory is
limited by the high-bulk, relatively low-value product.

The change from the coal furnaces to the gas and oil unit has
influenced local production. The Armstrong Furnace Company, the
largest producer of coal furnaces in the United States, has noted
a considerable drop in the demand for them. Much of the blame
for this is placed upon the costly coal strikes of recent years. The
cost of coal has steadily risen whereas gas and oil costs have remained
relatively stable. The Armstrong Company has supplemented the
loss by increased concentration in the gas and oil lines.

Shifting Markets—A geographical shift in the market has occurred. The Norman Products Company has enjoyed a large
business in gas conversion units especially in the south and south-

[5] Through such sales, some Columbus-made products commonly lose their identity
in the nation-wide markets.

west. Similarly, the Quad Stove Company's market has shifted from the mid-west to the growing southern market. Some companies are limited in their sales by their parent organization. This is true, for example, of the Lennox Furnace Company which confines all of its sales to the area west of the Ohio-Pennsylvania border since the eastern market is handled by its Syracuse, New York plant. In general, Columbus, at the junction of coal, gas, and oil facilities, and near the population center of the nation, is an excellent location for marketing these commodities.

Canadian sales are handled by three firms but overseas shipments are rare due to the bulk of the furnaces. For these reasons and because of competition with Canadian manufacturers, foreign sales are limited.

In addition to domestic and foreign sales, certain members of this industry have engaged in work on government contracts for space heaters for aircraft, tanks, and other military equipment.

Competition—The local firms compete but the major competition is from the Holland Furnace and the Bryant Furnace companies in Michigan, the Champion Furnace Company in Indiana and Illinois, the Olson Furnace Company in Sandusky, and other large firms. Stove manufacturers in Delaware, Newark, Mansfield, Hamilton, and Cleveland, offer competition. The Columbus Heating and Ventilating Company, which manufactures entire heating systems for schools, encounters strong competition in this somewhat specialized field.

Factors in Location—There have been two reasons for the location of these factories in Columbus: the smaller, native-owned plants were located to reach a local market, and the larger branch plants came here where greater production and procurement, through consolidation, permitted them to produce at lower costs for a national market.

With the Armstrong Furnace, Lennox Furnace, Buckeye Furnace Pipe, American Blower, and Surface Combustion companies, all branch plants, a consideration of their place in the structure of their parent companies was foremost. The first three are members of the Norris Industries of Iowa. The Armstrong plant, originally in London, Ohio, was moved here in 1928 to take advantage of

Columbus' labor supply. Excellent transportation facilities, favorable freight rates,[6] and an accessible supply of sheet steel at the Pittsburgh base price, were other factors involved.

In 1940, the Lennox Furnace Company occupied its large one-story factory on the Olentangy River Road to consolidate the company's operations. Favorable transportation to the highly competitive mid-western markets was a major permissive factor in this choice. Armstrong and Lennox then occupied adjoining buildings, but in 1947 the Armstrong Company moved to its new plant on West Third Avenue. By 1945, the Buckeye Furnace Pipe Company was organized for the express purpose of manufacturing pipe fittings and as another step in the consolidation of the Norris Industries in this area.[7] Buckeye Furnace has expanded its production considerably. The Armstrong and Lennox plants are competitors even though members of the same parent company. The only material gain resulting from the concentration of the three factories in Columbus has been in quantity purchasing of raw materials. Other bonds are weak.

The Surface Combustion Company, with its home plant in Toledo and other branches in New York, sought a location favorable to the sale and transportation of gas heating products in an area where freight rates were satisfactory. Columbus met these needs in 1930 at a time when a building was available.

The American Blower Company is one of the few large concerns in Columbus which located here primarily because of an available building. The city was regarded as a good rail center and a central shipping point, but it was the availability of a suitable building at a time of need that was a major factor in location. This firm is a subsidiary of the American Radiator Corporation in Detroit and was established in Columbus in 1938.

Raw Materials—Accessibility to raw materials is an outstanding advantage. While the city produces no light-weight sheet steel and stocks very little, this basic material is being obtained readily in Pittsburgh, Weirton, Wheeling, Youngstown, Middletown, Cleve-

[6] Freight rates are currently a major factor in the successful location of a plant. Railroad rates have increased by 76 per cent in the last seven years.

[7] Lennox earlier had manufactured pipe fittings.

The Armstrong Furnace Company: A Modern One-Story Plant in Northwest Columbus

land, and Gary. Gray iron castings are purchased locally and from foundries in Cleveland, Detroit, and Bloomington, Indiana. The Armstrong Company receives castings from a former Norris subsidiary in Jackson, Ohio. A variety of blowers and thermostats are used but Minneapolis-Honeywell equipment is best known; for these, Minneapolis, Detroit, and Cleveland are supply centers. Brass valves and brass products required by Quad Stove and Columbus Stove, are obtained in Cleveland, Detroit, Pittsburgh, and Chicago. The Johns-Manville organization in New Jersey supplies the asbestos required by the Columbus manufacturers.

Transportation—In the past ten years trucks have taken over much of the railroad's business. Eleven firms have good rail facilities with spurs on the Chesapeake and Ohio, Pennsylvania, or New York Central lines, but they ship 75 per cent of their goods by truck since smaller than car-load lots make up the majority of their shipments. Truck service is rapid and convenient. Recently, too, more customers specified truck shipment to ease their unloading problems and to assure quick service to distant points. Representatives of this industry asserted that more considerate public relations by the railroads serving Columbus would insure a greater volume of business in the future.

Utilities—Public utilities are satisfactory. New water mains in South Columbus and in the newly-settled Northwest have satisfied longstanding needs. The Columbus and Southern Ohio Electric Company provides adequate electric power. It has been most cooperative in an effort to meet industry's needs. Criticism of the gas supply has been voiced, however, and costly bottled gas has had to supplement the natural gas supply during critical winter months for some firms.

The Transportation Equipment Industry

A transportation equipment industry has been active in the city since the period in which the great carriage industry developed. The carriage industry was highly successful but with the changing market was replaced by the automobile and automobile parts industries. Since 1905, and until recent years, Columbus also achieved a national reputation in the manufacture of railroad cars. More recently the aircraft industry has been added to the field.

The transportation equipment industry is the fourth most important industry in the State.[8] In Columbus, where 26,457 persons are employed, it is the largest industry. Included in this group is the manufacture of aircraft (exclusive of engines), automobile parts, truck bodies, fire engines, and railroad freight cars. Both local and national firms are represented in the industry. It is another industry that has given Columbus a new national importance in manufacturing. The number of plants and workers in each of the industry groups at the time this study was made, and the periods during which the firms were established in Columbus are shown below.

Transportation Equipment Industry

Industry Group	Number of Workers	Number of Plants	Period of Establishment					
			1946–1953	1940–1945	1920–1939	1914–1919	1900–1913	Pre-1900
			Number of Plants					
Aircraft	17,040	1	1					
Automobile Parts	8,840	8	1		1	2	3	1
Fire Engines, Truck Bodies	447	6	1	1	2			2
Railroad Cars	130	1					1	
Total	26,457	16	3	1	3	2	4	3

Source: Appendix Table 1.

There is no single unifying feature that characterizes this industry. Plants vary in size from the truck body shops with fewer than 20 employees to the giant North American Aviation plant, largest employer in the city, with more than 17,000 workers. Also, the influences and factors promoting or retarding the growth of the several industry groups within the transportation field differ widely. This difference is reflected in the relative stability and permanence of automobile parts manufacture as compared with the declining importance of railroad freight car manufacture, and the uncertainty in the aircraft field. It is not known whether the nation's largest manufacturer of military aircraft is permanently located in Columbus, and the decline in railroad demand for freight cars has already lost for Columbus the national reputation that it once held in this field. Because of this diversity of factors affecting the transportation industries each major type will be discussed separately—aircraft (one

[8] *Ohio: An Empire Within an Empire* (Columbus: Ohio Publicity and Development Commission, 1950), p. 29.

plant with 17,000 workers), Railroad Freight Cars (one plant with 130 workers), and Automobile Parts, Fire Engines and Truck Bodies (14 plants with 9,287 workers).

Age and Plant Sites—Of the 16 companies in the transportation equipment field, the two oldest are the American Auto Parts Company established in 1894, and the Seagrave Corporation, in 1898. Two other companies were established in 1900—Clark Grave Vault Company and the A. L. Schodorf Company. The first decade of the century saw 2 additional plants established—The Ralston Steel Car Company in 1905 and Columbus Metal Products, Inc., in 1909. Four of the companies have been located in Columbus since the end of World War II—Stallman Gear Manufacturing Company

Transportation Equipment Companies

Company Name	Area Location	Year Located: In Columbus	Year Located: At Site	Number Employed 1953
American Auto Parts Company	North	1894	1939	19
Clark Grave Vault Company	North	1900	1922	855
Columbus Auto Parts, Inc.	North	1912	1927	494
Stitt Ignition Company	North	1916	1923	12
Timken Roller Bearing Company	North	1919	1919	4,134
Hoffman Auto Body Service	North	1923	1923	17
Seagrave Corporation	South	1898	1900	332
Henri La Prise and Company	South	1937	1952	49
Ralston Steel Car Company	East	1905	1905	130
Santeler Brothers	East	1933	1941	25
North American Aviation, Inc.	East	1950	1950	17,040
A. L. Schodorf Company	West	1900	1925	25
Stallman Gear Manufacturing Company	West	1945	1949	19
Timmons Metal Products, Inc.	West	1946	1949	29
General Motors Corp. (Ternstedt Div.)	West	1946	1946	3,217
Columbus Metals Products, Inc.	Northwest	1909	1948	60

Source: Appendix Table 1.

in 1945, Timmons Metal Products, Inc. and the Ternstedt Division of General Motors in 1946, and North American Aviation in 1950.

There is no major concentration of plants within the city although 6 of the 16 plants are in North Columbus, and 4 in West Columbus.

Aircraft

The North American Aviation Corporation of Los Angeles took over the government-built Curtiss-Wright plant in December

1950. It is leased from the Navy under the Naval Industrial Reserve Aircraft Plant (NIRAP) program, and is one of 13 such plants in operation throughout the country.

North American, as it is generally called, manufactures and assembles military aircraft on government contract. It is the only firm in central Ohio devoted to the production of aircraft, but functionally associated with it are more than a dozen machine shops which do sub-contract work.[9]

Factors in Location—The following statements explain, in large part, why the Curtiss-Wright plant was built in Columbus in 1941. They also indicate those favorable forces which influenced North American's location.

(a) Columbus, an inland city, fits into the plant dispersal program that was initiated in the war years and carried into the post-war period.

(b) Adequate rail and highway tranportation facilities are present. Tracks of the Pennsylvania and Baltimore and Ohio railroads lie to the south of the plant. Excellent main highways are nearby.

(c) The plant was built adjacent to Port Columbus on city-owned land. In addition to these facilities, good flying weather typifies the port.

(d) Columbus is within 70 miles of the Wright-Patterson Air Base at Dayton which carries on research and testing of aircraft.

(e) Most important, probably, Columbus was the only large city in Ohio which actually had a surplus of labor in 1940. An on-the-job training program provided the thousands of unskilled laborers with basic training. In 1950, North American could rely on many of these laborers returning to the plant from rural and urban areas in central Ohio, southeastern Ohio, West Virginia, and Kentucky. It was a semi-skilled labor force ready for use.

It is true that the North American organization considered other

[9] The machine shops engaged in the production of aircraft parts are included in a section on the Machine Shop Industry. They are not an integral part of the aircraft industry.

locations in Texas, Kansas, and Nebraska, but the exceptionally well-planned, modern physical plant which existed here was a deciding factor. It is doubtful whether the company would have built its own facilities here, considering that some other sites may have been more suitable in many respects for the peace-time aircraft activity.

Local Advantages and Handicaps—Public utilities, available space for expansion, and the physical lay-out of the plant, are satisfactory features. Most of the handicaps appear to be temporary. The absence of good access roads has been modified but the principal routes to the plant are jammed with traffic when shifts change. This has bothered other manufacturing concerns in the area and it has plagued residential commuters.[10] Public transit was not adequate for a number of months but this has been improved with bus service now available throughout the day. Relatively few workers use this service, however. Parking facilities remain inadequate even though large areas have been restricted for this purpose. The movement of workers from various points in the city and in the surrounding townships to the North American plant is shown in Map 5, and the accompanying picture shows that traffic congestion at the plant at the peak periods.

Markets and Raw Materials—Neither markets nor raw materials is a prime force in location. The market is the military service. Military personnel pick up the assembled craft and fly them to bases across the nation.

Aluminum and light metals are the basic raw materials. Sub-contrast work is extensive and has left its mark on the city with the establishment of many small shops whose existence depends upon it. Raw materials are purchased by the Government, tested by it, and then allocated to the individual sub-contractor who must use the supplied materials. No substitutions are allowed. The transportation of all local products is by truck. Rail service is important when distance, volume, and size justify it.

Employment—Peak employment at Curtiss-Wright during

[10] While more than $450,000 has been spent in improving the access roads and the parking facilities, it was announced on April 21, 1953, that new efforts would be made to alleviate the continuing traffic problem.

Traffic Flow at the North American Aviation Plant—The Suburban Location Has Not Eliminated Traffic Congestion

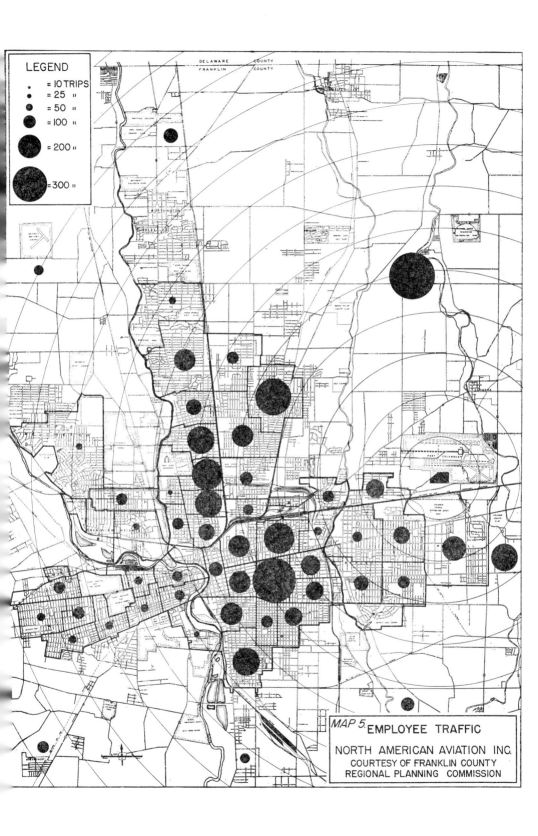

LEGEND

• = 10 TRIPS
• = 25 "
• = 50 "
● = 100 "
● = 200 "
● = 300 "

MAP 5. EMPLOYEE TRAFFIC

NORTH AMERICAN AVIATION INC.
COURTESY OF FRANKLIN COUNTY
REGIONAL PLANNING COMMISSION

World War II reached 25,000. North American has gradually increased its force to more than 17,000—four times as many being males as females. Women do wiring, riveting, and assembling of small parts; heavier machine work is done by men. The skilled mechanics, tool and die makers, draftsmen, and engineers are not readily available although Ohio leads the nation as a machine tool state.

Workers have been attracted to North American not only from Columbus but from many urban and rural areas of Ohio and adjacent states. The relatively high wage offered by the aircraft industry is the principal reason for this. These workers, essentially semi-skilled or untrained, have been given on-the-job training to fit them to their present jobs. While labor has been readily obtained by the North American Company, it is expected that continued industrial growth such as the establishment of the Westinghouse and General Motors plants will create local labor shortages.

Labor Competition — Practically every other manufacturing company in Columbus has complained about North American taking labor and bringing high wages to this traditionally low-wage town. Other firms, which often were anxious to grant wage increases or provide some other benefits, claimed that they did not receive the prompt attention from governmental agencies that North American did. Instead, they lost their workers to the aircraft industry.

Structure of Industry—It is difficult to see where the structure of the national industry played any role in the location of this plant in Columbus. The company's headquarters and three other plants are in southern California. The Columbus plant is the only one not closely tied to the parent company.

Effects upon Columbus—In the past ten years, the Aircraft Industry has helped in a most dramatic way to change the industrial character of Columbus. It brought a "foreign" type industry to the city and with it some changes in the basic structure of local industry. The dozens of small machine shops which dot the city owe much of their growth to the market created by this industry. Larger local firms can trace much of their expansion to contracts evolving from the aircraft firm's operations. In addition, large national manufacturers were attracted to Columbus as an industrial center in part because of the success of the aircraft industry. The surplus of semi-skilled labor, created by Curtiss-Wright, went a long way in bringing General Motors, Westinghouse, and even North American Aviation to the city. It is doubtful that any other single industry has done so much to attract national attention to Columbus as an industrial community.

Railroad Cars

It is almost incongruous to turn next to the section on railroad cars. While North American Aviation represents the dynamic growing industrial organization, the Ralston Steel Car Company is an example of the death of an industry. After 50 years of successful operation, this firm announced early in 1953 that it was closing.[11] That it is discussed here at all is due to the fact that it is a modern example of the transition that takes place in the industrial life of a city.

Location—The Ralston plant was located in East Columbus a few blocks from the North American plant. It was housed in a building that dated back to 1900. This building was originally constructed for the Rarig Engineering Company which made disappearing gun carriage for coastal defense and the first large pumps for public water works.

Ralston located here because the large building was available at a reasonable price and because an excellent railroad market was here. Five large railroads enter the city and four of these have local repair yards. The construction of railroad freight cars of all types was on a direct contract basis but, in recent years, the company did subcontracting work for other shops.[12]

Labor—The type of labor needed in this industry was not ordinarily found in Columbus. It congregated in steel centers but moved to Columbus whenever Ralston received car orders. The labor force was always transient and mobile. Generally it was unskilled; most of the work involved cutting and assembling steel sections for the cars. Much of it was heavy and dirty work,

[11] When this study was undertaken, Ralston Steel Car Company was still in business. It was sold and closed in 1953 but its development and decline are discussed here as an example of the death of an old, established local industry.

[12] At one time, an average of 25 cars were made in a day. A maximum of 40 were made in a day's time but this production rate was uneconomic.

thus many men were discouraged from seeking employment in the industry. At its peak, 700 men were employed by Ralston but the figure dwindled to an average of about 130 in recent years. Most recently, Ralston employed part-time farm labor in its shops since a steady working force could not be maintained.

Raw Materials—The company was well-situated for its raw materials. Steel was furnished by Pittsburgh mills and lumber came from the south. Some local foundry products were used but these were never important parts of the whole. The expected tie between Ralston and the Buckeye Steel Castings Company never materialized.[13]

Summary—Railroad cars had been built in Columbus since the middle of the nineteenth centry. The closing of the Ralston Steel Car Company's factory, after 47 years of operation, ended an important period in the city's industrial history. Ralston's inability to get much-needed allocated steel at the war's end, and its inability to keep pace with the fast-changing railroad industry brought about its closing. It illustrates what seems to be increasingly true—the specialized plant of local origin, which has typified the city's industry for many years, is slowly giving way to the branch plants of national organizations.

Automobile and Truck Parts

There are 8 companies engaged directly in the manufacture of auto parts, one company in the manufacture of fire engines and accessories, and 5 companies in the construction of truck bodies and accessories. In addition, many small machine shops do sub-contract work for these firms.

A. Automobile Parts Manufacture—No one dominating factor has influenced the location of these plants. The initiative of local men gave rise to the establishment of 6 of them, however. In some instances, a local invention affected the develoment of a company but this has been the exception rather than the rule. The Columbus Auto Parts Company originally made equipment for the carriage industry but it now manufactures connecting rods and parts of

---

[13] The absence of any bonds between the two firms was due to the specifications set forth in the contracts that Ralston handled. If the contracts did not specify Buckeye equipment, it could not be used.

universal joint assemblies for the auto industry. The American Auto Parts Company once produced hydraulic washing machines; the inventiveness of the owner eventually led the company into the manufacture of valve guides for the automotive industry. It is the third largest independent producer of these guides in the nation.

The Clark Grave Vault Company stamped metal burial vaults for many years, but government contracts in World War II boosted its output in other lines. It made extensive changes in the nature of its product so that the firm is an important manufacturer of auto parts at the present time.[14]

The Columbus Metal Products Company, now located in a modern plant in Northwest Columbus, is an old firm that has experienced many changes in product. From carriage parts to auto lamps and even to airplanes, the company has shown initiative and progress. It continues today as a manufacturer of auto and truck lighting equipment.

The two companies controlled by outside capital, Timken Roller Bearing and General Motor's Ternstedt plant, are branches of national organizations. Their location can be related to the internal structure of the individual firms. Each is the result of planning although the final choice of Columbus for the plant site was with respect to the national structure of the parent organization. Another firm, Henri La Prise Company, is a local firm recently brought under the control of a national firm. It was purchased in 1953 by the Summer Company, as part of an expansion and diversification program.

The Timken Roller Bearing Company chose Columbus for the site of a new plant in 1919. The Timken family began operations in St. Louis, moving to Canton, Ohio, in 1899. Canton was well-located with respect to coal, iron ore, and steel, and the new automobile market; its transportation facilities were inadequate, however. When the company considered expansion, it chose Columbus which, with five major railroads, had accessibility to all markets and to the raw material centers of the country.[15] Columbus also had

[14] To advertise the shift in products the company now is also known as the Clark Automotive Equipment Company.

[15] Both Canton and Columbus were mid-way between the raw material centers in the Pittsburgh district and the market in Detroit.

a very good labor supply at the time. It had been relatively un-disturbed by other industries or by unions. The new plant was located favorably with respect to the company's other operations in Ohio.

The move of the Ternstedt Division plant of General Motors to Columbus is a contrast in the location of industry. The eco-nomic considerations of the parent firm were more important than local geography. The General Motors organization considers the Great Lakes area the best in the nation for markets, raw materials, and the sale of scrap. This plant's operations are geared to materials sources and markets well beyond central Ohio. Its raw materials are obtained from different areas in the surrounding states, and its finished products are shipped to 22 General Motors plants across the nation.

Columbus was not the first choice for the location of this plant. A site in Chicago where a government-built plant was available near the Buick assembly plant was the first choice, but it was not pur-chased because the price was too high. Cincinnati was a second choice. Property was purchased and plans laid for a new building when petitions by the citizenry discouraged continuation. In this way, Columbus came to acquire a large, modern factory and a stable industrial concern.[16].

The geographical position of Columbus has been called its greatest resource. Certainly no other factor explains so well why the automobile parts industry has succeeded here. The city's posi-tion earlier influenced its development as a carriage center and as a minor manufacturing point for agricultural implements, but its advantages as an automobile parts supplier are even greater. Mid-way between the steel centers of Pittsburgh, Wheeling, Youngstown, and other Ohio steel towns, and the automobile market in north-western Ohio, southern Michigan, and northern Indiana, the city is a manufacturing-in-transit point for steel products.

Transportation—Transportation is almost entirely a permissive factor in location and yet the flexible transportation system in central Ohio is a principal reason for the establishment of large branch

[16] It would appear that GM considers its Columbus operation successful. In mid-1955, GM announced that the plant capacity in Columbus would be doubled in the near future.

plants here. Rail and truck are both widely used although the latter dominates when convenience or speed is desired. The General Motors factory has facilities for 16 railroad cars a day to assist in its great storage and shipping problem and to supplement truck service. Firms that operate on close schedules with Detroit automobile factories realize the time saved by the use of trucks.

Labor—For most local firms, labor is taken for granted but a national concern must evaluate the labor supply in terms of its long-range needs· The semi-skilled labor force that the Curtiss-Wright Company had trained provided a potential force in central Ohio in 1946. With little competition in the area or in southeastern Ohio from other industries, the new firms could draw upon this pool as they needed.

There are more than 9,200 workers in this section of the industry. About one-fourth are females who are employed to carry out light machine operations in the factories. The male workers operate lathes, drill presses, screw machines, stamping presses, or forges. Only a few jobs require true skills; most men are specialists in one or two tasks. They are trained for these tasks in a matter of a few days.

Products—These 8 firms whose diversified products range from valve guides, lights, lighting equipment, connecting rods, universal joints, roller bearings, and spark plugs, to auto body hardware, are not clustered in one community. Five of them are in North Columbus. Location has been accidental generally, but a planned location may take advantage of the accessible outgoing rail and highway facilities to the north.[17]

Community Ties—The Stitt Ignition Company which manufactures spark plugs for the automobile and petroleum industry, found Columbus a good location because of the influence of The Ohio State University. Training in ceramic engineering at the university has resulted in the orientation of the spark plug industry to this potential supply of ceramicists. This tie, while not a common one nor a strong one, nevertheless explains, in part, the continued operation of this firm in Columbus.

[17] Columbus Auto Parts, in North Columbus, has a location that gives it the advantage of an hour's shipping time over a location in South Columbus when shipping to the Detroit market.

There are few other local ties. Practically no purchases or sales are made in central Ohio. The only active suppliers are the foundries —Hertenstein and Chase foundries supply these firms with a large proportion of their gray-iron castings. National bonds are not much stronger except with the Timken and General Motors organizations.

B. Fire Engines and Accessories—The Seagrave Corporation is the largest manufacturer of fire-fighting equipment in the country. Employing about 310 males and 20 females, it builds a complete fire engine, including the motor.

The firm has a national market with any community a prospective customer. Its raw materials are readily available—steel from Pittsburgh, Youngstown, or Cleveland, and truck parts from Cleveland or Detroit. Cast products are either made in the plant or they are purchased locally. The company now casts its own engine block; these were formerly purchased.

Seagrave's began operation in 1881 in Detroit where it made ladders for apple-picking. Gradually the ladders began to sell to fire companies and more items were added to the stock. In 1898, a move was made to Columbus because the city was a better location for marketing the finished product; also it was the home of the firm's owner. A few years after the return to Columbus, the plant moved from West Lane Avenue at the C & O tracks to South High Street, just beyond the limits of the city. This move, typical of many made at that time, was undertaken to avoid the city's tax and zoning structure. Land was plentiful there in 1900 and a building and necessary capital were also obtainable.

The Seagrave Corporation is typical of the independent, specialized plant that was common to the older Columbus industrial community. It represents local inventiveness, initiative, and capital successfully at work.

C. Truck Bodies and Accessories—Four companies of local origin are engaged in the assembly of truck bodies and one, Stallman Gear Manufacturing Company, is a supplier of truck gears and parts. With this exception, this is not actually a manufacturing industry. These firms buy their raw materials from local warehouses and then assemble truck bodies for a local market. Because their orientation is completely local, they add little to the national structure of the automobile parts industry.

The Electrical Equipment Industry

This industry is similar to the Transportation Equipment Industry in that it too is represented by both local and national firms. It is, however, one of the newest industries in the city. With more than 7,700 workers, the Electrical Equipment Industry is the second largest industry-group in the city. Although it is the fourth youngest group, it is of growing importance to Columbus.

Age and Plant Sites—This is a relatively new industry since only 3 of the 9 plants were established before 1925, although, one plant, the Ebco Manufacturing Company was established as early as 1906. Four of the plants have come to Columbus since 1940, the most recent being the plant of the Westinghouse Manufacturing Company in 1953. The 9 plants are scattered throughout the city with 3

Electrical Equipment Companies

Company	Area Location	Year Located: In Columbus	Year Located: At Site	Number Employed 1953
Ranco, Inc.	North	1913	1936	883
Bell Sound Systems, Inc.	South	1932	1946	125
Acro Manufacturing Company	East	1940	1950	256
Ebco Manufacturing Company	West	1906	1906	225
Nippert Electric Products Company	West	1942	1946	116
Westinghouse Manufacturing Company	West	1953	1953	5,275
Buckeye Telephone and Supply Co.	Northwest	1921	1951	40
National Electric Coil Company	Northwest	1934	1934	733
Antenna Research Laboratories	Northwest	1948	1948	48

Source: Appendix Table 1.

plants each in the West and Northwest Areas. The 5 new plants are located beyond the old industrial agglomeration on the urban fringes. The firms such as Ebco in West Columbus, Bell Sound in South Columbus, and Acro Manufacturing Company in East Columbus, all in older industrial areas, have suffered some of the inconveniences of heavy traffic, inadequate parking, and crowded surroundings. There is no concentration of plants as there are no mutual bonds that attract or hold them to one part of the city.

Local Companies—The Ebco Manufacturing Company is an outgrowth of a foundry organized in Columbus in 1906. After many changes in products, and difficult financial conditions, the present management took over in 1935 and has successfully developed a nationally-known line of water fountains, coolers, air driers, juice dispensers, and refrigerator parts and accessories. The three-story plant on the original West Columbus site has been crowded recently because of increased industrialization. The Ebco Company has purchased acreage near Port Columbus in East Columbus for expansion in the future.[18]

Ranco Incorporated, dating from 1913 is also a local firm although control of the company is now with the Nash-Kelvinator organization. The founder of Ranco invented an automatic circuit breaker for use in coal mines while working at the Jeffrey plant. With other ideas in mind, he formed his own company supported by local capital. The present modern, one-story plant at West Fifth Avenue and the Olentangy River is on a site that was formerly a city dump and which was available at a reasonable price in 1936.

Ranco manufactures refrigerator, auto heater, and automatic temperature controls for national distribution. In addition to the home plant, two smaller units operate in Columbus, and, in line with the company's program of plant dispersal for economy's sake, separate plants operate in Delaware and Plain City. There is also a small plant in Scotland which handles overseas sales.

Established in 1921, the Buckeye Telephone and Supply Company is the third oldest firm in this industry. The modern and attractively landscaped plant, situated in the Northwest, was in a crowded Parsons Avenue building prior to 1951. A local entrepreneur organized this company which rebuilds and remanufactures telephone equipment for small telephone companies and for industrial firms. Competition is limited even though the firm sells to a national market as well as to several South American nations.

The Bell Sound Systems, a firm resulting from local inventions and initiative, was started in a garage at Mr. Bell's home in 1932. By 1946 it moved to larger quarters on Marion Road in South Columbus where it occupied part of the building of the Buckeye Stamp-

[18] Ebco moved into its modern one-floor plant early in 1955.

ing Company. A variety of sound equipment is produced including public address systems, tape recorders, inter-office communication systems, and custom electric products. Sales are national; competition is keen. In the fall of 1953, this firm was purchased by The Thompson Products Company of Cleveland.

Similar factors explain the humble beginnings of the Nippert Electric Products Company in 1942. In four years time, this firm moved from a downtown site to one just outside the city limits in West Columbus.[19] The move was underaken to avoid high rental costs and inadequate space. There is plenty of space for expansion at the new site and a large parking lot is present. Commutators and slip or collector rings used in the electrical and aircraft industries are the principal products. They may appear in electric mixers, generators, starters, or power tools. National sales, concentrated in the mid-west, are directed to manufacturers who use the product in a finished good. Plants in Dayton, Cleveland, Toledo, and Chicago offer the principal competition. Ohio is the leading producer of commutators in the nation.

The Antenna Research Laboratories is another native industry. This research organization, founded by research scientists in electronics at The Ohio State University does limited custom manufacturing. The plant, in a rural area in North Columbus, is free from obstructions and interference from other factories. This firm is also owned by Thompson Products of Cleveland; its research is geared to the program of the parent company although allied work is carried on with the Wright-Patterson Air Base.

Outside Interests—Of the three firms originally started by outside interests, the National Electric Coil Company, established in 1934, is the oldest. Its location was planned to take advantage of the accessibility of markets and raw materials. Other National Electric Coil plants are in Bluefield, West Virginia, and Harlan, Kentucky. This suggests two things: this company had located its plants in areas where wages are low—therefore, it is labor-oriented—or its plants have been located near the important coal mines of eastern United States—therefore, it is a market-oriented organization. Elec-

---

[19] The plant is just one foot beyond the city. This was done to avoid restrictive zoning regulations in this area.

tric windings and insulation for motors and generators used in the transportation, electric utility, and steel fabricating industries are the products of this firm, but re-winding operations are carried out in each plant, as well.

The Acro Manufacturing Company is the former Crise Company which began operations here in 1940. The Crise organization had operated in Mt. Vernon, Ohio, but an attractive financial offer brought it to Columbus. Acro, an eastern concern, bought control of the company in 1950 and now operates three branches under one roof: Crise Manufacturing, Acro Switch Company, and the Mu-Switch Corporation. They occupy part of the old multiple-story Holtzman piano factory on East Main Street.

A representative of the company indicated that its holdings were moved here to take advantage of the favorable tax rate which prevails for industries and individuals. A stable, nonunion labor force and a good location with respect to raw materials and markets were added incentives. Competition for labor and unionization are feared especially since the opening of the Westinghouse plant. The firm plans to move its facilities to Hillsboro, Ohio, in the near future to enjoy cheaper, more abundant labor which is free from union and industrial competition. Most of Acro's workers do precision work on electric snap-action switches (over 8,000 items), temperature controls, and shaded-pole motors, which are sold to original manufacturers. The Minneapolis-Honeywell Company is the principal competitor.

West Columbus has undergone a great physical change with the coming of the General Motors Ternstedt plant in 1946 (See discussion under Transportation Industry, p. 150), and the construction of the tremendous new Westinghouse Manufacturing Company's modern structure in 1952–1953. The choice of Columbus for the site of this appliance center was the result of months of careful planning and research by Westinghouse. Four reasons apparently were the prime forces in the location: (a) ideal transportation facilities are available and a favorable freight rate was in effect, (b) Columbus is centrally located for raw material supply, (c) sound labor and wage structures prevail, and (d) the city is situated to serve the major markets as a distribution center. Established manu-

The National Electric Coil Company, a Modern Branch Plant

facturers viewed the arrival of this plant with alarm. Westinghouse personnel, learned, through approximately 30 interviews, that two things worried the local concerns: what would Westinghouse do to the current favorable wage rate, and would Westinghouse take labor from the established firms? These questions have not yet been fully answered.

The plant was scheduled to manufacture jet aircraft for the Navy but in January 1953, it was announced that refrigerator equipment would be made here in the largest such unit in the Westinghouse organization. The plant site in suburban West Columbus was chosen because of (a) flat terrain ideal for construction, (b) 518 acres of land available in a large tract, (c) excellent rail facilities with four spurs each from New York Central and Pennsylvania railroads, (d) a suburban location away from congestion, and (e) the satisfactory utilities and housing units which were present or promised. Plans for schools, shopping centers, and housing units are in the making and utilities have been improved to meet the plant's needs.

Bonds—Each plant is independent of any other in the city. Local ties are insignificant, yet 5 plants are members of national firms. Some, such as Ranco Incorporated, are functionally tied to their parent firms but others such as Westinghouse, are branch manufacturing plants. Practically every firm sells to a national market; none is restricted to central Ohio. Within 500 miles are the major industrial and consumer markets of the nation: they are easily reached by highway, rail, and air. A favorable freight rate prevails for the shipment of electric products.

Raw Materials—These come from a variety of places; the central position of Columbus is a distinct advantage. Steel comes from Cleveland, Middletown, Sharon, and Pittsburgh. Copper and brass are usually obtained in Connecticut; mica, used by a number of companies for insulation, is imported through Boston and New York from India; and finished parts, such as motors and compressors, are purchased in Detroit, Dayton, Sydney, and Marion. The Westinghouse plant expects to get rock wool for insulation from Newark where the Owens-Corning plant is situated. Wool is purchased from western sources and plastics are obtained from other Westinghouse outlets. Some plastic products are being introduced for use in this industry by local companies.

Labor—Labor has been an advantage. About one-third of the 7,700 workers are women who are able to perform the repetitious and dexterous tasks better than men. More than half of the workers at Bell Sound and Acro Manufacturing companies are females; between a fourth and a third of the workers at Ranco, Westinghouse, Nippert Electric Products, and National Electric Coil. This is a complementary use of female labor, and it is possible in this community where many female workers are available. Few jobs require skill but each requires training until a routine is established.

In most of the plants, the male workers perform repetitive machine operations. Men are needed to cut, trim, and polish finished products, to assemble parts, to move and crate equipment. In some plants, and this will be true of the Westinghouse plant, operations are based upon an assembly line technique where each man may possess no skill but can doubtless do a routine job.

Summary—This industry has a bright future in Columbus. The principal advantage of the city is its position. Of a more local nature, a good supply of readily trained labor is a strong point. There are no serious handicaps to detract from the area. It would appear that other organizations within the industry might find Columbus a good location. Research facilities are present, industrial planning is gaining wider attention, and the community readily welcomes this type of diversified manufacturing. A sound and healthy future should be recorded for the Electrical Equipment Industry in Columbus.

CHAPTER VIII

THE CHEMICAL INDUSTRY

There are six separate industries classified under the heading, The Chemical Industry. Combined, they form the fourth largest industry-group in the city with 35 plants and 5,027 workers. Included are (1) chemical products (heavy chemicals, fertilizers, drugs, and paints), (2) ceramic products, (3) glass products, (4) dental products, (5) plastic products, and (6) rubber products. There are no bonds between these separate groups. There is no real basis for classifying them together except for convenience in discussion.

Periods of Establishment in Columbus

Three of these 6 industry groups were represented in Columbus by at least one plant before 1900—ceramic products, chemical prod-

TABLE 21—Chemical Industry: Number of Plants and Number of Workers in 1953, by Industry Groups, by Period of Establishment of Plants in Columbus

Industry Group	Number of Workers	Number of Plants	Period of Establishment					
			1946–1953	1940–1945	1920–1939	1914–1919	1900–1913	Pre-1900
			Number of Plants					
Ceramic Products	153	4			3			1
Chemical Products (Total)	1,290	16			8		1	7
Fertilizers	*373*	*4*			*1*		*1*	*2*
Pharmaceuticals	*320*	*4*			*3*			*1*
Paints	*310*	*4*			*1*			*3*
Miscellaneous	*287*	*4*			*3*			*1*
Dental Products	202	4		1	2		1	
Glass Products	2,631	3	1		1			1
Plastic Products	705	5		2	2		1	
Rubber Products	46	3	1	1	1			
Total	5,027	35	2	4	17		3	9

Source: Appendix Table 1.

ucts, and glass products (Table 21). In the chemical products group, 7 of the 16 plants were established before the turn of the century including 3 of the 4 paint manufacturers, 2 of the 4 fertilizer plants, one of the 4 pharmaceutical plants, and one of the 4 plants in the miscellaneous group. Almost one-half of the plants in this group (17 of 35, or 48.5 per cent) were established at intervals during the 19 years between the two world wars. Only 6 plants have been established since 1940, two of these, since 1946.

The Chemical Products Industry

The Chemical Products Industry is not large when compared with its national counterpart. It is important locally not only because it serves a local market but because it offers employment to 1,290 workers.

The industry is not a new one. In fact, Columbus has shared in no way in the "chemical revolution" which is so apparent in the Ohio River Valley or along the northeastern Lake Erie shore of the state. Nor is the future of this industry particularly bright in central Ohio. There are no chemical raw materials here to form the basis of an enlarged chemical industry; no cheap fuel offers an attraction; and an abundant water supply necessary to a large chemical installation is not available. It seems logical to predict that Columbus can anticipate no significant growth in this industry.

A specific definition of the Chemical Products Industry is required here. Alderfer and Michl subdivide the national industry into three parts: (a) the strict chemical industries, (b) the allied chemical industries, and (c) the chemical process industries.[1] In order to analyze the Columbus industry in detail it has been subdivided into four parts based upon products—fertilizers, drugs, paints, and miscellaneous products. Based upon the classification of the national industry, fertilizers, drugs, and the miscellaneous products are members of the strict chemical group; paints belong in the allied fields.

For the most part, the chemical companies in Columbus are oriented to an Ohio market and have few local or national bonds.

Fertilizers

Fertilizer manufacturers have been in Columbus since 1894; four concerns are now making these products. Three firms, Smith

[1] Alderfer, E. B., and Michl, H. E., *op. cit.*, pp. 216-217.

Agricultural Chemical Company, Farmers Fertilizer Company, and The Davison Chemical Company, produce commercial farm fertilizers. The fourth, Agricultural Laboratories, Incorporated, produces seed innoculants which are a type of plant fertilizer. The commercial farm fertilizers are usually sold by dealers or farm cooperatives in the Ohio, Michigan, and Indiana area. Seed innoculants reach a wider market in the corn and cotton belts.

Factors in Location—The Smith brothers recognized a growing market for fertilizer products in central Ohio in the late 1880's when they imported them by the barrel. By 1894, the Smith Agricultural Chemical Company was established, and these men began the manufacture of fertilizer in their own plant on Champion Avenue in East Columbus. This plant, within a block of the stockyards, served two purposes: it utilized the animal manures and waste products in the manufacture of organic fertilizers, and the farmers who brought livestock to the stockyards provided a potential market for the fertilizers.

The factors responsible for the development of the Farmers Fertilizer Company are not clearly known but it is believed to have been established in 1894 as a local cooperative. It originally handled many products for the farm trade but gradually gave them up and restricted its sale to fertilizers for which there was a large market in central Ohio.

The present Davison Chemical Company was originally the Welch Chemical Company, established in Columbus in 1911. This company, also, was oriented to the local market which it continues to serve as a subsidiary of the parent Baltimore firm.

Agricultural Laboratories, Incorporated is a fairly new company, organized in 1932. The original owner was a Columbus man who expanded this business through consolidations with similar businesses on the east coast and in Baltic, Ohio. The firm sells to farm cooperatives, grain stores, and farm supply stores.

Sites—All of the plants except Agricultural Laboratories, Incorporated, are in or near East Columbus and still occupy the same sites at which they were originally established. Each company was attracted to its site by cheap but abundant land adjacent to railroad lines. A factor that was not considered when those large plants

Fertilizer Manufacturers

Company Name	Area Location	Year Located: In Columbus	At Site	Number Employed 1953
Farmers Fertilizer Company	North	1894	1894	67
Davison Chemical Company	East	1911	1911	80
Smith Agricultural Chemical Company	East	1894	1894	200
Agricultural Laboratories, Incorported	Northwest	1932	1942	26

were built was zoning. Fortunately, two of the plants are beyond the residential areas. Dust, odors, and fumes are associated with the plants by their residential and industrial neighbors. The companies have taken steps to curb these nuisances; the continued expansion of residential areas has made this difficult.

The Agricultural Laboratories firm is located in Northwest Columbus where its two-story cement block building is shared with Detergents, Incorporated. There are no fumes or odors associated with this firm so that no zoning problems have developed.

Transportation of Materials—The bulky, low-value fertilizers are limited in the extent of their markets by freight rates. With the sale of a large volume of fertilizers at the local plant, truck transportation dominates in central Ohio. Raw materials are carried by rail, however. The combination of good markets and good railroads has made Columbus an ideal site.

Labor—To some extent labor has become scarce and wages have increased with the influx of new firms into Columbus but an acute labor shortage is not threatened. Of the 373 workers employed in the 4 plants, 210 are Negroes. The largest employer is the Smith Agricultural Chemical Company which employs 200 workers, half of them Negroes. The Agricultural Laboratories uses only 26 workers, mostly females, who prepare, label, and pack the products, in a plant where labor requirements are light.

Raw Materials—The most important raw materials are potash, obtained in New Mexico and California, and rock phosphate, obtained in Florida. Sulphuric acid is produced by a number of plants. Farmers Fertilizer buys its sulphuric acid from its neighbor, the American Zinc Oxide Company, and thereby establishes a bond of minor importance. Nitrogenous materials may be purchased from local farmers or from other chemical plants. The Agricultural Laboratories buys powdered humus from the Smith Agricultural Company and gets powdered charcoal in Tennessee.

Thus, while the basic raw materials must be transported more than 1,000 miles, this industry remains tied to its Ohio market. Well-established in an agricultural valley with economical transportation available, the industry's future seems assured. Future expansion of the city and/or stricter zoning regulations might lead to a relocation of the plants, however.

Pharmaceuticals and Serums

The four companies that form this division are completely unrelated. The Columbus Pharmacal Company and Warren-Teed Products Company are pharmaceutical concerns, the General Products Laboratory manufactures proprietary medicines, and the Columbus Serum Company produces hog cholera serum. These firms are primarily a result of local capital and initiative although the Columbus Serum Company was originally a state-owned organization.

Sites—The plants are scattered over the city since their locations were not selective but were due, in most cases, to the presence of an available building. The General Products Laboratories occupies a

Pharmaceutical and Serum Companies

Company Name	Area Location	Year Located: In Columbus	At Site	Number Employed 1953
Warren-Teed Products Company	North	1920	1937	150
Columbus Serum Company	South	1922	1922	30
Columbus Pharmacal Company	Downtown	1886	1915	130
General Products Laboratories, Inc.	Downtown	1920	1934	10

Source:Appendix Table 1.

large, old four-story building in the downtown area but the other firms are in far more modern structures in other sections. The General Products Laboratories was the only firm which noted a handicap to its present site and this was due to its crowded plant site and to inadequate parking facilities in the downtown.

Market—A major market is in central Ohio but each firm, except the Columbus Serum Company, also reaches a national market. The Warren-Teed organization has warehouses in Texas, California, Oregon, and Tennessee; the other companies have sales representatives in the national market.

Raw Materials—Chemical raw materials are obtained in the east coast port cities and in St. Louis and Chicago. The Columbus Serum Company buys hogs from the surrounding farm territory. Where chemicals and drugs are shipped, parcel post is used widely. Truck service is important but it is replaced by rail freight when bulkier or heavier items are shipped.

Labor Force—Approximately 165 of the 320 workers are women. The work is light but requires patience, agility, and speed. Plants range in size from the Columbus Pharmacal Company, with 130 workers, to the General Products Laboratories, with 10 workers. With respect to a labor force, as in practically every other respect, the Pharmaceutical Industry has been influenced in no significant way by the other industries in the city.

Paints

The state of Ohio ranks fourth in the nation in the value of its paint products; Columbus early was a leading manufacturing center with 2 of its 4 firms operating since the mid-1880's. The Columbus paint industry was developed to serve a market highly concentrated in this area. For the most part, the companies have remained local in character, oriented to central Ohio in many ways. Ties with the national paint industry are practically nonexistent. The Hanna Paint Manufacturing Company started in 1884, and the Dean and Barry Company a year later in 1885. These two firms were joined by the Shepard Paint Company in the 1890's. The newest firm, the Frey-Yenkin Paint Company was organized in 1923.

Paint Companies

Company Name	Area Location	Year Located: In Columbus	At Site	Number Employed 1953
Shepard Paint Company	West	1890's	1935	12
Dean and Barry Company	Downtown	1885	1900	78
Hanna Paint Manufacturing Company	Downtown	1884	1913	171
Frey-Yenkin Paint Company	Northwest[a]	1923	1928	49

[a] Has moved to East Columbus.

Source: Appendix Table 1.

Sites—The firms are concentrated in or near the downtown area. Hanna and Dean and Barry are both in the heart of the Downtown: both firms have branches outside the city. Hanna Paint Company has a large industrial paint plant in Pittsburgh and smaller plants in Birmingham, Alabama, and Dallas, Texas. The Dean and Barry Company operates a small plant in Dennison, Ohio. Frey-Yenkin and Shepard Paint have their main plants in Northwest and West Columbus, respectively, near the Downtown; neither has national branches.[2]

Products—Each firm produces secondary products in addition to its major line of house paints. The Pittsburgh branch of the Hanna Company produces industrial paints (60 per cent for the steel industry), while Dean and Barry is now engaged in wallpaper design and production, and Frey-Yenkin sells varnishes, resins, and enamels. Sales are through retail outlets, hardware stores, or jobbers. The Dean and Barry Company maintains its own retail stores throughout Ohio and West Virginia. Local competition is on friendly terms but there is increased national competition.

Factors in Location—The Hanna Company was started by two brothers, originally from Columbus, who worked for the Sherwin-Williams Company in Cleveland and returned to Columbus to start their own business. The site of the Hanna building, in the heart of the Downtown, resulted from forward planning by the company's management. The building is many-storied and appears to be poorly designed for paint manufacture. Actually it was designed so that it could be converted into an office building. In the fall of 1952, the company announced its plans to expand facilities at a new location on Windsor Avenue in North Columbus. This move would consolidate all holdings in Columbus and would mean the abandonment of the downtown building which was purchased by the neighboring electric company for office use.

The other companies have located in or near the Downtown for various reasons. Dean and Barry did so at a time when the area was partially residential; they have remained in their original lo-

[2] Both companies have had to move their plants to allow for civic progress. Frey-Yenkin's modern plant is in East Columbus.

cation. Frey-Yenkin felt that its location at the junction of the rivers gave it access to the Downtown without the handicaps of the Downtown location.

Markets—The prime market is within 150 miles of the city, yet almost all of the raw materials used are brought in from beyond Ohio's borders. Linseed oil, probably the single most important raw material, is imported from the northwest, from Texas, and from warehousing centers in the mid-west. Tung oil comes out of the south, turpentine from the naval stores industry in the southeast, fish oils from coastal areas, and other oils from a variety of sources. Pigments, spirits, lead, and zinc are usually purchased from chemical companies with headquarters in the east.

These bulk items are shipped by railroad tank car to the plant's door. Prevailing freight rates usually determine the method of transport. About 90 per cent of the outgoing products are shipped by truck on the short hauls.

Labor—Approximately 310 workers are employed by these firms with 264 of these men. The Hanna Company has a working force of 171 (25 women) that is reliable and stable. Dean and Barry has 78 employees, many of them commuters from rural communities. This firm's labor is stable, turnover is low, the workers are reliable, and cooperation between workers and management is fine. The company distributes a bonus every year to its workers— no labor union has ever been organized. The Shepard Paint Company, with 12 employees, is the smallest firm in this group.

Miscellaneous Chemicals

Widely diversified and unrelated are the 4 companies in this group. The Ironsides Company, founded in 1883, makes special preservatives and lubricants; The American Zinc Oxide Company, a subsidiary of the American Zinc, Lead, and Smelting Company, was founded in 1920 and produces zinc oxide; The G. F. Smith Chemical Company established in 1929 produces analytical chemicals; and the Barneby-Cheney Company, founded in 1920, makes activated carbon products.

Sites—The companies are scattered in 4 industrial areas. Two of the companies are on their original sites—American Zinc Oxide (1920), and Smith Chemical Company (1929).

Miscellaneous Chemical Companies

Company Name	Area Location	Year Located: In Columbus	At Site	Number Employed 1953
American Zinc Oxide Company	North	1920	1920	173
Barneby-Cheney Engineering Company	East	1920	1940	51
Ironsides Company	Downtown	1883	1929	53
Smith Chemical Company	West	1929	1929	10

Source: Appendix Table 1.

Factors in Location and Markets—The American Zinc Oxide Company on Windsor Avenue is a branch of a national organization. Its location in Columbus is tied to the national industry. Four factors affected its location here; perhaps the first is most important: (1) a balance was maintained between the raw materials (zinc ore or concentrate from the company's holdings in Tennessee) and the market (rubber, paint, ceramic, and chemical industries), (2) good railroad facilities were here, (3) a good supply of bituminous and anthracite coal is available, and (4) a good supply of labor is present.

Balanced between the raw materials of Tennessee and the coal of Pennsylvania, the plant can also easily reach by rail the major markets in the industrial lake states. It sells by-product sulphuric acid to the Farmers Fertilizer Company. The plant is just beyond the city's limits in Clinton Township where it can avoid restrictive zoning measures.

Natives of central Ohio started the other 3 firms. The Ironsides Company makes lubricants for the steel or wire-drawing industries from refined vegetable and animal oils. While located in a cluttered hodge-podge in the Downtown, its facilities are adequate.

The G. F. Smith Company has no bulk sales but its analytical chemicals reach world-wide markets. The company, started by a research chemist, ships its low-bulk, high-value products by parcel post.

The Barneby-Cheney Company, here since its founding, was organized by Columbus men. The activated carbon product requires domestic and foreign nut shells for raw materials. Black walnuts from Tennesse, pecans from Texas, peach pits from California, and coconuts from Java are some of the shells used. Because of the long haul to its major markets in the Texas and California oil fields, railroad transportation is used. The company has been closely tied to the American Solvent Recovery Corporation. On January 12, 1953, an announcement was made that the two firms had consolidated as the Barneby-Cheney Engineering Company; a Solvents Recovery Division will still manufacture air purification systems.

The Ceramic Products Industry

The availability of abundant raw materials in Ohio for the ceramic industry played only an indirect role in the establishment of the 4 ceramic products companies now operating in Columbus, all of which are essentially equipment-making industries rather than manufacturers of clay products. The pioneer company in this field, Orton Ceramic Foundation, was established in 1896, followed in 1920 by the Harrop Ceramic Service Company. Sixteen years later, in 1936, two other companies were established—

Ceramic Products Companies

Company Name	Area Location	Year Located: In Columbus	At Site	Number Employed 1953
Orton Ceramic Foundation	North	1896	1932	33
Harrop Ceramic Service Company	East	1920	1950	20
Industrial Ceramic Products, Inc.	Northwest	1936	1936	90
Pereny Equipment Company	Northwest	1936	1947	10

Source: Appendix Table 1.

Industrial Ceramic Products, Inc., and Pereny Equipment Company. All of the companies are relatively small, the largest—Industrial Ceramic Products, Inc., employing around 90 workers.

Factors Influencing Location—The principal factor which has influenced the establishment of these companies in Columbus is not a conventional one; it may be termed *institutional*. More specifically, it is the influence of The Ohio State University and its department of ceramic engineering. Through its early program in this field, the university trained men who are at present successfully engaged in work in the Ceramic Products Industry. The continuing research carried on at the university supplements industrial experiments and offers new techniques and ideas to the private industries just as the training program supplies technicians. While this force is specifically related to the presence of the ceramic products industries in Columbus, the interests of The Ohio State University in this field are related to the natural resources of the state. Clay, coal, and gas were the initial raw materials which stimulated the ceramic industry in the state. Westward-moving markets, which were developed during the ceramic industry's initial period of growth, added further incentive. The nation's largest clay manufacturing centers were established in the Plateau counties of eastern Ohio yet there was no established center of research in that area.

The Ohio State University answered the challenge and, unwittingly perhaps, assumed a dominant role in influencing the location of ceramic products manufacturers.

There are growing bonds between the industry and the university. Ceramic art classes (fine arts), teacher training groups, and pottery training for the layman have increased these bonds. The Battelle Memorial Institute is available to tackle problems of private industry in this field, as well as in others. That the entire program has been useful is proved by the continuing research at the university and at Battelle, by the success of local firms, and by the increasing interest on the part of the public in ceramic art.

All 4 of the companies in this industry-group relate their origins to the university. The oldest firm is the Orton Ceramic Foundation which was established by Edward Orton, Jr. Mr. Orton had organized the Ceramic Engineering Department at the university in 1894 and, while a member of the faculty, began the production of pyrometric cones for use in determining temperatures in furnaces and kilns. Earliest products were made prior to 1900 but the Standard Pyrometric Cone Company was not founded until a few years later. The business was a sideline to university work but gradually it dominated Orton's activities and he left university teaching.

The successful operation of the company, once the sole producer of the cones in the United States, led Orton to establish a research foundation to continue after his death. Its purpose was two-fold: to continue to make and supply cones to the ceramic industry, and to use all profits to continue research and to supply financial grants for research in this country. The Foundation was organized in 1932. Its location in residential North Columbus was permitted on special condition that it conform to the zoning laws. It is an attractive addition to the neighborhood.

Each of the other 3 firms can relate its development to the university's influence also. It was the prime factor in their location: other factors of market, raw materials, and/or labor, have been permissive; none has been impelling.

The Harrop Ceramic Service Company was started in 1920 by local men as an engineering service. Manufacturing was secondary but it gradually grew in importance and, in 1950, a new building was occupied in East Columbus with adequate space for manufacturing facilities. Three graduates of the university, with degrees in ceramic engineering, combined their skills and capital to form the Industrial Ceramic Products Corporation in 1936. Originally, designers of kilns and plants, they now produce supports for dinnerware in the glost (or glaze) fire as well as a few specialty items. The firm's modern, one-story plant on West Fifth Avenue in the Northwest, was one of the first manufacturing plants to be established in the area. Pereny Equipment Company was organized by a native of Detroit who received his degree in ceramics at the university. While he originally operated a pottery shop, the demand for equipment stimulated the organization of the present company. Electric furnaces, kilns of varying sizes, and a variety of other equipment, are produced for schools and industry. Expansion was rapid; the company moved to a site in Northwest Columbus which was zoned for light industry and had railroad facilities adjacent.

Competition—Competition is not great. The Orton Company has two competitors; one is in nearby Pataskala and the other in East Liverpool. Both firms were started by men who learned their profession while working for the Orton Foundation. The other firms have no strong competition.

Markets—While market accessibility was not a principal factor in location, it is doubtful whether a better location could have resulted with careful planning. Although the local firms sell to international markets, Ohio and its neighboring states absorb the bulk of production. California has been increasingly important as a market because of the strong interest in pottery-making in that state. International sales are not sought by most companies because handling costs are high and breakage is common. The Orton Foundation sells to firms in Europe, Asia and South America.

Raw Materials—A large part of the raw materials used are brought in from out of state. Orton and Industrial Ceramics use earth materials. Kaolin is obtained in the southern Piedmont and Florida, ball clays in Kentucky and Tennesse, quartz from Illinois, feldspar from Canada, and specific minerals from the source areas possessing the desired qualities. The other two firms which manufacture furnaces and kilns have entirely different raw material needs. Steel and electrical supplies are purchased locally and refractory brick comes from Pennsylvania.

Practically all transportation is by truck although the available storage space at a plant will determine how much can be stockpiled. Outgoing products are trucked since they are generally fragile and require careful handling.

Labor—Labor has been no problem since the number of workers required is small. About 155 workers are on the combined payrolls. Pereny Equipment Company has a small force of 10 but Industrial Ceramics Products employs nearly 100. About one third of the employees are women who are engaged in light, repetitive tasks. Most of the women are married and come from the neighborhoods adjacent to the plants. They are a reliable and economical working force.

Prestige—With the reputation established by The Ohio State University and by the four manufacturing firms, Columbus has gained considerable prestige as a ceramic center. A further tribute to its importance has been the erection of the new national headquarters of the American Ceramic Society on North High Street.

The Glass Products Industry

A glass industry has been important in Columbus since prior to the turn of the century when natural gas was discovered in Licking

County. At that time a number of glass companies moved to central Ohio; one of these, Federal Glass Company, remains. With the decline of the central and southeastern Ohio gas fields and the shifting market, central Ohio lost some of its earlier importance.

Glass Products Companies

Company Name	Area Location	Year Located: In Columbus	Year Located: At Site	Number Employed 1953
Federal Glass Company	South	1900	1900	1,055
Kimble Glass Company	South	1932	1932	1,568
Columbus Porcelain Metals Corp.	East	1946	1946	10

Source: Appendix Table 1.

Today, three firms produce glass products. These 3 firms, two in South Columbus and one in East Columbus, generally have sufficient space for parking and for possible limited expansion. Kimble Glass faces the major threat of encroachment by residential units. Many of its members must park on the narrow streets of South Columbus which become congested at rush hours. Federal Glass possesses over 20 acres of land in South Columbus for possible expansion.

Factors Influencing Location—The Federal Glass Company was organized in Columbus in 1900. It was founded by men who had worked in the glass industry in Fostoria, Tiffin, and Steubenville. They chose to locate in Columbus for two specific reasons: (1) the plentiful supply of natural gas then present in central Ohio was a distinct lure, and (2) land values were low at the turn of the century and some land, in South Columbus, was donated free of taxes to the company. Currently, Federal employs over 1,000 workers and reaches a nationwide market with its table and miscellaneous glassware.

The Kimble Glass Company, a subsidiary of Owens-Illinois, is a more recent addition to the Columbus industrial scene. It came to Columbus in 1932 when the parent firm sought room in which to expand. At that time the facilities of an old-line Columbus glass producer were for sale. The major product of the Kimble plant is television tubes.

The Columbus Porcelain Metals Corporation was founded in

1946. This small plant on East Fifth Avenue employing about 10 workers is an example of a planned location. The owners recognized a market in Columbus and central Ohio—there is no comparable plant within 50 miles. The company does not manufacture in the strict sense; it applies porcelain enamel to fabricated metal parts. A major customer is the White Castle System (with headquarters in Columbus) which has its metal buildings porcelainized.

The two large glass plants are handicapped, to some extent, by the limited supply of natural gas still available. As residential and industrial consumers increased in number, shortages became more critical especially during winter months. Presently, gas is piped in from the southwest. Other raw materials must also be imported although the position of Columbus is more favorable, in most cases. Sand is purchased in the lake states and soda ash and lime in Ohio. From the standpoint of accessibility to market, one firm contends that it would be difficult to be more strategically located.

Freight rates determine which type of carrier will be used, railroad or truck. Much of the bulky raw material requirements are shipped in by rail. On the other hand, trucks are utilized more frequently on out-going shipments. One estimate places 60 per cent of all shipments by rail.

Labor—An ample labor supply has been an asset to the glass firms in the past but these industries have felt the impact of the more recent industrial expansion in Columbus. Of the more than 2,600 workers employed, 868 are women who are readily available to industry in the South Columbus industrial area. They have afforded a relatively cheap labor supply in the past. Most of the labor is now unskilled. When the glass industry first came to central Ohio, it brought with it its own skilled craftsmen. No skilled crafts group has developed over the years, but increasing competition for labor has caused wages to rise. It has been stated that high labor costs in Columbus will ultimately drive the glass industry from the city. Labor requirements are such that both of the major companies could easily relocate.

Bonds—Local bonds between the glass industry and other firms are weak. Federal Glass Company controls the operations of the Hercules Box Company but the bonds between the two plants have diminished over the years. Kimble Glass, as a subsidiary of Owens-Illinois Glass Company, has its policy set by a national manufacturing firm.

The Dental Products Industry

Whenever a list of the diversified products of Columbus manufacturers is compiled, the heavy industrial commodities are stressed but the list usually ends with the phrase ". . . and even artificial teeth." A Columbus firm is one of the world's largest manufacturers of inter-changeable artificial teeth and backings for bridgework. The dental products industry in Columbus is primarily the Columbus Dental Manufacturing Company which is the only firm of four that sells to a market beyond central Ohio. The other companies are dental laboratories which serve the dental trade at a pro-

Dental Products Companies

Company Name	Area Location	Year Located: In Columbus	At Site	Number Employed 1953
Columbus Dental Manufacturing Co.	South	1903	1915	150
Alban-Theado Dental Laboratory	Downtown	1930	1930	22
Cranfill Dental Laboratory	Downtown	1945	1947	18
National Dental Company	Downtown	1930	1932	12

Source: Appendix Table 1.

fessional level. The three dental laboratories are located in the Downtown area. The Columbus Dental Manufacturing Company started operations in 1903. By 1915, it had outgrown its old quarters and moved to new quarters on Wager Street in South Columbus. The founder of the firm, Thomas Steele, was originally a watchmaker in New England. Through experience gained with a friend who made an unsuccessful artificial tooth, Mr. Steele produced a highly satisfactory one which was a modification and improvement of the earlier design. The name Steele is synonymous with the term inter-changeable teeth. Mr. Steele, who left New England when he could find no backing there, was financed in Columbus and for this reason established his shop here.

The dental laboratories produce restorations for the dental profession. They are market-oriented in the strictest sense. The Alban-Theado Laboratory was established in 1930 near the Medical

Center on East State Street. The National Dental Company began its operations shortly afterwards and, in 1932, moved to its present quarters on the sixth floor of a High Street building. The third laboratory, Cranfill Dental Laboratory is also downtown in a second floor building. This company started here in 1945 and expanded to its present quarters in 1947.

Markets—The professional market and the desire by local men to establish their own firms determined the locations of the dental laboratories. Each firm sells its finished product to the dentist who ordered the item. Competition is keen and a high degree of efficiency is required to meet standards.

The Columbus Dental Manufacturing Company, on the other hand, meets a world-wide market. Local sales are negligible; the majority of its sales are confined to the United States but may reach all continents. The company does not work in the denture field—its only product is the inter-changeable type tooth.

Raw Materials—The dental laboratories buy plastics, precious metals, and other supplies from local supply houses. The larger firm buys on a national market. The teeth used by this firm are molded and fired in eastern Pennsylvania (Philadelphia is the center of the industry) and the local firm prepares them and their backings. Gold, silver, paladium, and platinum purchased in New York and Chicago, are widely used.

Transportation—Most finished products are shipped by parcel post but the laboratories use messenger service for local deliveries. Incoming goods are shipped by parcel post or express, the nature of the product and the urgency of the need determines the method.

Labor—Each small dental laboratory must train its own working force which is a technical one that is relatively well paid. Because of the skills involved, this labor is noncompetitive. On the other hand, the Columbus Dental Company does not need highly trained workers. Its wages are lower, on the average, and labor is much more competitive. This firm employs about 150 workers of which 50 per cent are women. The three laboratories have a total of 52 workers, including 8 women.

Bonds—The companies are independent organizations and there appear to be no functional ties in Columbus although two of the firms have ties beyond the city. The National Dental Company is associated with a larger organization having 6 laboratories in Ohio and West Virginia, and The Columbus Dental Manufacturing Company has recently expanded its interests to include outlets in California and the Industrial Aluminum Foundry in Columbus. A machine shop within the main building, opened during the war, can supply small precision machined parts that are needed. A complete polishing and plating department is also maintained. Chrome, nickel, and copper plating is done for company use and for local contracts. In this way, the company keeps its minor functions in operation profitably throughout the year.

While the Columbus Dental Manufacturing Company is a well-known name in the field, no real prestige exists for the industry in Columbus. It is a specialized industry that has added to the city's importance as a diversified manufacturing center, but the real "prestige" centers are in Philadelphia and Chicago.

The Plastic Products Industry

The Plastic Products Industry is one of the newest in Columbus. Yardley Industries, the parent firm of the Yardley Plastics Company has been operating in Columbus since 1902, but only recently has it engaged in the manufacture of plastic products. The other companies have been established here since 1938. Each firm was developed by natives of the area who had ideas and capital to back them.

The Yardley organization was known for years as a manufacturer of insulating materials, weather-stripping, and screening. With new management in 1941, the firm began the fabrication of plastic wall tiles, pipe, and tubing.

The Columbus Plastic Products Company, the largest company in the local industry and one with an important national reputation, was established by Columbus natives to produce household items of injection molded thermoplastics. The Plastex Corporation makes plastic parts which are sold to other manufacturers who utilize them in a finished product. Sales to the refrigerator industry, to lamp manufacturers, and to sign and billboard firms indicate the diversity of products. The S and W Molding Company, originally a sales organization, is now an independent unit of the Yardley Industries. It finishes aluminum and plastic molded parts. Welch Plastics, a producer of custom molds to the specification of other concerns, is the newest firm.

Plant Sites—The plants are scattered over the city with three of them in the older industrial-commercial sections. The other two are on the urban fringes. The Columbus Plastic Products Company was formerly on Dublin Avenue in the heart of an old indus-

Plastic Products Companies

Company Name	Area Location	Year Located: In Columbus	At Site	Number Employed 1953
S and W Molding Company	South	1941	1946	38
Yardley Plastics Company	South	1902	1933	177
Plastex Corporation	Downtown	1939	1939	88
Columbus Plastic Products, Inc.	West	1938	1947	402
Welch Plastics Company	Northwest	1946	1946	30

Source: Appendix Table 1.

trial area but it now has a modern and spacious plant on West Mound Street. Adequate parking facilities are available and the modern, single-story plant provides economic manufacturing space. Welch Plastics has a small plant in Grandview, west of the Olentangy River. The Yardley Plastics Company now occupies a series of old, residential buildings but plans to build a new factory on a large tract in South Columbus.

Markets—These companies have the largest percentage of their sales within mid-western United States and three firms sell to foreign areas as well. New and diversified plants in the city have created a larger home market, however. About 98 per cent of the Plastex market is out of the state. The S and W Molding Company reaches the building and construction industry throughout the nation. Products include wall tiles and moldings for kitchens and bathrooms.

Raw Materials—Chemical plastics from Dow, Du Pont, Celanese, Monsanto, Bakelite, Goodrich, and Koppers companies are imported from out of state. Usually raw materials are shipped by truck but the railroads carry their share of bulk goods. Truck facilities offer faster, more convenient, and cheaper service, according to industry representatives.

Labor—Of the 705 workers, approximately 200 are women who are preferred to men primarily because they demand a lower wage and are usually more readily available. Yardley, Columbus Plastic, Welch Plastics, and S and W Molding, all use women for light repetitive jobs.

Skilled workers are not particularly needed. Simple feeding, cutting, handling, and packing operations are typical of the extrusion companies. Some stamping operations are performed in the plastics plants but most goods are molded. Even though the jobs do not require skill, the workers must be adept at their specified tasks.

Utilities—Public utilities are satisfactory in general. For the plants within the city, parking is a problem. Most plants use the neighboring streets; this is an inadequate but necessary step. The firms on the fringes have adequate parking space but in contrast lack good transit service. The same applies to expansion; those plants within the city are in older buildings which have been utilized to capacity. New plants, wisely anticipating future needs, have located in fringe areas where expansion is possible.

Summary—Columbus is not a plastics center and yet none of the companies would leave here. Each is Columbus owned and operated so that its identification is with the city. A better location might be found from a market or supply standpoint but Columbus remains a stable community in an excellent location with respect to markets and raw materials. This is an expanding industry nationally; its continued growth in Columbus seems assured.

The Rubber Products Industry

This industry consists of three small firms whose locations in Columbus are related to the local market. Their products, few in number, are assembled or fabricated rubber goods.

Sites—The companies are all small and occupy small buildings not particularly adapted for manufacturing. The Allen Company

Rubber Products Companies

Company Name	Area Location	Year Located: In Columbus	At Site	Number Employed 1953
Allen Manufacturing Company	South	1943	1946	15
Clarite of Great Lakes, Inc.	East	1950	1950	9
Fournier Rubber and Supply Company	Downtown	1933	1938	22

Source: Appendix Table 1.

has its own small, cement block building in South Columbus. The other two firms rent their buildings—one in East Columbus, and one in the Downtown area.

Factors in Location—The oldest company, the Fournier Rubber and Supply Company, was organized in 1933 when the owner, a salesman for the Goodyear Rubber Company, recognized the need for a rubber supply house in the area. In 1945, the company began to manufacture cut rubber gaskets which now constitutes one-third of the business.

The Allen Manufacturing Company formed by natives of central Ohio in 1943, is also market-oriented. It employs about 20 women who stuff shredded foam rubber into cotton ticking. The rubber is bought in Akron and the ticking from southern mills. Columbus supplies the low-wage labor to assemble the finished product. The principal urban markets are easily reached.

The third firm, Clarite of the Great Lakes is actually a battery assembly plant. It is the only firm with ties beyond the area. Established here in 1945, it is a branch of a Salt Lake City organization which has other plants in California, Kansas, and Oklahoma. The bonds are financial since all plants are independent operating units which have no ties with one another. The company chose to locate this assembly plant in Columbus since the city is a good distribution point. Its principal sales territory is in Michigan, Ohio, Indiana, and Illinois.

Raw Materials—These are few in number. Paper, cork, and asbestos are purchased by the Fournier Company from suppliers in Detroit, Pittsburgh, and Lancaster, Pennsylvania. The company hopes to manufacture metal gaskets before long; its material requirements will increase. The Clarite firm buys all of its materials. Hard rubber battery boxes are purchased in Indianapolis from the Richardson Rubber Company and battery tops are obtained in Chicago. Lead, for the battery plates and posts, comes from the National Lead Company.

Eighty per cent of the shipping is done by truck since over-night deliveries can be made at much lower rates and in shorter periods than prevail for rail hauls.

The fact that the city is a good distribution point with an extensive transportation network, and is a good labor town seems to make it an ideal location for these firms. Otherwise, there is nothing in particular in Columbus to attract or retain these firms.

CHAPTER IX

THE WOOD AND PAPER PRODUCTS INDUSTRY

Included in the Wood and Paper Products Industry are the manufacturers of caskets (5 companies), of paper and paper containers (7 companies), and of showcases and furniture (8 companies). Among the 20 companies in these industries are several of the oldest and most stable industries in the city, although the industry group as a whole is next to the smallest in the city, employing only about 1,760 workers. Only 3 of the companies employ as many as 200 workers, employment in the other 17 companies ranging from 14 to 150 workers.

TABLE 22—Wood and Paper Products Industry: Number of Plants and Number of Workers in 1953, by Industry Groups, by Period of Establishment of Plants in Columbus

Industry Group	Number of Workers	Number of Plants	Period of Establishment					
			1946–1953	1940–1945	1920–1939	1914–1919	1900–1913	Pre-1900
			Number of Plants					
Casket Industry	381	5		1	2	1		1
Paper and Paper Container Industry	845	7	2			2	1	2
Showcase and Furniture Industry	537	8	2		1		1	4
Total	1,763	20	4	1	3	3	2	7

Source: Appendix Table 1.

Almost one-third of the companies were established before 1900, 4 of them in the showcase and furniture group, 2 in the paper and paper container group and one casket manufacturer. During the 40-year period between 1900 and 1940, 8 of the companies were established at irregular intervals; one was established during the World War II period, and 4 in the post-war period.

The Casket Industry

Columbus has long enjoyed a reputation as a center for the manufacture of caskets. Although there are at present only 5 companies engaged in the manufacture, two of them are among the largest and best known in the nation.

Age and Plant Sites—The oldest company, the Columbus Coffin Company, was established in 1880; the next oldest, the Belmont Casket Company, in 1916. Two other companies were established in the 1920's—Buckeye Casket Company in 1921, and Boyertown Burial Casket Company in 1924. The fifth company, Advern Casket Company, was established in 1943 when the present owner purchased the Swetland Casket Company which was then closing.

Casket Manufacturing Companies

Company Name	Area Location	Year Located: In Columbus	Year Located: At Site	Number Employed 1953
Advern Casket Company	North	1943	1943	14
Belmont Casket Manufacturing Co.	North	1916	1916	151
Buckeye Casket Company	North	1921	1933	98
Columbus Coffin Company	North	1880	1880	41
Boyertown Burial Casket Company	South	1924	1924	77

Source: Appendix Table 1.

Four of the companies are concentrated in the North Columbus industrial area with one located in South Columbus. Four of the 5 companies have remained in the industrial area in which they were originally established although 3 of them have moved from their original locations within the area (Appendix Table 1). The Columbus Coffin Company occupies the old, multiple-story building that it erected in 1880 and subsequently enlarged in the crowded industrial area on Buttles Avenue. When the Belmont Casket Company moved into Columbus in 1916, the Columbus Chamber of Commerce was instrumental in obtaining the Peters' Buggy plant for them. The site in North Columbus is still used although considerable expansion has occurred. The establishment in Columbus in 1924 of the branch plant of the Boyertown Burial Casket Company whose offices are in eastern Pennsylvania coincided with the closing of the local Ohio Casket Company. Because of an inadequate building, the new firm moved to the Immel Body and Coates Steam Car Companies' building on South High Street where it has remained.

Factors Influencing Location—In each instance, the geographic position of Columbus, near the center of population and the national market, has been the principal factor in location although of almost equal importance has been the availability of an adequate relatively low-wage labor force. The Columbus Coffin Company moved to Columbus in 1880 from Zanesville, Ohio. The founders of the company were originally from Columbus and, recognizing the growing market in central Ohio, relocated their operations in Columbus. The Belmont Casket Company is a branch plant of a Bellaire, Ohio firm which moved most of its operations from Bellaire in 1916 because that city was poorly located with respect to markets and transportation. Columbus was chosen for its urban market, excellent rail facilities, and ready supply of low-cost labor. The labor force was considered "ideal" at the time. The Boyertown Burial Casket Company in eastern Pennsylvania established a branch plant in Columbus in 1924 coincident with the closing of the locally owned Ohio Casket Company in order to contact the mid-western market.

The Buckeye Casket Company and the Advern Casket Company were formed by local entrepreneurs with Columbus capital backing them. The Buckeye Company was started in 1921 by a man who had formerly worked for other casket firms in the city. He located in Columbus because of personal contacts in this accessible market territory.[1] The Advern Casket Company was established in 1943 when the present owner purchased the Swetland Casket Company which was then closing. The geographic location was ideal for the distribution of the company's low-priced caskets primarily to the rural communities of Ohio, West Virginia, and Kentucky.

Products—All types of caskets are made ranging from cheap wooden ones to those of expensive bronze. The Belmont Casket Company, which specializes in high-quality metal caskets and considers itself the pioneer in this field, makes lead-coated steel, copper, and bronze caskets in addition to wooden caskets. The Boyertown Burial Casket Company makes only wooden caskets in its Columbus plant with the parent factory in eastern Pennsylvania supplying

[1] The Buckeye Casket Company suspended operations in 1955.

metal cases and hardware. Both the Columbus Coffin Company and the Buckeye Casket Company produce metal and wooden caskets. The smallest and newest firm, Advern Casket Company, buys the wooden shells and finishes them.

Competition is keen but it is usually restricted to specific price ranges and individual styles. The high-priced caskets reach a national market and have relatively little competition. In contrast, the cheaper caskets are rarely shipped more than 150 miles, but competition is great.

Markets—The market, the motivating force in the location of the companies in this industry, varies greatly with each firm as well as with the product. The Belmont Company sells throughout the United States; Ohio is its major sales territory, however. The Buckeye Casket Company reaches markets in 36 states in the east, south, and mid-west. Local sales are not important. On the other hand, Columbus Coffin, Boyertown Casket, and Advern Casket companies concentrate their sales in Ohio and neighboring states.

Raw Materials—The casket industry has been at no disadvantage in obtaining raw materials. Practically all of the textiles are purchased in New York City where eight textile firms cater exclusively to the casket companies. Casket woods are purchased in the nearby forested areas with oak coming from the Appalachians of Kentucky, West Virginia, and Tennessee, cherry from Pennsylvania, birch from the Adirondacks, and tulip and walnut from Ohio. Cheaper grades of wood, such as cypress, used in the construction of covered caskets, are purchased on the west coast or in the south.

Metal products come from many sources: copper from the Revere Copper Company in the Connecticut River valley, and zinc, aluminum, and lead from Chicago. Steel is purchased in Ohio from Armco Steel in Middletown, or from the Youngstown Sheet and Tube Company. Belmont Casket buys its lead-coated steel from the Wheeling Steel Compny and uses it in its stamping operations at Bellaire. Hardware supplies for the other firms are purchased out of the city with Richmond, Connersville, and Elmwood, Indiana, the centers.

Transportation—Transportation facilities are adequate for the needs of these companies. Rail service dominates this industry because it gives a better freight rate than the trucking industry. A few firms have their own trucks which insure the safe, convenient, and economical transportation of their raw materials and finished products.[2]

The Showcase and Furniture and Fixtures Industry

No company in this group has bonds with national organizations nor with other concerns in the city. All are local firms and their histories in this area are fairly long.

Age and Plant Sites—The major development in the manufacture of furniture and fixtures and of showcases had occurred by the beginning of the century. Of the 8 companies now operating, 4 were established in the 1880's or 1890's, and a fifth, in 1901. The

Showcase and Furniture and Fixtures Companies

Company Name	Area Location	Year Located: In Columbus	At Site	Number Employed 1953
Showcase Companies				
J. S. MacLean Company	Downtown	1885	1925	28
Columbus Showcase Company	Northwest	1895	1923	247
Schwartz Showell Corporation	Northwest	1899	1920	71
Furniture and Fixtures				
Franklin Lumber and Fixture Co.	North	1901	1933	47
General Furniture Corporation	North	1948	1948	58
Josephinum Church Furniture Co.	South	1882	1912	26
Boss Display Fixtures Company	West	1932	1932	15
Lerch Industries	Northwest	1951	1951	45

Source: Appendix Table 1.

other three companies, all in the furniture and fixtures group, have been established since 1932, the most recent, in 1951. Five of the plants are now located in the North and Northwest industrial areas and one each in the Downtown, West, and South Areas. All of the companies have changed their sites at some time during their histories, but only 4 of them have moved out of the industrial area in which they originally located. (Appendix Table 1.) The present plant of the Columbus Showcase Company, the second largest firm of its type in the nation, is located in the Northwest

[2] Boyertown Burial Caskets Company has its own specially-built trailers which were designed to carry casket shells between the plants and to carry finished caskets to markets.

industrial area. This plant was built to meet the specific needs of the company, reflecting the interest of the company in locational planning in relation to present and future needs. This is the only plant in the group occupying facilities especially designed for its use. The J. S. MacLean Company, manufacturers of custom show-cases, started operations in the Downtown area in 1885, but moved into an old brewery in West Columbus in 1925 where it has op-erated successfully since. The Schwartz Showell Corporation is lo-cated in Northwest Columbus where it has occupied the same site since 1920 when it moved there to gain railroad facilities and space for expansion. The Franklin Lumber and Fixture Company started operations in the Downtown area but moved into North Columbus and presently occupies cramped quarters in the crowded section of that area. The Josephinum Church Furniture Company operates in a crowded, old shop in an alley (Merritt Street) in South Co-lumbus. The General Furniture Company in North Columbus and Lerch Industries in Northwest Columbus, the two most recently established firms, started operations in available buildings not par-ticularly well suited to their needs.

Factors in Location—Accessibility to the market for the finished product has been the principal factor in the location of these com-panies in Columbus. Three of the 8 companies located in Columbus specifically to be near a growing market. The others were estab-lished here with the market as a permissive factor in their develop-ment. Access to raw materials, woods, glass, hardware and steel was a strong secondary factor, as was also good transportation facilities.

When the Columbus Showcase Company was established in Columbus in 1895, the principal manufacturers of showcases, out-side of the eastern seaboard cities, were located in Chicago, Quincy, Rockwell, and St. Louis. The founder of the Columbus Showcase Company operated a plant at Quincy but decided to move eastward to meet the market in the lower lake states. His first choice was Buffalo, but Columbus was finally chosen after the railroad facilities and the accessibility to raw materials were considered. In 1895, Columbus had a large number of rail lines entering the city that could bring in prize oak from the forests of southern Ohio and

Indiana and glass and hardware materials from the Pittsburgh area. With the addition of an adequate force of skilled, low-wage labor the combination was hard to beat. The other two showcase and display producers—Schwartz Showell Corporation and the J. S. MacLean Company, established in 1885 and 1899, respectively, were locally owned and largely oriented in their early days to Columbus and neighboring markets although more recently more distant markets have been tapped.

The Josephinum Church Furniture Company whose history goes back to 1882, was originally part of a Catholic home for boys. When the manufacturing phase of its operations was ordered separated from the church, a group of Columbus businessmen saw the possibilities for investment. The General Furniture Corporation, manufacturer of dinette furniture, and Lerch Industries, a manufacturer of custom living room furniture, are both new companies. The latter was started by a man who had successfully operated the Crise Manufacturing Company (electric products) in Columbus. He started this company after retiring from the Crise organization. General Furniture centered its activities here so as to reach the markets within Ohio.

Markets—Markets range from central Ohio to the entire nation. In most cases, stock items are produced by each shop but custom production is a considerable part of the business. Some companies, the Columbus Showcase Company for instance, have regular customers for whom they make showcases. One such customer is the Parker Pen Company which uses the local firm's showcases in its retail store displays. The showcase market is expanding—80 per cent of the firm's market was in Ohio 20 years ago, but only 20 per cent is now centered here.

Church furniture is sold nationally but the other furniture firms are more limited. Only the Franklin Lumber and Fixture Company sells overseas. Minor sales are made in South America and Asia.

Raw Materials—Wood is the principal raw material; the quality of wood needed depends upon its application in the finished product. The Josephinum Company uses the finest quality oak from the Appalachians and elm from Michigan and Wisconsin. Cherry and walnut, once favorites, have gone out of style and are no longer readily available. The showcase firms once used Ohio oak almost exclusively for the finished wooden cases, but Appalachian and west coast areas supply the requirements today. Glass is still purchased in Pittsburgh and in Mt. Vernon, Ohio. Hardware comes from Chicago and Grand Rapids; the latter is an important supply center because of the furniture industry there.

Steel is purchased by the Franklin Lumber Company for its refrigerated cases in Pittsburgh, Middletown, and Cleveland. The Lerch firm buys finished wooden frames from shops in Grand Rapids, springs and felt from a variety of sources, and textiles in New York City.

Transportation—While practically 90 per cent of the finished goods is shipped by truck because of speed and convenience, it was railroad transportation that was a factor in location 50 years ago. Railroads are rarely used today; usually only for the importation of wood. Most of the large plants have sidings and plenty of dock and storage space.

Labor—From a labor standpoint, this is a small-scale industry. A total of 537 persons is employed. The largest employer is the Columbus Showcase Company with about 250 workers. No other firm employs more than 71 workers. With a large percentage of the work requiring skilled carpenters and wood-working craftsmen, there is a shortage of good labor. The Josephinum Company, which requires a four-year apprenticeship for its workers, finds it difficult to interest young men in this work. Frequently, the showcase plants attract the partially trained apprentices with the lure of higher wages. The Lerch Company imported its essential laborers from Grand Rapids before it began operations here.

The Paper and Paper Container Industry

Age and Plant Sites—The three oldest companies in this industry were established near the turn of the century, Columbus Paper Box Company in 1890, Frankenberg Brothers, Incorporated in 1895, and the Dobson-Evans Company in 1902. Two companies have been established since the close of World War II—Pollock Paper Company in 1946, and Puritan Products Incorporated, in 1951.

Paper and Paper Container Companies

Company Name	Area Location	Year Located: In Columbus	Year Located: At Site	Number Employed 1953
Corrugated Container Corporation	North	1916	1946	140
Hercules Box Company	South	1919	1919	200
Pollock Paper Company	South	1946	1946	200
Puritan Products Incorporated	South	1951	1951	22
Frankenberg Brothers, Incorporated	Downtown	1895	1923	102
Columbus Paper Box Company	West	1890	1920	92
Dobson-Evans Company	Northwest	1902	1938	89

Source: Appendix Table 1.

Three of the plants are located in South Columbus, with one each in the North, West, Downtown, and Northwest areas.

Factors in Location—A market-oriented industry, dependent upon distant sources for its raw materials, is the Paper and Paper Container Industry. The Columbus shoe industry created an important local market at an early date and was a principal factor in the location of the four container companies. A generally favorable market influenced the location of the three remaining firms.

The oldest firm, The Columbus Paper Box Company has been here since 1890. It is distinctively market-oriented toward the shoe industry. The set-up and folding paper boxes it makes, although light, are high in bulk and, therefore, costly to ship. A plant here was well-situated for the markets in neighboring Chillicothe, Washington Court House, Lancaster, Nelsonville, Xenia, Logan, and Portsmouth shoe centers.

Frankenberg Brothers, Incorporated, founded in 1895, manufactures folding boxes for the retail trade that is found within 500 miles of the city. The founders were natives of the area who recognized a growing market in central Ohio. The business has expanded so that less than 20 per cent of its sales are now in Columbus; the majority is in Ohio and adjacent states.

The Corrugated Container Company is one of two firms which was located in the city by outside interests. Eastern investors chose to build here in 1916 when they sought a good location in the heart of the growing mid-west. About 65 per cent of the company's sales remain in central Ohio with the majority of the corrugated products going to the consumer goods industries.

The Hercules Box Company, on Marion Road in South Columbus since 1919, is a fully-owned subsidiary of the Federal Glass Company. All of its production originally went to the parent firm but today very little does. The growth of the company resulted from the parent firm's desire to consolidate its facilities in South Columbus where space was available and good transportation present.

The largest paper plant in the city, and the only one with bonds beyond the city, is the Pollock Paper Company on Frebis Avenue in South Columbus. This plant which came to Columbus in 1946, makes wax paper for bakeries. It is one of 5 plants owned by a Texas group which has a wide market throughout much of southern and eastern United States. Originally, the plant was in Cincinnati but when that factory was forced to close, Pollock decided to buy a "going" concern rather than to build a new plant and be forced to shut down operations entirely. The Ohio Wax Paper Company, in Columbus, was for sale at this time. It was bought by Pollock interests and its building was occupied. Most of the Cincinnati operations were moved here but, later, some were moved to Middletown. In addition to the two Ohio factories, two branches serve the southwest from Dallas and Houston.

The remaining two firms are natives in all respects. The Dobson-Evans Company, a manufacturer of cut paper products for an Ohio market, first set up operations in 1902 in the Downtown. It now occupies a modern building in Northwest Columbus. The newest and smallest firm, Puritan Products, Incorporated, was founded in South Columbus in 1951 to make cellophane and polyethylene bags. About 70 per cent of its market is in central Ohio with the remainder in states west to the Mississippi.

Transportation Problems—Handling of goods is a problem in this industry. Many box firms ship to their principal customers as frequently as once a day because purchasers usually do not have storage space and can make only limited purchases. The necessary frequent shipments can be most conveniently handled by truck. The Pollock Paper Company has its own handling problem. Wax paper requires careful handling. It must be shipped by refrigerated truck or car so that it is satisfactory for immediate use. The company uses its own trucks and it trains crews for the delivery and handling work. The firm imports its raw materials by rail, however.

Raw Materials—While markets are concentrated in central Ohio, none of the raw materials is obtained locally. Paper is purchased from scattered mills in the United States and Canada; cardboard comes from plants in Middletown, Toronto, Urbana, and Franklin; paper board and kraft paper, used in corrugated boxes, is bought in the South Atlantic and Gulf states. Chip board, used by one firm, comes from Middletown, Lancaster, and sources in Pennsylvania and New York. The petroleum industry in Texas and Indiana supplies Pollock with wax; printing ink is bought in central Ohio. Cellophane and polyethylene, used by Puritan Products, is obtained from chemical companies such as Du Pont.

Labor—There is a better supply of semi-skilled workers in Columbus than in most cities. Even so, labor is tight. About 845 workers are employed and 248 of these are women. The Pollock Paper Company and Hercules Box Company are the largest employers each with 200 workers. Puritan Products has only 22 workers. Heavy female employment is found at the Columbus Paper Box and Frankenberg Box companies. Women are well-suited for work in this industry.

Unions are present in four plants but activity is at a minimum. The average wage is about $1.25 to $1.75 an hour with incentive systems in force. The South Columbus firms find that the dependable labor of the past is no longer abundant. Good plant and secretarial help is scarce.

Local Handicaps—Similar handicaps as those that have appeared in other groups are common here. Gas service is not adequate. Plants in the South Columbus area were unanimous in agreeing that poor transit service was a major handicap to the development of that area. All of the plants have adequate parking space, even in the crowded industrial areas, but such space is obtained at high costs.

Prestige—This is not a prestige industry but it is another example of a distinctively market-oriented industry that has prospered.

CHAPTER X

THE SHOE AND TEXTILE PRODUCTS INDUSTRIES

The Shoe and Textile Products Industries are older in Columbus than the founding dates of most of the firms now operating would indicate. The Shoe Industry has had a colorful history in Columbus and the city remains a minor shoe center today with 9 plants employing about 2,350 workers, and with one company, the H. C. Godman Company, tracing its history back to 1865[1] The

TABLE 23—Shoe and Textile Industries: Number of Plants and Number of Workers in 1953, by Industry Groups, by Period of Establishment of Plants in Columbus

Industry Group	Number of Workers	Number of Plants	Period of Establishment					
			1946–1953	1940–1945	1920–1939	1914–1919	1900–1913	Pre-1900
			Number of Plants					
Shoe Industry	2,348	9		3	4	1		1
Textile Industry	2,224	14	2	1	5	3	2	1
Total	4,572	23	2	4	9	4	2	2

Source: Compiled from Appendix Table 1.

Textile Products Industry as represented in Columbus might well be found in any city the size of Columbus. The 14 firms in this group manufacture a variety of unrelated products. Three of the companies have been operating in Columbus since the beginning of the century. The oldest, National Glove Company, was established in 1899, and in 1900 the Columbus Coated Fabrics Company and the J. P. Gordon Company were established. Six of the companies have located in Columbus since 1940—3 in the shoe industry and 3 in the textile products industry, two of which have been established in the post-war period. The Barry Corporation established in 1947 is the largest company in the group, employing about

[1] Since this study was completed the Godman Company has closed its manufacturing plant in Columbus.

1,800 workers. A relatively large proportion of the workers in these industries are women who are adept at the type of work involved, and are available at relatively low wages.

The Shoe Industry

The Shoe Industry, originally concentrated in New England, and specifically in Massachusetts, has spread over much of the midwest and eastern south. The concentration of the industry in New England had occurred because of a variety of factors: an early start, an export market, availability through imports of hides, and the abundance of cheap labor trained in this work.[2] With unionization of labor and the leasing of shoe-making machinery,[3] which introduced mechanization and increased the division of labor, the industry moved closer to the center of population. Cheap, nonunion labor and access to the important mid-western markets have made Columbus an excellent location.

Age and Plant Sites—Although Columbus was an early center for shoe manufacturing, with the exception of the Godman Shoe Company established in 1865 and the Jones Heel Manufacturing Company, in 1916, all of the companies now operating have been

Shoe Companies

Company Name	Area Location	Year Located: In Columbus	Year Located: At Site	Number Employed 1953
Jones Heel Manufacturing Company	South	1916	1916	20
Dickerson, Walker T., Shoe Company	Downtown	1930	1930	350
Godman, H. C., Company	Downtown	1865	1923	351
Joyce, Incorporated	Downtown	1941	1941	253
Julian and Kokenge Company	Downtown	1932	1932	911
Hollywood Products, Incorporated	Downtown	1945	1945	29
Prima Footwear, Incorporated	East	1940	1948	360
Leighton Heel Company	West	1931	1938	41
Leighton Fiber Products Company	West	1938	1938	33

Source: Appendix Table 1.

[2] The term *trained* is used in preference to *skilled*. Workers in this industry are trained to a job—they are not skilled craftsmen.

[3] Machinery in the shoe industry is leased. This permits a small shoe manufacturer to start in the business with a minimum of capital. It also allows for much mobility within the industry.

established since 1930, 3 or one-third of them, during the period from 1940 to 1945. The plants are concentrated in or near the heart of the Downtown Area where expansion is limited and parking difficult. Characteristically they are housed in multiple-story buildings which, generally, have been given good care.

Factors in Location—Shoes have been made in Columbus since the early 1800's but never on a large scale until the 1880's. The H. C. Godman Company, which had started as a leather-finishing business at the close of the Civil War and began to make shoes after the McKay Automatic Stitcher was invented, became one of the nation's biggest shoe manufacturers. In 1890 the firm left one factory in Columbus and moved other facilities to Lancaster. Later, labor difficulties brought it back to West Columbus where a very large five-story plant was erected. This company had two other factories here and one each in Xenia and Logan; the firm was one of the four largest in the country. As a result of over-expansion and the subsequent depression the firm held only the two local plants and its Logan factory in 1940. The West Columbus building was sold to the Federal Government during the war. All other manufacturing facilities in the city have since been abandoned. In 1949, a large plant in Marion, Indiana, was purchased and is now used as the company's headquarters. A retail system of about 100 stores still operates consuming nearly 50 per cent of the company's output.

The Godman Company's experiences are typical of the shoe industry. Because it is a low-wage, labor-oriented industry, any disturbance of labor may affect its location. Commonly, the movement of a large shoe firm from an urban center to a rural community is a reflection of this sensitivity. In addition, the leasing of machinery permits much easier and cheaper movement than would otherwise occur.

The Jones Heel Manufacturing Company, the second oldest in the city, has also experienced such moves. It was first organized in Pennsylvania at the turn of the century, but the firm moved to Columbus in 1916 to consolidate factories located in Williamsburg, Batavia, and Dayton. In addition, its principal market—H. C. Godman Company—was here, and a secondary market in Cincinnati was accessible. Trained labor was relatively plentiful and wages were low. Today, a market remains in Ohio (locally and in Portsmouth) but the growing market is in the south.

Labor has influenced the moves of the Julian and Kokenge Company also. This Cincinnati firm was represented in Columbus by its subsidiary, the Lape and Adler Company, from 1921 until 1932 when the parent firm came here. Labor problems in Cincinnati in the form of unionization and the demand for higher wages forced this move.

Walker T. Dickerson, a man trained in the Julian and Kokenge organization, started his own company in 1930 when he purchased the Reilly Shoe Company. He recognized the fine physical facilities here, the presence of a trained, low-wage labor force, and the national market for women's shoes. Today, the Dickerson Shoe Company and Julian and Kokenge compete in the sale of quality women's dress and health shoes.

Two relatively new firms manufacture dance and ballet shoes. Prima Footwear, Incorporated and Hollywood Products, Incorporated were established here in 1940 and 1945, respectively. The former company has occupied its South Columbus factory since 1948 and has recently expanded. Hollywood Products was organized by a couple who had previous experience in other shoe factories. Their plant on North High Street, is in a crowded, inadequate building.

Joyce, Incorporated, a California manufacturer of women's shoes and the originator of the platform shoe, moved most of its facilities to Columbus in 1941 to be nearer its raw materials and to reduce shipping costs to the major markets. With experienced, low-wage labor present, the company felt the move a wise one. It began operations in Pasadena, California, and still retains offices and sales rooms there. Its principal manufacturing plants are in Columbus but there is also a small factory in Xenia and shoes are made under contract by a New Hampshire firm.[4]

Industrial linkage was a factor in the location in Columbus of

[4] The Joyce organization has been merged recently with The United States Shoe Corporation, with headquarters in Cincinnati.

two separately organized firms owned by the same New England firm. The Leighton Heel Company, a branch of Leighton Industries of Lynn, Massachusetts, Auburn, Maine, and Lynchburg, Virginia, was organized here in 1931 to produce fiber heels. It came to Columbus because a large percentage of its business was with the Godman Company. In 1938, the firm bought a Godman-owned building in West Columbus and, with it, purchased the fiber production facilities of the Godman Company. Through this functional tie-in, the Leighton Fiber Products Company produces fiber board used by the Leighton Heel Company and other manufacturers of shoe heels.

Labor—The principal force attracting this industry has been labor. Currently it is tight and wage demands are higher than usual. Approximately 2,350 workers are employed—more than 1,350 are females. Women workers are commonly associated with the shoe industry because they form a mass of cheap labor in communities where men are employed in other industries. The shoe industry is a symbolic industry in Columbus making complementary use of available female labor.[5] Unions exist in only 2 of the 9 plants— the H. C. Godman Company and Julian and Kokenge, two of the larger firms. Less than 50 per cent of the labor in the national industry is unionized due largely to the many moves the companies have made.

Much of the labor requires no more than repetitive skills. It is largely handwork done at cutting, sewing, stitching, or shaping machines. Some operations are carried out while seated at a machine although such jobs as cutting or shaping counters are done at upright machines. Frequently the work is on an incentive basis with a base wage established and increments added for extra production. Most of the machines in any shoe plant are leased from the United Shoe Machinery Company. Leasing of machinery is further important as a factor in the location of plants[6] since it not only permits a company with little capital to enter the business, but makes it

[5] In northeastern Pennsylvania, where the male workers were employed in the anthracite mines, the shoe industry located to use the cheap female working force that was available.

[6] Alderfer, E. B., and Michl, N. E., *op. cit.*, p. 494.

easier for companies to move away from tight labor areas. Thus, the availability of cheap labor and the leasing system are basic factors in the location of the shoe industry.

Market—There is another consideration in a review of the factors which influence the location of this industry. It is the role of market. The H. C. Godman Company attracted at least three other firms to the city. The Godman Company purchased as much as 100 per cent of their production at times.

Central Ohio is a good distributing point for the major national markets. The Jones Heel, Leighton Heel, and Leighton Fiber Products companies sell their specialized supplies to manufacturers locally and nationally. All other firms manufacture shoes for the retail trade. Of these, only the Godman and Julian and Kokenge organizations have their own retail outlets. Competition is very keen.

Markets vary. The Godman, Julian and Kokenge, and Prima Footwear companies sell beyond the United States to South American and Pacific nations. The supply houses are more restricted. The Jones plant concentrates sales in central and southern Ohio but also reaches Kentucky, Tennessee, and West Virginia. Fifty per cent of Leighton Heel's sales are in Ohio with neighboring states, Missouri (largely St. Louis), and the Pacific coast absorbing the remainder. Fiber products are even more restricted. About 50 per cent of their production goes to the heel plant and the remainder to the Williams Shoe Company and the Selby Shoe Company in Portsmouth.

Raw Materials—For a century or more, raw material supply centers have been in the New England and Eastern Seaboard states. Leather, cloth, and findings are still obtained there. Pennsylvania, Ohio, and Wisconsin have recently become important centers. St. Louis, probably the nation's leading shoe center, is another big supplier of findings. The scrap product used by the heel and fiber companies is difficult to obtain. It is found occasionally in this area but ordinarily it must be imported from the east.

A large percentage of imported goods are carried by rail since the long haul of supplies and scrap is more economical this way. Finished shoes are shipped by truck. Smaller lots and shorter distances dictate the type of carrier used.

Summary—Labor has been the immediate impelling force in the location of the Shoe Industry in Columbus, but the growing western market has affected the national regional shift. There have been many permissive forces. Some of them have assumed impelling characteristics at various periods in the industry's development. The growing western market and the presence of the H. C. Godman Company in the city attracted factories. The leasing system, within the industry itself, permits the easy establishment of a shoe factory in any community with a satisfactory labor force. And lastly, because shoe plants have been here for almost 90 years, the city has gained some prestige in this industry. This, too, may be a permissive force in the location of a new plant.

The Textile Products Industry

The 14 companies comprising this group manufacture a great variety of textile products the most widely advertised of which is oil cloth. Among other products are sheepskin and coated gloves, automobile seat covers, burlap and cotton bags, trousers, suits, uniforms, dresses, fabric notions, knapsacks, and burial slippers. For the most part, products are sold directly to retail houses or are handled through wholesale houses or jobbers. In most cases sales are nationwide although the United Woolen Company, Joseph and Feiss, and the smaller bag firms have more limited markets. The Columbus Coated Fabrics Company, manufacturing a variety of oil cloth, is one of the few to sell to a world-wide market.

Age and Plant Sites—The oldest company in the group, the National Glove Company, was established in 1899 and has been located at its present site in East Columbus since 1901. The largest company, the Columbus Coated Fabrics Company, employing more than 1,000 workers, was established in 1900. Since its establishment it has remained at the same site in North Columbus in a large factory which when built in 1900 was on the outskirts of Columbus. Industrial and residential expansion has since hemmed in this plant.

The plants are largely concentrated in the older industrial areas of the city, primarily in the Downtown, where they occupy rented space on the second and third floors of the downtown buildings, and East Columbus areas.

Textile Products Companies

Company Name	Area Location	Year Located: In Columbus	At Site	Number Employed 1953
Columbus Coated Fabrics Company	North	1900	1900	1,073
Practical Burial Footwear Company	North	1915	1920	29
Hercules Trouser Company	South	1921	1921	89
Central Ohio Bag and Burlap Company	East	1937	1950	10
Columbus Glove Manufacturing Company	East	1932	1946	46
Gordon, J. P., Company	East	1900	1932	78
National Glove Company	East	1899	1901	56
Simon and Haas Company	East	1917	1946	26
Barry Corporation	Downtown	1947	1950	180
Capital Bag and Burlap Company	Downtown	1918	1936	20
Joseph and Feiss Company	Downtown	1945	1945	138
Rudolph Stern Dress Company	Downtown	1931	1946	29
United Woolen Company	Downtown	1924	1924	350
White-Bush Manufacturing Company	Downtown	1950	1950	100

Source: Appendix Table 1.

Factors in Location—A variety of factors have influenced the location of these firms in Columbus. The three older companies, National Glove, Columbus Coated Fabrics, and the J. P. Gordon Company, were all started here more than 50 years ago. The latter two were, in effect, out-growths of the important buggy industry. The first made buggy tops and aprons and the latter made horse covers, storm fronts, and other items. The J. P. Gordon Company more recently had been widely known for its automobile seat covers. (Early in 1954 the firm closed its plant). This pioneer in the seat cover field had faced growing competition with over 400 firms. In addition, the use of man-made synthetic fibers in new automobiles might well forecast the decline of the entire industry in the near future.

Between 1915 and 1920, the Practical Burial Footwear, Simon and Haas, and the Capital Bag and Burlap companies were organized to take advantage of the westward-moving market. The first two have now expanded to meet a national market.

Three firms moved into Columbus. The Hercules Trouser Company, an industry that makes complementary use of cheap labor, came to Columbus in 1921 from Zanesville.[7] In 1935, a de-

[7] Labor difficulties, principally unionization efforts, continue to plague this company locally and in the neighboring communities, where its branches operate. The situation is similar to that in the Shoe Industry.

centralization program was initiated to establish plants in nonindustrial communities where cheap female labor could be employed. Wellston, Manchester, Hillsboro, and Jackson, Ohio, are manufacturing outlets; the Columbus plant is largely a warehouse and office.

The United Woolen Company came to Columbus in 1924 when the company's plant in Parkersburg, West Virginia burned. The location here was based principally on the accessibility to markets. The Rudolph Stern Dress Company moved here from Toledo at this time.

The only other outside firm, and the only branch plant, is the Joseph and Feiss Company of Cleveland. The firm has been in existence since 1841 but it came to Columbus only in 1945. The principal reasons for this move were the availability of an adequate building and presence of cheap labor. The local plant makes men's trousers which are then shipped to the home plant where they are matched with suit coats made in a Rochester, New York, plant.

Local investment and initiative are responsible for the growth of the four remaining firms which were established since 1936: the Columbus Glove Manufacturing Company, the Central Ohio Bag and Burlap Company, the Barry Corporation, and the White-Bush Manufacturing Company. (It is significant that the textile firms are still coming here. Whether the recent industrialization in the city will discourage these moves remains to be seen.)

Labor—Cheap, nonunion labor that was once a principal force in permitting the successful development of textile factories is now less abundant. The new industries which have located in Columbus in recent years have greatly affected the availability of this help. Textile firms charge that "pilfering" and "pirating" of labor has been extreme. The easy labor market is gone.

Of the 2,224 workers, approximately 1,100 are employed by the Columbus Coated Fabrics Company. The two bag companies are the smallest employers with fewer than 20 workers each.

Female workers, comprising one-third of the work force, are used in those plants which do not normally operate at a full schedule. Where lay-offs are frequent, male workers cannot be retained, hence the heavy use of females. In these cases, many of the women are married; they work for "pin money." Where the male ratio is high, as in the Columbus Coated Fabrics factory, heavy and steady work is involved. Here huge machines, which print and coat fabrics, are handled by men. In the Columbus Glove plant men dip, dry, and pack industrial gloves.

Raw materials—A variety of textiles and accessories is purchased in east coast cities. The National Glove Company, one of the few firms manufacturing sheepskin gloves in this country, buys skins in France, Australia, and Iran. The Columbus Glove Company does not make a glove. It buys cloth gloves from firms in Chicago and Detroit and then coats them with various protective agents. The Columbus Coated Fabrics Company buys its textiles and oils in the east and south, although the rotogravure work is done in an adjacent plant.

Utilities—Without exception, public utilities are satisfactory. The water supply is adequate, the gas supply is sufficient, and the electric service, to this large consumer, is very good. Public transit facilities are available at every plant, largely because of their near Downtown locations. Expansion space and parking facilities are not satisfactory in most cases, particularly in the Downtown area.

Summary—The Textile Products Industry, while not as homogeneous as the Shoe Industry, is a fairly large one in Columbus. Its great diversification of products binds it to no single market. The historic bonds between the producer and the eastern and southern mills remain a characteristic feature. It can trace its successful development to the initiative and investment of local men, and to the satisfactory labor market that has prevailed in central Ohio for more than 50 years.

CHAPTER XI

MISCELLANEOUS INDUSTRIES

There remain four companies (or industries, in this case) that can not be grouped satisfactorily with the other industry-groups. They are included in the study because they are basic manufacturing companies. (Certain entire industry-groups were purposely omitted from the study because they were not engaged in manufacturing activities in the metal, chemical, wood and paper, shoe and textile industries which are more representative of the maturing industrial community). The firms of the Miscellaneous Industries group are borderline firms that might justifiably fit into one of the other 20 groups. Each firm's activities are discussed, the forces in their development analyzed and their role in the industrial community considered.

Three of these companies are among the oldest in the city, having been established by 1900, and the fourth company has been operating in Columbus since 1935. All but one are located at sites in the older industrial sections of the city.

Miscellaneous Industries

Company Name	Area Location	Year Located: In Columbus	Year Located: At Site	Number Employed 1953
Weinman Pump Manufacturing Company	North	1877	1908	125
Commercial Paste Company	North	1900	1920	29
Franklin Glue Company	Downtown	1935	1945	27
Columbus Sucker Rod Company	Northwest	1900	1923	24

Source: Appendix Table 1.

Pumps—The Weinman Pump Manufacturing Company was situated along the banks of the Scioto River from 1877 to 1908 when the city took the site for river improvements. Then the company produced hydraulic water pumps; now centrifugal pumps for water units are made. Once many pump shops were in Columbus but 90 per cent of the business is now handled by this firm which reaches national and international markets.

Minor local handicaps, such as the lack of space and limited accessibility to railroads, are outweighed by advantages. The mines of central United States are the principal markets and they are easily reached. All of the major industrial markets are served quickly by the good railroad and highway systems. It would be hard to find a better location for this small firm's specialized operations.

Bronze and aluminum castings are made in the factory; grey-iron castings come from Poulton Foundry which has been closely associated with Weinman's for more than 50 years. Steel and monel metals for machine parts are purchased in Pittsburgh and Marion, Ohio. With no immediate access to the railroads, more than 90 per cent of all shipping is by truck.

About 125 men, 25 Negroes, are employed. The Negro workers are used in the core and foundry rooms. A large machine shop is also maintained in the factory where planing, boring, shaping, and other operations are performed by skilled workers on the finished pumps.

Sucker Rods—A local man organized the Columbus Sucker Rod Company more than 50 years ago to make wooden sucker rods for the oil industry. Since that industry has shifted to deep drilling and since most of its activities have shifted from Ohio, the company now makes the rods for water wells.

Competition is light since only a firm in Delaware, Ohio, and one in Texas compete. The Columbus firm supplies all of the metal couplings for its competitors. While the company might be better situated in Texas for its market, raw materials, excellent transportation facilities and favorable freight rates are all present in Columbus. Texas is the important market for water rods since much of the range land depends upon well water. Over 80 per cent of all products are moved by rail—this includes the finished rods which are shipped in carloads, the lumber which comes from the South, and the steel which comes from Pittsburgh and Youngstown.

Only 24 workers are connected with the firm but some of them have been with it for more than 40 years. There is little labor turnover and new firms have had virtually no effect upon this company's operation.

It is adequately served by all public utilities at its attractive Northwest site. No expansion is anticipated since the market is stable.

Glues and Adhesives—Neither the Commercial Paste Company, organized here in 1900, nor the Franklin Glue Company, founded in 1935, located here because of raw materials supplied by the meat-packing industry. Both firms are the product of local initiative and investment. The older firm had the backing of natives from the start, and available capital was a prime factor in the location of the Franklin Glue plant. The present buildings, even though multiple-storied and in a crowded area, offered superior facilities when occupied in 1920 and 1945, respectively.

The Commercial Paste Company makes school pastes, hardware pastes, and industrial glues (newspapers, printers, etc.). Franklin Glue produces glue for wood industries and for over-the-counter sale in hardware stores.

Franklin Glue depends upon animal hides for its raw materials but the Commercial Paste Company uses vegetable dextrones, flour, and chemicals. Local warehouses supply some needs but the majority of materials are shipped in from Chicago and east coast centers.

The two firms employ between 20–25 male workers each. In addition, the Commercial Paste Company uses 7 women to pack, fill, and label the product. Of the 27 workers at Franklin Glue, about 20 are Negroes. Neither firm has felt any competition for workers resulting from the industrial expansion in Columbus.

CHAPTER XII

CONCLUSIONS

The foregoing geographic analysis of the industrial development of Columbus, Ohio has indicated that the changes which have occurred have been *evolutionary* in character. During the century and a half of economic development, the growth of manufacturing activity was gradual; at no time was there a significant change in the economic base of the city.

The events since 1940 have greatly modified the pattern of industrialization in the city which had evolved since the middle 1800's. The traditional factors of plant location have been appraised and re-evaluated. New factors, frequently the result of the changing economy, have been uncovered and their impact upon the future industrial growth of Columbus has been assessed.

A consideration of these factors alone lends credence to any statements regarding the continued industrial growth of the city. But it is important that Columbus be considered in the major frame of reference—as an Ohio city, and as an important industrial center in the heart of the American manufacturing belt. The industrial future of Columbus cannot be assessed except in this larger framework.

Ohio's position as the nation's second state in manufacturing weighs heavily in any consideration of Columbus' future. The growth of the steel industry in Ohio, and the state's increasingly important role as a supplier of automobile parts is reflected in the types of industry currently experiencing growth locally. That the St. Lawrence Seaway should benefit Ohio and not Columbus is unlikely. And certainly the development of atomic power facilities in the state, and the growth of two great chemical centers—on the east lake shore and in the Ohio valley—will affect the future of Columbus.

In this concluding section, attention will be paid to these events as well as to the traditional geographic factors of plant location in an effort to suggest the main outlines of the pattern of future industrialization in Columbus.

206

CHART 5

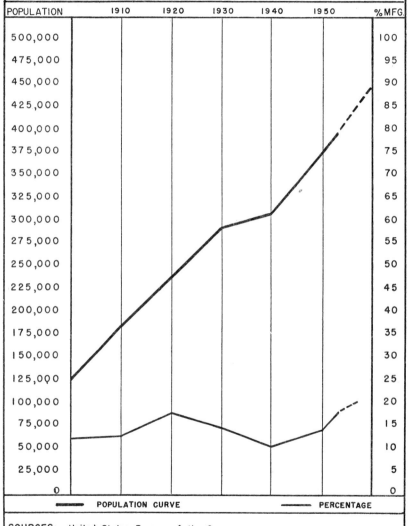

POPULATION GROWTH IN COLUMBUS, OHIO, 1900-1960:
WITH PERCENTAGE ENGAGED IN MANUFACTURING

POPULATION	1910	1920	1930	1940	1950	%MFG.
500,000						100
475,000						95
450,000						90
425,000						85
400,000						80
375,000						75
350,000						70
325,000						65
300,000						60
275,000						55
250,000						50
225,000						45
200,000						40
175,000						35
150,000						30
125,000						25
100,000						20
75,000						15
50,000						10
25,000						5
0						0

POPULATION CURVE   PERCENTAGE

SOURCES: United States Bureau of the Census
           Research Department, The Columbus Chamber of Commerce

H.L.H.'53

Prior to 1940, Columbus failed to keep pace with Ohio's growth in population and manufacturing. The city's position was enhanced, however, by the rising transfer costs of raw materials and finished products. It began to attract new industry. Between 1939–1947, Columbus experienced a 67 per cent increase in the number of production workers. This was a larger percentage increase than that recorded for the nation, state, or central Ohio region.

The growth pattern has not stopped although the sharp increases of the last decade have leveled off. A population of approximately 625,000 is forecast for Metropolitan Columbus by 1960. With about 45 per cent of the large (more than a million dollars in value) new plants in the United States being located in cities the size of Metropolitan Columbus, the growth in manufacturing may parallel that of population. The most significant result, and also a prime cause of this growth, is expected to be the continued location of branch plants in central Ohio.

The *geographical position* of Columbus has been called its major resource. More specifically, it has been the geographic position of Columbus with respect to the major national markets that has enhanced the city's growth. Historically, an expanding local market was the prime factor in industrial evolution; currently, the city's position has improved as population and industry have expanded in the west and south, and as new industrial opportunities have materialized in the lake states.

A local market is frequently the principal force affecting the development of native industry. The small manufacturing establishments of early Columbus were strictly local-market oriented. Limited by inadequate transportation facilities, the products of these shops were restricted to central Ohio markets. A sequence of changing local markets—the farm market, the railroad shops, the carriage industry, the bituminous coal mines of southeastern Ohio, and eventually the automobile industry—provided the incentive for local manufacturing activity.

Columbus firms were slow to develop a market to the north. It was not until the so-called automobile "revolution" that local manufacturers turned attention to the manufacturing centers from Pittsburgh to Chicago; it is to this area that Columbus firms look for their major markets today.

Columbus has assumed an increasingly important role as an automobile parts supplier. As further expansion by automobile manufacturers continues in Ohio and neighboring states, this city's share in the final product should increase. The expansion of steel production within the state—notably in Cleveland, Youngstown, and certain Ohio River cities—is intimately related to the expanding automobile centers. An important share of the consumers' goods of the nation are produced in this area, as well, reflecting both the increased demand for steel and a larger market for Ohio suppliers.

What influence the St. Lawrence Seaway will have upon Columbus manufacturers is a matter for conjecture. It can be assumed, however, that local firms can expect to share in any expansion of northern Ohio industries which are directly affected by the Seaway. Columbus firms which now engage in foreign trade will probably appreciate some measure of growth if the St. Lawrence Seaway is as effective in fact as is anticipated in the planning stage.

The geographical position of Columbus in the heart of the expanding midwestern market has not gone unnoticed. The most obvious example of the interest and attention devoted to the city is in the development of branch plants of national organizations.[1] The city is an excellent distributing point for both consumer and industrial markets. Within 500 miles of Columbus are the major markets for automobile parts, electrical products, industrial and mining machinery, furnaces and heaters, shoes, textiles, and such diversified products as the city makes. Two diverse examples will illustrate this point. The General Motors' Ternstedt plant manufactures hardware for General Motors' plants across the entire nation; the Westinghouse plant manufactures consumer goods which, in turn, are marketed nationally from this central distributing point.

[1] About 10 per cent of the plants in Columbus are branch plants of national organizations and another 5 per cent are firms of local origin that are now controlled by outside capital.

There remain in Columbus many industries whose activities are oriented strictly to a market within 50 to 100 miles of the city. Generally high-bulk, low-value industries, they may include local firms or branch plants of national organizations. The importance of the central Ohio market is usually great enough to keep an established industry active here, but alone it is not of such an order as to stimulate new interests or to attract new firms.

Recognition of Columbus' position with respect to the major markets of the nation was belated. In fact, an entirely unrelated event set the stage for later industrial development. Directly, and indirectly, the construction of the Curtiss-Wright aircraft plant in Columbus in 1941 has been a major cause of Columbus' post-war industrial growth. This plant, erected by the Federal Government on city owned land, broke the long hold on industrial progress that had been maintained by a few firms for more than a half century. This event was the opening wedge. The city emerged from the war period with a new kind of manufacturing activity which employed far more workers than any other industry.

The Federal Government is a powerful *institutional factor* in plant location. Its role in the localization and character of manufacturing activity has increased immeasurably in the last 15 years. Government influence, which once meant the application of government services and regulations to business, was extended during World War II and the Korean conflict to include the construction and operation of necessary war-time manufacturing facilities. Other inducements were made to defense industries, such as certificates of necessity and tax write-offs, during these periods. Some emergency measures of the war years have become accepted practices today. A number of the government-owned plants have continued in operation, either under private ownership or by leasing. (See Table 5 for a break-down of government-financed facilities in Franklin County during the war years.)

Until the Federal Government's construction of the Curtiss-Wright plant, Columbus was not well known nationally as a manufacturing center. With the war's end, Curtiss-Wright's operations were curtailed sharply and employment dropped. The large number of semi-skilled workers proved to be a lure, along with other factors, to national firms seeking to relocate branch facilities.

In locating the Curtiss-Wright plant in Columbus, major consideration was given to the presence of a small local labor surplus, and to the pool of labor which could be drawn to the city from southeastern Ohio, West Virginia, Kentucky, and other southern states. At its peak, the aircraft industry employed more than 25,000 persons—many of them not native to central Ohio. With the cessation of hostilities, thousands of Curtiss-Wright workers were without employment. This surplus of semi-skilled labor helped attract other national manufacturers to Columbus. General Motors was the first company to develop a branch plant in the city; Westinghouse Manufacturing Company has followed. In addition, local firms experienced considerable expansion.

The results of the aircraft industry's operations have not all been well received. Other manufacturers believed that the higher wage rates and the increased union activity in the city had their start in this industry. In the past, a moderate wage rate and a minimum of union activity had given Columbus little labor trouble. Neither can be ignored in a study of the future industrial development of the city, however.

In a sense, the aircraft industry stimulated local manufacturing activity. Curtiss-Wright, and North American at the present time, were dependent upon sub-contractors; dozens of new machine shops sprang up in Columbus to serve it. Established manufacturers found large contracts available with this industry. Many such firms expanded facilities and diversified products at this time. In this way, the government became a major force in industrial progress.

When Curtiss-Wright withdrew its local operations, Columbus was faced with the loss of its largest industry. The huge building first attracted the ill-fated Lustron Corporation, a maker of porcelain steel houses. A more significant move occurred in 1950, however, when the building was leased from the Navy by the North American Aviation Corporation. Columbus has profited by the presence of this large firm. It seems to be a stable addition to the industrial community, and as of this date, its future in Columbus appears sound. However, caution must be exercised in predicting the future since the aircraft industry has been notoriously unstable, and the North American company's ties with Columbus are not strong.

The factors reviewed above combined to give Columbus generally favorable national publicity. The expansion of capacity by local firms, the diversification of products, the attraction of large branch plants of national organizations to the city, and the continuing industrial growth of the city—all of these can be tied to the influence of the Federal Government in its decision to locate a single plant in the city in 1941. This institutional factor would, indeed, seem to be a principal one in effecting a change in Columbus' economic base.

There are also other institutional forces in the city which, although they have not, in the past, played such a dynamic role as the Federal Government, may be more influential in the future. Research facilities may be considered an institutional force: they may affect the location of modern manufacturing plants which depend upon advanced research to keep abreast of industrial developments. Research facilities now present in Columbus have been directly responsible for the establishment of four plants and they have indirectly influenced the location of many other concerns.

The basic facilities are The Ohio State University and the Battelle Memorial Institute. The University serves a principal purpose of training men for work in engineering, electronics, chemistry, ceramics, and similar technical fields. It also trains young people for management and sales work. It carries on fundamental research through its contracting agency, the Research Foundation. Perhaps its best known influence locally has been in connection with the emergence of the Ceramic Products Industry. Much has already been said of this. The four companies in this industry developed here because the University trained their leaders who regarded Columbus as a favorable location. Continuing research into problems of ceramic engineering and other phases of ceramic research has proved beneficial to local as well as national firms.

The Battelle Memorial Institute aids private industry, through sponsored research, in overcoming research obstacles, in cutting production costs, in establishing new processes and operations, or in designing effective machines and plants. For the national or local firm which lacks capital or has a small clientele, Battelle offers assistance in research.

Such facilities not only attract and hold local industry, they have attracted outside industries. National research organizations have recently moved to Columbus giving added weight to its significant role as a research center. The headquarters of the American Ceramic Society and a branch of the Bituminous Coal Research Institute have been opened here recently. The American Chemical Society has long concentrated its *Chemical Abstracts* staff on the campus of The Ohio State University.

Rarely do manufacturers or industrial planners consider tranportation facilities to be an impelling force in the location of industry. With rail, air, and truck lines readily accessible to most parts of mid-western United States, transportation accessibility assumes a permissive role in plant location. On the other hand, the absence of adequate facilities is enough to limit the industrial growth of certain areas. However, the position of Columbus with respect to market and raw material accessibility is enhanced by exceptionally good transportation facilities. Maps 6 and 7 show the network of transportation facilities available in Columbus—railroads, highways, and air. Five major railroad lines of inter-regional scope enter the city. Three of these provide both passenger and freight service; two are freight roads. These roads rank among the major lines of the east-north-central states. They carry more than 50 per cent of the bulk goods coming to the city although more than 80 per cent of the finished products leave by truck.

Highway facilities are generally very good. Columbus is located on a main east-west highway—Route 40—and on, or adjacent to, the north-south routes 23, 42, 33, and 3. The contemplated toll road between Cincinnati and Conneaut would be within a few miles of Columbus. Access to most parts of the city by these routes is generally adequate.

In addition to rail and highway facilities, Port Columbus, as the nation's fifth busiest airport, offers good passenger and freight

MAP 6—Trade Areas and Airline Routes of Columbus

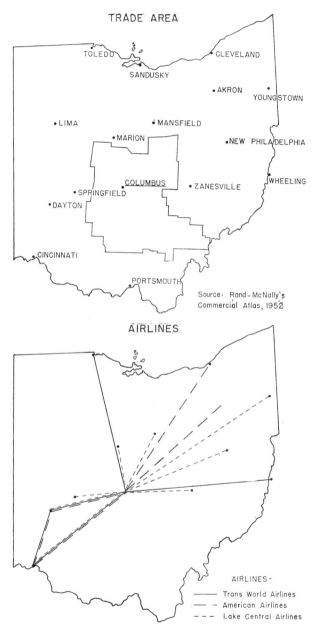

TRADE AREA

TOLEDO

CLEVELAND

SANDUSKY

AKRON

YOUNGSTOWN

LIMA

MANSFIELD

MARION

NEW PHILADELPHIA

COLUMBUS

ZANESVILLE

WHEELING

SPRINGFIELD

DAYTON

CINCINNATI

PORTSMOUTH

Source: Rand-McNally's
Commercial Atlas, 1952

AIRLINES

AIRLINES-

———— Trans World Airlines
— — American Airlines
– – – Lake Central Airlines

MAP 7—Highway and Railway Trade Routes of Columbus

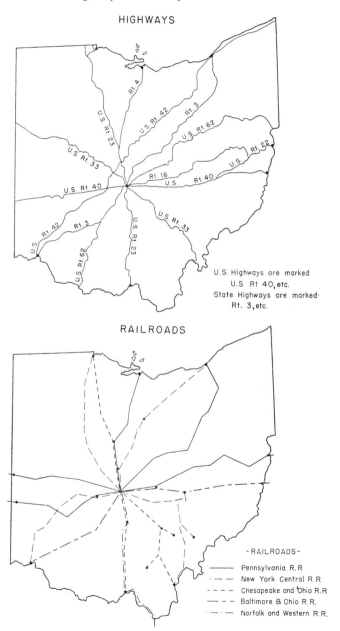

HIGHWAYS

U.S. Highways are marked
U.S Rt 40, etc.
State Highways are marked·
Rt. 3, etc.

RAILROADS

-RAILROADS-

———— Pennsylvania R.R
—·—— New York Central R R
— — — Chesapeake and Ohio R.R
— — — Baltimore & Ohio R.R.
—·—·— Norfolk and Western R.R.

service. The airport facilities have, no doubt, played a significant role in bringing such industries as Curtiss-Wright (and now North American) to the city.

The role of transportation facilities in the location of industry appears to be increasingly permissive. That is, with the exception of a handful of large manufacturing organizations in Columbus, it would appear that satisfactory transportation facilities are taken for granted. Certainly every manufacturer is aware that his ability to secure raw materials or to reach his market satisfactorily is dependent upon adequate transport. Even so, given adequate transportation facilities, most organizations give more serious thought to other factors.

Coal, iron ore, natural gas, and timber were the basic raw materials which attracted industry to central Ohio from 1870 to 1900. Satisfactory deposits of these materials are no longer available locally nor have any other materials basic to modern industry taken their place. Consequently, there are few firms in central Ohio that are raw-material oriented. It is unlikely that any new firm requiring cheap access to high quality earth materials will locate here.

Columbus is not sharing in the growth of heavy industry which is currently underway in other sections of the state. Neither the heavy metals industry nor the chemical industry has displayed interest in this area. The chemical industry's growth has been outstanding in the Ohio valley and in northeastern Ohio. Both areas possess important brine deposits, ground water, surface streams, and adequate coal for power to serve their needs. Central Ohio has neither the chemical raw materials nor the combination of these factors to encourage the expansion locally of this dynamic industry.

The geographical position of Columbus with respect to the major manufacturing centers, and therefore the major supply centers of industrial raw materials, more than off-sets the dearth of earth materials. Steel from western Pennsylvania, Cleveland, Youngstown, and the Ohio River towns is economically transported to central Ohio; manufactured metal parts are brought into the city from Cleveland, Chicago, Detroit, Pittsburgh, and many other midwestern manufacturing centers. For many commodities, Columbus has become a manufacturing-in-transit point. This is especially true in the auto parts industry. Steel and related metallic raw materials move from the production center to Columbus for processing and fabrication; the fabricated part is then shipped north to the automobile centers of Michigan and Indiana. Well balanced between supplier and purchaser, Columbus should experience further growth in the metal fabricating industry.

The traditional location factors are too often presumed to be the principal factors influencing the location of industry. By reviewing the traditional factors alone, a good case can be established to explain the location of manufacturing activity in any community. If this method of analysis were to be followed exclusively in Columbus, the case would be built upon circumstantial evidence.

Initiative and inventiveness have played an impelling role in the location of nearly 65 per cent of the Columbus manufacturing establishments. One hundred and twenty-five firms (60 per cent of the 204 firms included in the study) now operating in Columbus virtually ignored the traditional factors in determining their locations. These companies developed in Columbus for the simple reason that the owners lived in the community. It should be emphasized, however, that they have persisted because the traditional factors were generally favorable to industry.

Many such firms developed as individual mechanics or skilled machinists opened their own shops. A few of these have expanded to become large concerns. For the most part, they remain dependent upon a local market.

Fewer in number, perhaps, but more spectacular in development and success are those firms which grew out of local inventions. Many stable, old-line firms were started here through the combination of inventiveness and initiative of a few individuals. The Jeffrey Manufacturing Company and the Jaeger Machine Company are examples. There are new companies, too, whose locations in Columbus are related to local inventive genius, at least in part. Such an example is the Industrial Nucleonics Company.

Men trained in the operations of a manufacturing organization may in turn leave that organization to establish their own companies after they have accumulated the necessary skills and capital. An excellent example in Columbus is the Tool Industry where such "splintering" has occurred many times. In this case, a trade—manufacturing quality saws—was carried from the parent firms to smaller companies. Many machine shops have resulted from such "splintering," and most of the smaller shoe firms trace their origins to the training their owners received in the larger factories.

The availability of local capital has declined as a location factor, but in the past it has been responsible for the location of a number of important companies in the Columbus industrial area. The small firm's success frequently can be based upon its ability to secure capital during its formative years. In contrast, the branch plants which have more recently located in Columbus have not had to consider local capital in their plans. These firms have expanded because their parent companies had sufficient capital to launch a building program, or else capital was available nationally.

The examples of local capital attracting outside companies to Columbus are few indeed. Where this factor has played a role, it has been considerable. On the other hand, local capital has had much to do with the growth of native industries. It is unfortunate, however, that much of the timidity of local capitalists, recognized 100 years ago, persists today. Columbus can not hope to attract and keep the small manufacturer whose prime need is capital unless local lending agencies are more willing to invest in industry. Capital as a factor in plant location has been largely a negative influence in Columbus.

A force of increasing importance in plant location is represented in the national structure of a given industry. The role national structure has played in the location of industry in Columbus becomes most apparent when branch plants of national organizations are considered. The motivating factor in the location of these plants has been the dictate of the parent firm. The traditional factors of geographic planning may have been considered by the parent firm for many locations. The final choice of Columbus as a site may have been in light of the company's national distribution of manufacturing facilities, or as an outgrowth of a company's diversification policy. In a sense, the structure of the parent organization controls the choice of the branch plant site in Columbus.

When more than one unit of an industrial organization is found in a community, the functional ties between these units are probably the principal reasons for the location of added facilities. As the trend towards diversification continues, it would seem that this inter-relationship of manufacturing units would play a greater role in future plant growth. With the expansion of Columbus' industry, and with the continued development of large manufacturing concerns locally, the national structure of industry should assume greater importance as a force in the localization of industry.

There is another kind of structure—industrial structure within the city, or linkage. Linkage results when a firm locates near an already established plant either to sell to that plant or to buy a raw material from it. Linkage, as a factor in the location of industry, is perhaps most apparent in the modern chemical industry in which a producer of basic chemicals may find several processors locating nearby to make economical use of the needed materials. Linkage has not been a significant locational factor in Columbus, nor does the future seem to indicate increased importance.

The influence of labor, in one form or another, continues as a dynamic force in plant location. Columbus has offered a relatively low-wage labor force throughout its history. For the third largest city in the state and the eighth largest in the number of manufacturing employees, the prevailing wages have been low. The area (the city and Franklin County) currently ranks fourteenth among the 21 economic areas of the state in average wages paid. The trend, however, is towards higher wages.[1] This trend will cause some turnover among the manufacturing plants already established in Columbus, and it will tend to limit the types of industry which might locate here.

Although the city's rates are on a par with those of southern Ohio communities, Columbus pays wages lower by 5 to 15 cents an hour than either the large or small communities in northern Ohio. Columbus is on a line that divides the high-wage (north) and low-wage (south) areas of the state. The Ohio State Employment Service listed the following hourly wage rates offered to beginning workers by Columbus manufacturers as of March 1953:

[1] *Monthly Business Review*, Federal Reserve Bank of Cleveland, Vol. 34, No. 1, Supplement, pp. 22–23.

Males	Rating	Females
$1.00-1.20	Unskilled	$ .75-1.05
$1.15-1.35	Semiskilled	$ .85-1.15
$1.30-2.00	Skilled	$1.10-1.50

Source: *Labor Market Information,* Bureau of Unemployment Compensation, Ohio State Employment Service, March 1953.

Generally, a low-wage labor force proves attractive to most industries. It should be remembered, however, that the prevailing wage rates in this community, while now relatively low, are increasing. Such new firms as General Motors and Westinghouse were able to tap a relatively low-wage labor force by their moves to Columbus, but other firms, more sensitive to the changing labor costs, have already begun an exodus from the city. The Shoe Industry, perhaps more than any other local industry, is highly sensitive to the demands of labor. More than 50 years ago, shoe firms began a move to Columbus to enjoy the advantages of a low-wage, nonunion labor force; today, they are leaving because of the threat of competition for labor at higher rates. This competition has been a natural outgrowth of the increasing role national firms play in the economic life of Columbus.

In addition to labor costs, the presence or absence of skilled workers may be a strong factor in location. Columbus has never supported a skilled labor force; less than one-tenth of its workers were classified as skilled in 1954. With increasing industrialization, a better *trained* labor force is probable. Columbus lacks the manufacturing experience necessary for the rapid development of a relatively skilled force.

Undoubtedly a major factor influencing plant location in central Ohio at the outset of World War II and in the immediate post-war period was the availability of labor. Southeastern Ohio was a surplus labor area in 1940. The Curtiss-Wright plant was situated here, in part, to utilize this labor. North American Aviation and other national firms have continued to draw upon this pool.

National organizations consider this labor supply to be a major impelling factor in location. Southern Ohio remains the only area of surplus labor in the state.[2] In April 1953, the Ohio State Em-

[2] "Ohio Labor Market, April 1953," Bureau of Unemployment Compensation, Ohio State Employment Service, No. 32, April 1953.

ployment Service estimated that more than 7,000 workers were available in the Columbus area alone. Of this number, approximately one-fourth would come from the surrounding towns and rural areas.[3]

Industry has benefited by the absence of labor competition either within industry itself or by labor unions. This has been due, in large measure, to the diversification of manufacturing activity in Columbus. Furthermore, the influence of national firms and of national unions has been at a minimum until recently. The combined effect of national industry and national unions has been to upset the labor stability of the past. Such a combination tends to bring national wage rates, national labor issues, and large, national unions to the city.

A final characteristic of Columbus' labor is the abundance of female workers and the complementary use made of them. Male workers, attracted to higher paying jobs, leave many lower paying jobs to women. As the labor market tightens, females become a more critical factor. There is, however, no good example of true symbiosis in Columbus.

In summary, labor has proved to be a definite factor in the localization of industry in Columbus. Wage rates, skills, worker availability, competition, unionization, and other factors complicate the picture. Nonetheless, labor has been the impelling force in the location of many new manufacturing concerns; it has been a strongly permissive force in the location of many others.

Columbus has never attracted power-oriented industries. Cheap fuel is missing from central Ohio, although large reserves of steam coal are present in southeastern Ohio and neighboring West Virginia. Unless abundant supplies of low-cost fuel are made immediately available to Columbus, it is unlikely that the city will prove attractive to major power consuming industries in the future.

Suggestions have been made that Columbus will profit from atomic power or as a result of the increased steam generation of electricity which has occurred in Ohio in connection with the Pike County atomic plant. If current forecasts are reliable, it is unlikely that atomic energy will be available to private industry at com-

[3] *Labor Market Information, op. cit.*

petitive costs for some years to come. Even then, it is doubtful that this area, lying adjacent to the major bituminous coal fields of the nation, would profit immediately. Cheap power or abundant industrial power appear to be minor factors in the future industrial growth of Columbus.

The water supply of Columbus is adequate for present needs, with the exception of occasional dry spells during the summer months. The city may still be faced with a water shortage in the future if residential and industrial expansion continues at current rates. The limitations placed upon industry by the absence of an abundant surface or ground water supply, however, may be a major factor in setting limits on future industrialization. Heavy water consuming industries have not located in Columbus in the past; it is not conceivable that they will in the future.

Currently, the Griggs and O'Shaughnessy reservoirs on the Scioto River, with a combined capacity of 6.8 billion gallons, supply the city with its water. There are some wells in operation but they add a relatively insignificant amount of water to the city's total. The average daily water consumption in Columbus is approximately 58 million gallons: the reservoirs can yield an average daily supply of only 42,350,000 gallons in a very dry year.

Action is being taken to meet the growing demands of the city but there is question whether it will be adequate in terms of the long-run. The new Hoover Dam, on Big Walnut Creek, will increase estimated storage capacity of 19.7 billion gallons and the daily yield, by 50 million gallons.[4] The dam was dedicated in September 1955 with the filtration plant put into use in mid-1956.

Additional storage dams are planned for a site at the junction of the Scioto River and Mill Creek and for somewhere along the Big Darby Creek, west of Columbus. Greater capacity north of the city along the Scioto River is a necessity, according to city water officials. The key to such planning is the development and realization of these projects *before* the real need arises.

Nowhere in the county is ground water used extensively by industry. This is due partly to lack of information about ground water supplies in some areas, and to inadequate supply in other

---

[4] With added gates the gross yield is estimated to be 63.5 million gallons per day.

areas. No manufacturing plant in Columbus relies upon ground water for more than a fraction of its operations; some utilize it for cleaning and cooling operations where constant temperatures are a requirement.

In 1945 it was recommended that a survey of ground water potential should be made since areas possessing large quantities of ground water would prove to be good locations for water-consuming industry.[5] Not much action was forthcoming; no new large water-consuming industry has come to the city, either.

The only large supply of ground water in the area is believed to be found about eight miles south of the city at Reese Station. There is an estimated daily supply of 30 million gallons available there. If heavy water users are to enter the Columbus industrial community, it would seem most likely that their interest would center in that area. It appears unlikely that Columbus will attract major water-consuming industries to any other part of the area until an abundant and cheap supply of water can be assured.

The service offered by the major public utilities in Columbus is considered to be generally satisfactory. Neither the electric nor the gas companies has openly sought to attract new industry to the central Ohio area; few new manufacturing concerns have come to Columbus within the past 25 years because of an advantage reflected in either utility.

Winter-time shortages of industrial gas have hampered the operations of some large industries. A number of new manufacturing concerns reported having difficulty in obtaining sufficient quantities of gas for satisfactory operations. If this is true and if it continues, it seems safe to suggest that no large gas-consumer can afford to risk a location in Columbus under these conditions.

There is doubt whether the city can retain all of its current large gas-consumers. The glass plants have always considered cheap fuel a prime requisite for economical operations; the dependence upon fuels from beyond Ohio does not make central Ohio an ideal site.

The electric supply has been more satisfactory although rarely

[5] *Water for Columbus,* The Columbus Chamber of Commerce, Columbus, 1945. (The report was prepared by The Jennings-Lawrence Company, Civil and Municipal Engineers.)

MAP 8

PEAK HOUR
TRAVEL TIME

NOTE: TRAVEL TIMES SHOWN
ARE BASED ON AN ORIGIN AT
BROAD AND HIGH STREETS.

SOURCE: FRANKLIN COUNTY
REGIONAL PLANNING COM—
MISION.

NORTH

1/2   0   1 Mile

20 MIN.

15 MIN.

10 MIN.

5 MIN.

1 MILE

2 MILES

3 MILES

4 MILES

5 MILES

10 MIN.

15 MIN.

20 MIN.

20 MIN.

20 MIN.

more than adequate for most manufacturing organizations. Very few concerns do not receive good service but high cost and service limitations are sometimes restrictive. No doubt the electric service will continue to satisfy current consumers but as a single factor it is unlikely to attract new firms to Columbus.

Public transit facilities are another type of public utility. For the most part, public transit service to Columbus manufacturers has proved adequate. A major weakness is the transit system's failure to penetrate the built-up areas beyond the political limits of the city. Many plants lying on the fringe of the urban center do not receive transit service. This has proved to be a minor handicap in the location of some firms. A transit franchise which would permit the extension of service into adjacent residential and industrial communities is a necessity.

The exaggerated cross-roads pattern of Columbus continues to aggravate highway accessibility to various parts of the city. All parts of the city are not equally accessible either from without or from within. Consequently, accessibility to a plant site has become a factor of considerable significance in the location of industry in Columbus.

The outstanding advantage of the two newer industrial areas, Northwest and suburban West Columbus, is their accessibility. These areas are readily accessible to traffic traveling on state routes, and a well-developed street pattern provides accessibility within the communities. In contrast, South Columbus has access to only one main highway, Route 23; the absence of through streets has handicapped local shipping, according to manufacturers in the area. The limitations placed upon transportation by narrow streets, numerous dead-ends, and limited through streets has naturally handicapped the growth of the area. Downtown Columbus and part of North Columbus experience similar problems of local accessibility. Map 8 illustrates one of the problems. It shows how long it takes to travel a number of miles from the heart of the city through each major area. The bottlenecks are clearly shown as are the areas of apparent ready accessibility.

Improved transportation facilities within the city and county are required not only to support the growing industrial population but also to handle more adequately the mass of goods which moves into the city daily. New highways now in the planning stage, and the improved street program now envisioned promise increased highway accessibility in the future.

Railroad accessibility was once a prime factor in the location of industry. Accessibility to a major railroad could place a firm in a strong competitive position with respect to markets or raw materials. Columbus is especially well-served; five major railroads have important lines through the city (Map 7) and freight facilities are maintained here by each line. The three east-west routes connect Columbus with the raw materials centers to the east and the markets to the north and west. The two north-south routes—the Chesapeake and Ohio and the Norfolk and Western—carry raw materials, primarily coal, towards northern markets. These lines are freight transporters as well.

At the present time, the majority of the Columbus manufacturers interviewed revealed that rail shipments account for less than 20 per cent of their volume. On incoming goods, and especially where bulk goods are handled, the railroads account for nearly 50 per cent of the volume. Trucks have made the difference with their obvious advantages for many small manufacturers.

Local manufacturers were asked what factors were responsible for the relative decline in the use of railroad freight services. Two factors dominated their thinking: competitive costs for services rendered were more satisfactory from the trucking interests, and there is a resentment expressed locally towards the type of services rendered by the railroads. Generally, rail and truck freight rates compare favorably, but the railroads lose favor when small items are shipped, when short hauls are involved, when speed is essential, or when special handling is desirable.

A major complaint lodged against the railroads has been over the delayed movements of freight within Columbus' rail yards. The suggestion has been made that a belt-line railroad around the city, connecting the various lines, would relieve this problem. It is unlikely that such a program will win enthusiastic support from the

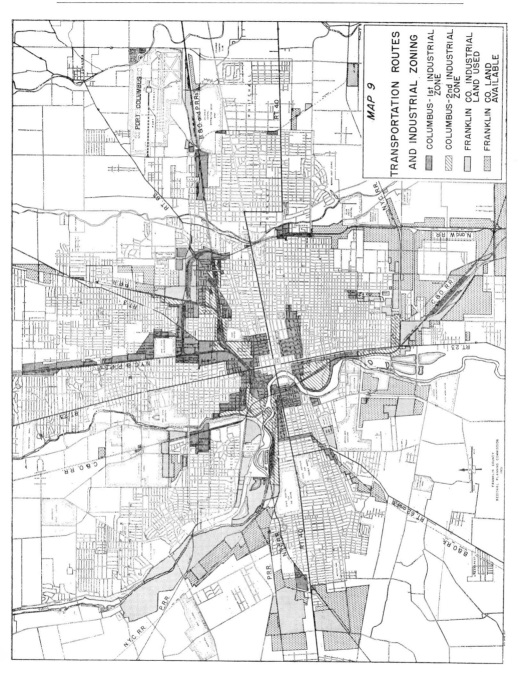

MAP 9

TRANSPORTATION ROUTES
AND INDUSTRIAL ZONING

COLUMBUS - 1st INDUSTRIAL ZONE
COLUMBUS - 2nd INDUSTRIAL ZONE
FRANKLIN CO. INDUSTRIAL LAND USED
FRANKLIN CO. LAND AVAILABLE

railroads, and the relocation of railroad lines seems to be many years off. Map 9, showing transportation routes and industrial zoning, illustrates some of the complications arising from the varied pattern of railroad lines in the city. With five major railroads entering the city from any number of directions, a badly cut-up urban pattern has resulted.

The advantages of the railroads to the city's industrial future need to be re-appraised in light of the changing pattern of industrial growth.

The differences in the zoning and tax structures between the city and adjacent townships have affected the choice of plant sites. In South Columbus, for instance, most of the large manufacturing plants lie beyond the city's limits in Marion Township. Marion Township had no restrictive zoning measures on industry in the past; in addition, its industrial tax rate was very low. The combination attracted manufacturers. They received most of the benefits of a Columbus site without having to pay for them. Today a similar situation exists in West Columbus where General Motors and Westinghouse are situated just outside the city. Annexation efforts in these areas are strong, due to the tax duplicate borne by these large manufacturing firms.

A shortage of industrially zoned land currently exists. While there is large acreage favorably zoned, the land is in such poor condition, or in such inaccessible places as to be unattractive for most industries. Inadequate water supply, poor sewerage, and unsatisfactory utilities limit the potential of other areas.

Along the Scioto River south and northwest of the city, industrially zoned land is available; this land consists of abandoned quarries, for the most part. In Marion Township, to the south, land is zoned for industry but it has been so badly subdivided as to be uneconomical for industrial purchase or for most other uses. Within the city there is practically no good industrial land.

The zoning problem requires attention if the industrial development of the city is to continue. Re-zoning of the entire county might be the answer. Certainly adequate land for industry, supplied with the major utilities, must be made available if continued industrialization is to be realized.

With some exceptions, taxation has not appeared to be a limiting factor in plant locations in this area. In a few instances, the favorable tax rate, which exists in Ohio for industry, was instrumental in bringing plants here from other states.

There is present in Columbus another factor which discourages industry. Columbus does not possess sufficient and suitable manufacturing space for the new firm that cannot afford to build a plant.

A small firm, just getting started in manufacturing, is usually short of capital. It cannot afford to build; it must find suitable space already constructed which can be rented or purchased. Downtown Columbus possesses the greatest number of potential sites, and as was seen earlier, has been the cradle-area for many new firms. The loft-type manufacturing building is frequently used there, but this is not adequate for every manufacturer's needs. In the newer sections of the city, there is limited space available; this has resulted in the construction of many temporary, concrete block buildings which are intended to "make do" until the firm can afford the construction of larger quarters.

Space for expansion of existing facilities is also limited in Columbus. Well-established firms which have enjoyed growth, particularly in the last 15 years, are frequently limited in their planned expansion by the shortage of high-quality building space available. Parking facilities are limited, especially in the older industrial areas. These factors are emphasized by the relocation of older firms in suburban areas, and by the location of branch plants in the suburban industrial areas. No large branch plant has moved into the older and more crowded South, North, and Downtown Columbus areas. A number of relatively large firms originally centered in or near the Downtown community have moved to suburban sites, and other firms, now operating in cramped and outmoded quarters, are considering such moves.

Unless Columbus can satisfy the building and spatial requirements of its own firms, the exodus of manufacturing facilities from the central city to surrounding areas will undoubtedly continue. Outside interests which seek building sites have rarely considered locating within the city. Part of the answer to this is the limited space available for industrial construction. The city cannot afford to lose more industry to the surrounding county. Making space available through a revamped zoning plan might be an impressive step in the right direction. One such method, proved in many other communities, is the *industrial park* concept. Considerable acreage, zoned for industry and supplying the necessary goods and services, could satisfy the demand for space. Such a "park" might be locally financed, or railroad interests might develop it. An industrial park would go a long way towards answering the criticism about space and zoning difficulties in Columbus, and it would stabilize industrial growth in a given area.

In summary, Columbus must face up to both strong and weak points in the future if it is to continue industrial growth. Both must be recognized and dealt with realistically. It is possible, of course, that what appear to be weaknesses can be strengthened by changes that are as broad as national policy, or as limited in scope as the annexation of suburban territory. The seemingly strong points may be weakened through an improper evaluation of their role in the local manufacturing community. Following are some general predictions which consider both the strong and weak points.

1. Columbus can expect continued growth due to its geographical position in the heart of the major industrial and consumer markets of the nation, and with respect to the major suppliers of industrial raw materials. The city is becoming a manufacturing-in-transit point—processing industrial raw materials for markets in other areas —and growth in this activity should continue.

2. Branch plants will share in an even larger part of the community's manufacturing. This will result from continued national recognition of central Ohio's geographical position. This means, concurrently, that "home" or Columbus-developed industry will be decreasingly important in shaping local industrial policy.

3. Columbus will share increasingly in the state's industrial progress. With increased steel production in Ohio, metal fabricators should find Columbus to be a good location. The St. Lawrence Seaway should mean, eventually, increased activity for those local firms engaged in export.

4. Diversification of manufacturing activity, which has been a

strong feature of local manufacturing interests, will continue but with the dominance of a few major industries—primarily those in automobile, aircraft, and electrical equipment manufacturing.

5. The research organizations—as represented by The Ohio State University and Battelle Memorial Institute—will play a greater role in future industrialization. Manufacturers requiring research knowledge and facilities should find Columbus an excellent location; more research-oriented concerns will locate here in the future. Research facilities may be the modern equivalent of local initiative.

6. While it is doubtful that any firm will locate in Columbus specifically because of transportation facilities, it cannot be denied that the excellent highway and railroad network radiating from Columbus will influence plant location. The accessibility to markets and raw materials provided by the present facilities is a strong permissive factor in the location of industry.

7. Earth raw materials are not readily available locally; it is highly unlikely that Columbus will attract either heavy or basic industries, such as steel or chemicals. On the other hand, access to industrial raw materials, and especially steel, should provide an impetus to the location of more fabricating plants in this area.

8. Local initiative, management, and capital will play a decreasing role in determining industrial development, policies, and programs in the future. This is in line with the growth of national firms in the area. This is bound to affect the city which, in the past, has been extremely conservative.

9. Industrial immaturity is evident locally with the absence of integration and/or linkage in manufacturing operations. Both factors can generate new industry. Unless this condition changes, Columbus cannot count on these forces to promote industrial growth.

10. The complexion of labor is undergoing a change. New industry has failed to develop a skilled labor force but a better-trained one has resulted. The regional labor surplus that once attracted industry to central Ohio is apparently on the decline and should, therefore, be of little consequence in the future. Increased wage rates, the result, in part, of national industry's appearance on the scene, will create disharmony for awhile. It will result, as it already

has, in the exodus of some low-wage firms. Increased union activity has done much to change the traditional labor picture locally. Labor competition, missing in the past, is on the upswing and will continue. National labor standards are assured for the future. Columbus' former strong point—cheap labor—is now all but an illusion.

11. Columbus has never attracted power-oriented industries and it is unlikely that it will in the future unless cheap and abundant fuel is made readily available. It is doubtful that atomic power will be widely utilized in this coal-rich area for many years.

12. Utilities—water, gas, electric, and transit facilities—are adequate. Singularly, they have not attracted industry to the city nor has any major utility openly solicited new industry. The role of local utilities as a factor in location will remain purely permissive. On the other hand, it is important that the utilities anticipate future needs and begin to prepare adequately for them now.

13. Railroad accessibility between Columbus and national points has been exceptionally good but within the city the hodge-podge of railroad lines has resulted in poor service and delayed handling of goods. On a local level, there is definite need for a reorientation of these facilities, with a belt-line railroad perhaps the answer to immediate problems.

14. The current shortage of good land zoned for industry must be corrected in the future if political Columbus is to continue its growth. Inadequate industrial facilities within the city have forced new firms to locate in suburban areas. This movement must be limited if the urban core is not to stagnate. A complete re-appraisal of industrial zoned lands on a county-wide basis would perhaps be a starting point.

15. The needs of industry with respect to adequate building space and satisfactory parking facilities must be re-assessed. Within political Columbus, inadequate building facilities and crowded streets have limited industrial expansion. The desire for space has been the prime factor in the relocation of many urban firms in suburban areas. The concept of the industrial park might be an answer to several of these problems. The park would provide large acreage and all needed facilities for the expansion of local and national in-

dustry, large and small. It would keep industry within the Columbus area by offering all of the national advantages of a central Ohio location combined with the conveniences of local services on an urban site.

Columbus, a relatively stable industrial community and one subject to a minimum of change until 1940, will continue to experience the change that comes from maturity. Certain industries—notably those in the low-wage group or those that are extremely unstable—will be lost. But the city will experience an actual and relative growth in manufacturing. While it is unlikely that heavy industry or industry oriented to power or earth raw materials will locate in Columbus, the city should enjoy a considerable expansion in metal fabrication (especially for the auto industry) and metal processing industries. Undoubtedly, diversification will continue as a major characteristic of the local industrial scene.

The rapid growth of the past 15 years has subsided to some extent but moderate industrial expansion will continue into the future. There is every reason for optimism in Columbus if some basic handicaps to industrialization are overcome.

APPENDICES

APPENDIX A

LIST OF
COMPANIES VISITED AND INTERVIEWED

Company Name	*Address*
Accurate Manufacturing Company	945 King Avenue
Acro Manufacturing Company	2040 East Main Street
Advance Tool Stamping and Die Corp.	642 East Fifth Avenue
Advern Casket Company	687 Henry Street
Agricultural Laboratories, Inc.	1145 Chesapeake Avenue
Alban-Theado Dental Laboratory	247 East State Street
Allen Manufacturing Company	88 West Kossuth Street
American Auto Parts Company	919 Bonham Street
American Blower Corporation	666 Marion Road
American Solvent Recovery Corp.	Eighth and Cassady Avenues
American Zinc Oxide Company	1363 Windsor Avenue
Antenna Research Laboratories	797 Thomas Lane
Armstrong Furnace Company	851 West Third Avenue
Artcraft Ornamental Iron Company	724 East Hudson Street
Art-Mil Machine & Manufacturing Company	170 Hosack Street
Atlas Brass Foundry Company	32 West Deshler Street
Auld Company, D. L.	1209 North Fifth Street
B and T Metals Company	425 West Town Street
Banner Die-Tool and Stamping Company	1300 Holly Avenue
Barneby-Cheney Engineering Company	Eighth and Cassady Avenues
Barry Corporation	78 East Chestnut Street
Bell Sound Systems, Incorporated	555 Marion Road
Belmont Casket Manufacturing Co.	330 West Spring Street
Berry Brothers Iron Works	250 East First Avenue
Blade Saw Company	909 West Third Avenue
Bonney-Floyd Company	2176 South Third Street
Borger Brothers Boiler Works	611 Marion Road
Bonded Scale and Machinery Company	800 Curtis Avenue
Boss Display Fixtures, Inc.	856 McKinley Avenue
Boyertown Burial Casket Company	1675 South High Street
Brightman Manufacturing Company	659 Marion Road
Buckeye Casket Company	1249 Essex Avenue
Buckeye Engineering and Manufacturing Co.	368 West Park Avenue
Buckeye Furnace Pipe Company	897 Ingleside Avenue
Buckeye Pump and Manufacturing Company	415 South 18th Street
Buckeye Stamping Company	555 Marion Road
Buckeye Steel Castings Company	2000 South Parsons Avenue

Company Name	Address
Buckeye Telephone and Supply Company	1250 Kinnear Road
Buckeye Wire and Iron Company	203 South Gift Street
Capital Bag and Burlap Company	83 West Fulton Street
Capital Die, Tool and Machine Company	456 East Fifth Avenue
Capital Elevator & Manufacturing Company	424 West Town Street
Capital Machine Company	815 Grandview Avenue
Capital Manufacturing and Supply Co.	153 W. Fulton Street
Capitol City Manufacturing Company	857 West King Avenue
Central Automatic Company	1591 East Fifth Avenue
Central Ohio Bag and Burlap Company	715 Curtis Avenue
Central Ohio Welding Company	253 East Spring Street
Chase Foundry and Manufacturing Co.	2300 South Parsons Avenue
Clarite of Great Lakes, Incorporated	804 Mt. Vernon Avenue
Clark Grave Vault Company	375 East Fifth Avenue
Columbus Anvil and Forging Company	117 West Frankfort Street
Columbus Auto Parts Company	E. Hudson Ave. and Penn. R.R.
Columbus Bolt and Forging Company	291 Marconi Boulevard
Columbus Brass Manufacturing Company	1284 Edgehill Road
Columbus Coated Fabrics Company	1280 North Grant Street
Columbus Coffin Company	Ingleside and Buttles
Columbus Conveyer Company	869 West Goodale Boulevard
Columbus Co-op Foundry	310 West Poplar Avenue
Columbus Dental Manufacturing Company	634 Wager Street
Columbus, Die, Tool & Machine Company	955 Cleveland Avenue
Columbus Engineering Company	480 West Broad Street
Columbus Forge and Iron Company	544 West First Avenue
Columbus Glove Manufacturing Company	1836 East Fulton Street
Columbus Heating & Ventilating Company	182 North Yale Avenue
Columbus Malleable Iron Company	760 Curtis Avenue
Columbus Metal Craft Company	146 South Yale Avenue
Columbus Metal Products, Incorporated	1341 Norton Avenue
Columbus Paper Box Company	338 West Town Street
Columbus Pharmacal Company	330 Oak Street
Columbus Plastic Products, Incorporated	1625 West Mound Street
Columbus Porcelain Metals Corp.	3760 East Fifth Avenue
Columbus Serum Company	2025 South High Street
Columbus Showcase Company	850 West Fifth Avenue
Columbus Stamping and Manufacturing Co.	95 North Glenwood Avenue
Columbus Steel Industries, Inc.	768 East Eleventh Avenue
Columbus Stove Company	827 Reynolds Avenue
Columbus Sucker Rod Company	1281 Edgehill Road
Commercial Paste Company	Buttles at Michigan
Corrugated Container Company	640 Shoemaker Avenue
Cranfill Dental Laboratory	244 South Third Street
Cream Cone Machine Company	1195 Essex Avenue

Company Name	Address
Davison Chemical Company	3355 East Fifth Avenue
Dean and Barry Company	296 Marconi Boulevard
Denison Engineering Company	1160 Dublin Road
Dickerson Company, The Walker T.	326 South Front Street
Dobson-Evans Company	1100 West Third Avenue
Dresser-Ideco Company	875 Michigan Avenue
Ebco Manufacturing Company	401 West Town Street
Edwards Company, J. T.	1241 McKinley Avenue
Eldred Company	2305 Cleveland Avenue
Exact Weight Scales Company	944 West Fifth Avenue
Farmers Fertilizer Company	1380 Windsor Avenue
Federal Glass Company	515 East Innis Avenue
Federal Steel Fabricators, Incorporated	500 North Stanwood Avenue
Fournier Rubber and Supply Company	459 North High Street
Frankenburg Brothers, Incorporated	479 Ludlow Street
Franklin Brass Foundry	776 East First Avenue
Franklin Glue Company	119 West Chestnut Street
Franklin Lumber and Fixture Company	878 Michigan Avenue
Frey-Yenkin Paint Company	251 Sandusky Street
General Furniture Corporation	509 Charles Street
General Machine Products Company	3871 Sullivant Avenue
General Motors Corp., Ternstedt Div.	Georgesville Road
General Products Laboratories, Inc.	137 East Spring Street
Godman Company, H. C.	37 East Fulton Street
Gordon Company, J. P.	232 Neilston Street
H and E Machine Company	1646 Fairwood Avenue
Hanna Paint Manufacturing Company	95 West Long Street
Harrop Ceramic Service Company	3470 East Fifth Avenue
Hatco Corporation	947 West Goodale Boulevard
Hearn Die, Tool and Machine Company	115 Vine Street
Henri La Prise and Company	550 E. Mound Street
Hercules Box Company	521 Marion Road
Hercules Trouser Company	570 South Front Street
Hertenstein Company, M.	1409 South High Street
Hoffman Auto Body Service	1480 North Grant Street
Hollywood Products, Incorporated	288 North High Street
Industrial Aluminum Company	660 St. Clair Street
Industrial Ceramic Products, Incorporated	965 West Fifth Avenue
Industrial Nucleonics Corporation	1205 Chesapeake Avenue
Ironsides Company	270 West Mound Street
Jaeger Machine Company	540 West Spring Street
Jeffrey Manufacturing Company	East First Avenue

Company Name	*Address*
Jones Heel Manufacturing Company	843 South Front Street
Josephinum Church Furniture Company	351 Merritt Street
Joseph and Feiss Company	107 North Sixth Street
Joyce, Incorporated	212 North Fourth Street
Julian and Kokenge Company	280 South Front Street
Kilbourne and Jacobs Company	Lincoln and North Fourth Street
Kimble Glass Company	711 Southwood Avenue
Klein and Company, H. L.	2237 Tuttle Park Place
Krouse Testing Machine Company	573 East Eleventh Avenue
Lattimer-Stevens Company	715 Marion Road
Leighton Fiber Products Company	433 West State Street
Leighton Heel Company	433 West State Street
Lennox Furnace Company	1711 Olentangy River Road
Lerch Industries	1080 West Goodale Boulevard
Leukart, J. Machine Company, Inc.	195 Hosack Street
Lilley-Ames Company	257 East Broad Street
MacLean Company, J. S.	470 South Front Street
Metalcrafters, Incorporated	740 Jenkins Avenue
Mid-West Machine Company	2128 Eakin Avenue
Miller Glass Engineering Company	148 South Glenwood Avenue
Modern Tool, Die and Machine Company	1201 Essex Avenue
Morris Steel Company, C. E.	731 Curtis Avenue
National Aluminum Company	1133 Alum Creek Drive
National Dental Company	82 North High Street
National Electric Coil Company	800 King Avenue
National Glove Company	924 East Main Street
Nippert Electric Products Company	1759 West Mound Street
Norman Products Company	1150 Chesapeake Avenue
North American Aviation, Incorporated	4300 East Fifth Avenue
Ohio Machine Products, Incorporated	3077 Beulah Road
Ohio Malleable Iron Company	1343 Fields Avenue
Oran Company	2222 South Third Street
Orton Ceramic Foundation	1445 Summit Street
Peerless Saw Company	571 South Third Street
Pereny Equipment Company	893 Chambers Road
Pfening Bakery Machinery Company	1075 West Fifth Avenue
Plastex Corporation	402 Mount Vernon Avenue
Pollock Paper Company	780 Frebis Avenue
Porcelain Steel Buildings Company	555 West Goodale Boulevard
Poulton, Edwin, Foundry Co., The	1071 Goodale Street
Practical Burial Footwear Company	1397 Essex Avenue
Prima Footwear, Incorporated	705 Ann Street
Puritan Products, Incorporated	2319 South Sixth Street

Company Name	*Address*
Quad Stove Company	78 East First Avenue
Ralston Steel Car Company	2901 East Fourth Avenue
Ranco, Incorporated	601 West Fifth Avenue
Rockwell Tools, Incorporated	1314 Kinnear Road
Rudolph Stern Dress Company	337 South High Street
S & W Moulding Company	980 Parsons Avenue
Santeler Brothers	950 East Main Street
Schodorf Company, A. L.	370 West State Street
Schoedinger Company, F. O.	322 Mt. Vernon Avenue
Schwartz Showell Corporation	842 West Goodale Boulevard
Scott Viner Company	1224 Kinnear Road
Seagrave Corporation	2000 South High Street
Shepard Paint Company	338 West Broad Street
Simon and Haas Company	939 East Main Street
Simplex Foundry Company	681 Michigan Avenue
Smith Agricultural Chemical Company	618 North Champion Avenue
Smith Chemical Company	867 McKinley Avenue
Stallman Gear Manufacturing Company	527 West Rich Street
Stanwood Industries	1455 East Fifth Avenue
Stitt Ignition Company	86 East First Avenue
Superior Die, Tool and Machine Company	1432 Parsons Avenue
Surface Combustion Company	400 Dublin Avenue
Thompson Metal Fabricating Company	1266 West Goodale Boulevard
Thurman Machine Company	156 North Fifth Street
Timken Roller Bearing Company	1205 Cleveland Avenue
Timmons Metal Products Company	845 Harrisburg Pike
Triumph Brass Company	557 Wager Street
Union Fork and Hoe Company	500 Dublin Avenue
United Seal Company	450 South Pearl Street
United Woolen Company	78-84 East Spring Street
Warren-Teed Products Company	582 West Goodale Boulevard
Weinman Pump Manufacturing Company	290 Spruce Street
Welch Plastics Company	814 West Third Avenue
Westinghouse Manufacturing Company	300 Phillipi Road
White-Bush Manufacturing Company	97 North Sixth Street
Wright and Company	1999 Bryden Road
Yardley Industries	138 Parsons Avenue

APPENDIX B

INTERVIEW PATTERN

1. Company Name...

2. Present Location ....

3. Date Located Here...

4. Previous Location............................... Date...........
   Reasons for Change..

5. Type of Product..
   Producer or Consumer Goods....................................
   Competitors in Central Ohio.....................................

6. What factors influenced the location of this company in Columbus?
   (a)
   (b)
   (c)

7. (a) What are the handicaps to the present location?
      In Columbus.................. In Central Ohio...............

   (b) What are the advantages to the present location?.................

   (c) Has the change of Columbus from a commercial to an industrial city *promoted* or *retarded* the particular company's development?

8. What has been the role of the following factors in the location of industry in Columbus, Ohio?

   (a) Market: % sales in Columbus......; % sales in Central Ohio......

   (b) Raw materials: % purchased in Columbus............

   (c) Transportation: Shipped by truck.....; Imported by Truck......
                        Shipped by Rail......; Imported by Rail.......
      Type of goods shipped or imported by either service:

   (d) Labor: Males employed..........; Females Employed.........
              Negroes employed.......; Active Union.............
      Any particular reasons for the use of female or Negro labor?........
      Wage rate:............. Compared to city average:...........
      Has a surplus of labor (W.W. II labor pool) been important?
      Have new companies affected the labor supply?

(e) Water supply: ....
    Costs of land: ....
    Expansion facilities: ....
    Parking facilities: ....
    Public transit: ....

(f) Power facilities: ....

(g) Presence of building:.............. Who previously occupied site?

(h) Place of company in Columbus in structure of the nationwide industry:
    Functional convenience—is the location in Columbus a result of convenience with respect to other industries for market, raw materials, etc.:

(i) Other factors:
    Zoning: ....
    Prestige value of Columbus:..............................

9. Value added to product by manufacturer:..........................

10. Role of company in foreign trade:................................

APPENDIX C

TABLE 1—Basic Data for 204 Manufacturing Companies, Columbus, Ohio, Classified by Major Industry Types, by Industrial Groups and Sub-Groups: Year Established in Columbus and Year Located at Present Site, Original and Present Location by Industrial Areas, and Number Employed, 1953

(x) = Present Area Site: (—) = Original Area Site

Industry Group and Company Name	Industrial Area						Year Located:		Number Employed—1953		
	North	South	Down-town	East	West	North-west	In Columbus	At Site	Male	Female	Total
Ceramic Products											
Harrop Ceramic Service Co.				x	—		1920	1950	20	0	20[a]
Industrial Ceramic Products, Inc.	x—					x—	1936	1936	60	30	90
Orton Ceramic Foundation			—				1896	1932	10	23	33
Pereny Equipment Company						x	1936	1947	10	0	10[a]
Total									**100**	**53**	**153**
Chemical Products							CHEMICAL INDUSTRY				
Fertilizers											
Agricultural Laboratories, Inc.	—					x	1932	1942	12	14	26
Davison Chemical Company				x—			1911	1911	80	0	80[a]
Farmers Fertilizer Company	x—			x—			1894	1894	65	2	67
Smith Agricultural Chemical Co.				x—			1894	1894	194	6	200
Total									**351**	**22**	**373**
Pharmaceuticals and Serums											
Columbus Pharmacal Co.			x—				1886	1915	76	54	130
Columbus Serum Co.		x—					1922	1922	25	5	30
General Products Laboratories, Inc.			x—				1920	1934	4	6	10
Warren-Teed Products Co.	x			—			1920	1937	50	100	150
Total									**155**	**165**	**320**

TABLE 1—(Continued)

(x) = Present Area Site: (—) = Original Area Site

Industry Group and Company Name	Industrial Area						Year Located:		Number Employed—1953		
	North	South	Down-town	East	West	North-west	In Columbus	At Site	Male	Female	Total
CHEMICAL INDUSTRY (Continued)											
Paints											
Dean and Barry Co.			x—				1885	1900	69	9	78
Frey-Yenkin Paint Co.					—	x	1923	1928	37	12	49
Hanna Paint Manufacturing Co.			x—				1884	1913	146	25	171
Shepard Paint Co.					x—		1890's	1935	12	0	12[a]
Total									264	46	310
Miscellaneous Chemicals											
American Zinc Oxide Co.	x—						1920	1920	165	8	173
Barneby-Cheney Engineering Co.				x			1920	1940	51	0	51
Ironsides Co.			x—				1883	1929	47	6	53
Smith Chemical Company					x—		1929	1929	9	1	10
Total									272	15	287
Dental Products											
Alban-Theado Dental Products			x—				1930	1930	17	5	22[a]
Columbus Dental Mfg. Co.		x	—				1903	1915	75	75	150[a]
Cranfill Dental Laboratory			x—				1945	1947	15	3	18[a]
National Dental Co.			x—				1930	1932	12	0	12[a]
Total									119	83	202
Glass Products											
Columbus Porcelain Metals Corp.				x—			1946	1946	8	2	10
Federal Glass Co.		x—					1900	1900	598	455	1,053
Kimble Glass Co.		x—					1932	1932	1,157	411	1,568
Total									1,763	868	2,631

TABLE 1—(Continued)
(x) = Present Area Site; (—) = Original Area Site

Industry Group and Company Name	North	South	Down-town	East	West	North-west	In Columbus	At Site	Male	Female	Total
CHEMICAL INDUSTRY (Continued)											
Plastic Products											
Columbus Plastic Products, Inc.	—				x		1938	1947	297	105	402
Plastex Corporation			x—				1939	1939	56	2	58
Welch Plastics Co.						x	1946	1946	5	25	30
Yardley Industries		x					1902	1933	115	62	117
S and W Moulding Co.	—	x—					1941	1946	27	11	38
Total									**500**	**205**	**705**
Rubber Products											
Allen Manufacturing Co.		x	—				1943	1946	3	12	15
Clarite of Great Lakes, Inc.				x—			1950	1950	7	2	9
Fournier Rubber and Supply Co.			x—				1933	1938	18	4	22[a]
Total									**28**	**18**	**46**
Total Chemical Industry									**3,552**	**1,475**	**5,027**
METAL INDUSTRY: FABRICATING											
Electrical Equipment											
Acro Manufacturing Co.	—			x—			1940	1950	80	176	256
Antenna Research Laboratories		x				x—	1948	1948	45	3	48[a]
Bell Sound Systems, Inc.			—			x	1932	1946	50	75	125[a]
Buckeye Telephone and Supply Co.					x—		1921	1951	35	5	40[a]
Ebco Manufacturing Co.			—				1906	1906	180	45	225
National Electric Coil Co.					x		1934	1934	439	294	733
Nippert Electric Products Co.			—				1942	1946	84	32	116
Ranco, Inc.			—				1913	1936	558	325	883
Westinghouse Manufacturing Co.	x				x—		1953	1953	3,975	1,300	5,275[b]
Total									**5,446**	**2,255**	**7,701**

TABLE 1—(Continued)

(x) = Present Area Site: (—) = Original Area Site

Industry Group and Company Name	Industrial Area						Year Located:		Number Employed—1953		
	North	South	Down-town	East	West	North-west	In Columbus	At Site	Male	Female	Total
METAL INDUSTRY: FABRICATING (Continued)											
Heating and Cooling Equipment											
American Blower Corp.		x—					1938	1938	440	31	471
Armstrong Furnace Co.						x—	1928	1947	460	42	502
Borger Brothers Boiler Works				x			1859	1946	18	2	20
Buckeye Furnace Pipe Co.	x—				—		1945	1945	46	22	68
Columbus Heating and Ventilating Co.	x—				x—		1874	1937	60	9	69
Columbus Stove Co.					—		1939	1939	72	3	75
Lattimer-Stevens Co.		x					1920	1927	84	6	90
Lennox Furnace Co.						x—	1940	1940	520	39	559
Norman Products Co.						x—	1945	1945	116	12	128
Oran Co.							1937	1937	67	7	74
Quad Stove Co.	x—						1904	1904	21	1	22
Schoedinger Co., F. O.			x—				1890	1921	74	19	93
Surface Combustion Co.	x—						1931	1931	700	140	840
Total									**2,678**	**333**	**3,011**
Industrial Machinery											
American Solvent Recovery Corp.				x—			1919	1919	72	10	82
Bonded Scale and Machinery Co.		x					1932	1936	35	7	42
Capital Elevator and Mfg. Co.			—		x—		1918	1923	40	2	42
Columbus Conveyor Co.						x	1919	1920	24	3	27
Cream Cone Machine Co.	x—						1948	1948	10	30	40ᵃ
Denison Engineering Co.			—			x	1935	1942	396	43	439

TABLE 1—(Continued)

(x) = Present Area Site: (—) = Original Area Site

Industry Group and Company Name	Industrial Area						Year Located:		Number Employed—1953		
	North	South	Down-town	East	West	North-west	In Columbus	At Site	Male	Female	Total
METAL INDUSTRY: FABRICATING (Continued)											
Industrial Machinery (Continued)											
Eldred Co.	x—						1946	1946	15	0	15[a]
Exact Weight Scales Co.			—			x	1916	1930	102	11	113
Industrial Nucleonics Corp.						x—	1950	1950	93	20	113
Jaeger Machine Co.	x		—				1903	1910	862	81	943
Jeffrey Manufacturing Co.	x				—		1876	1888	2,306	250	2,556[a]
Kilbourne and Jacobs Co.	x—				x—		1865[e]	1870	138	13	151
Krouse Testing Machine Co.	x—						1937	1941	24	2	26
Miller Glass Engineering Co.						x	1935	1935	60	2	62
Pfening Bakery Machinery Co.						x	1927	1937	32	3	35
Scott Viner Co.			—				1926	1951	83	2	85
Total									**4,292**	**479**	**4,771**
Tools and Implements											
Blade Saw Co.						x—	1946	1946	24	0	24
Peerless Saw Co.		x—					1931	1931	24	0	24
Rockwell Tools, Incorporated						x—	1951	1951	188	29	217
Union Fork and Hoe Co.	x—						1860[d]	1907	197	36	233
Total									**433**	**65**	**498**

TABLE 1—(Continued)

(x) = Present Area Site; (—) = Original Area Site

Industry Group and Company Name	Industrial Area						Year Located:		Number Employed—1953		
	North	South	Down-town	East	West	North-west	In Columbus	At Site	Male	Female	Total
METAL INDUSTRY: FABRICATING (Continued)											
Transportation Equipment											
Aircraft											
North American Aviation, Inc.				x|—			1950	1950	13,720	3,320	17,040
Automobile Parts											
American Auto Parts Co.	x		|				1894	1939	12	7	19
Clark Grave Vault Co.	x		|				1900	1922	845	10	855
Columbus Metal Products, Inc.	—|					x	1909	1948	51	9	60
Columbus Auto Parts Co.	x|						1912	1927	454	40	494
General Motors Corp., Ternstedt Div.					x|—		1946	1946	2,107	1,110	3,217
Henri La Prise & Co. (Summer & Co.)		x			|		1937	1952	45	4	49
Stitt Ignition Co.	x|						1916	1923	6	6	12
Timken Roller Bearing Co.	x|						1919	1919	3,039	1,095	4,134
Fire Engines, Trucks Bodies, and Accessories											
Seagrave Corporation		x					1898	1900	310	22	332
Hoffman Auto Body Service	x					|	1923	1923	17	0	17
Santeler Brothers		|		x			1933	1941	25	0	25[a]
Schodorf Co., A. L.					x		1900	1925	25	0	25
Stallman Gear Mfg. Co.			|		x		1945	1949	18	1	19
Timmons Metal Products Co.			|		x		1946	1949	29	0	29
Railroad Equipment											
Ralston Steel Car Co.				x|—			1905	1905	130	0	130[a]
Total									20,833	5,624	26,457
Total Metal Fabricating									33,682	8,756	42,438

TABLE 1—(Continued)

(x) = Present Area Site: (—) = Original Area Site

Industry Group and Company Name	North	South	Down-town	East	West	North-west	Year Located: In Columbus	Year Located: At Site	Male	Female	Total
METAL INDUSTRY: PROCESSING											
Forging Industry											
Berry Brothers Iron Works	x—						1881	1881	65	0	65
Brightman Manufacturing Co.		x—					1895	1895	51	3	54
Columbus Anvil and Forging Co.		x—					1900	1900	45	4	49
Columbus Bolt and Forging Co.			x—				1852	1852	900	231	1,131
Columbus Forge and Iron Co.	x—						1898	1898	93	3	96
Total									1,154	241	1,395
Foundry Industry											
Iron and Steel Foundries											
Bonney-Floyd Co.		x—					1904	1904	508	18	526
Buckeye Steel Castings Co.		x					1886	1902	1,797	64	1,861
Chase Foundry and Mfg. Co.		x—			—		1896	1896	43	2	45
Columbus Co-op Foundry	x—			x—			1938	1938	11	1	12
Columbus Malleable Iron Co.				x—			1936	1936	241	6	247
M. Hertenstein Co.		x	—				1880	1892	67	1	68
Ohio Malleable Iron Co.	x—		—				1902	1905	518	22	540
Poulton Foundry Co., The						x	1921	1921	24	1	25
Total									3,209	115	3,324
Nonferrous Metals Foundries											
Atlas Brass Foundry Co.	—						1907	1907	85	6	91
Buckeye Pump and Mfg. Co.		x					1897	1913	40	0	40[a]
Columbus Brass Mfg. Co.					—	x	1936	1952	20	1	21
Franklin Brass Foundry	x—			x—			1925	1927	29	2	31
Industrial Alumnium Co.	x—						1945	1945	14	1	15
Simplex Foundry Co.		x					1907	1925	10	0	10
Triumph Brass Co.	x—						1850	1919	15	8	23
Total									213	18	231
Total Foundry Industry									3,422	133	3,555

TABLE 1—(Continued)

(x) = Present Area Site; (—) = Original Area Site

Industry Group and Company Name	Industrial Area						Year Located:		Number Employed—1953		
	North	South	Down-town	East	West	North-west	In Columbus	At Site	Male	Female	Total
METAL INDUSTRY: PROCESSING (Continued)											
Machine Shops											
Accurate Mfg. Co.	x—					x—	1942	1945	24	3	27
Advance Tool, Stamping & Die Corp.		x—					1940	1942	24	0	24
Art-Mil Machine and Mfg. Co.		x—					1949	1949	55	2	57ᵃ
Buckeye Engineering and Mfg. Co.					x—	x—	1943	1949	15	0	15ᵃ
Capital Machine Co.	x—					x—	1942	1948	70	20	90
Capital Die, Tool and Machine Co.	x—						1897	1928	20	1	21
Capital City Mfg. Co.	x—						1952	1952	30	0	30ᵃ
Central Automatic Co.	x		x—				1944	1948	8	2	10ᵃ
Central Ohio Welding Co.	x		—				1911	1930	20	0	20ᵃ
Columbus Die, Tool and Machine Co.		x	—				1906	1914	100	4	104
Columbus Engineering Co.					x—		1938	1940	107	23	130
General Machine Products Co.		x			x—		1951	1951	15	14	29
H and E Machine Co.					—		1944	1949	11	0	11
Hatco Corp.						x	1942	1946	33	8	41
Hearn Die, Tool and Machine Co.	x—						1893	1893	22	0	22
Klein, H. L. and Co.	x—						1946	1951	36	1	37
Leukart, J., Machine Co., Inc.		x—					1896	1948	146	2	148
Metalcrafters, Inc.		x					1950	1952	80	3	83
Mid-West Machine Co.			—		x—		1951	1951	78	53	131
Modern Tool, Die and Machine Co.	x						1915	1950	40	1	41
Ohio Machine Products, Inc.	x—						1943	1948	53	2	55
Stanwood Industries	x—						1949	1949	16	0	16
Superior Die, Tool and Machine Co.		x				x	1928	1952	65	2	67
Thompson Metal Fabricating Co.			x—				1951	1952	40	2	42
Thurman Machine Co.			x—				1917	1942	85	11	96
Wright and Co.	—			x—			1941	1944	10	0	10
Total									1,203	154	1,357

TABLE 1—(Continued)

(x) = Present Area Site: (—) = Original Area Site

Industry Group and Company Name	Industrial Area						Year Located:		Number Employed—1953		
	North	South	Down-town	East	West	North-west	In Columbus	At Site	Male	Female	Total
METAL INDUSTRY: PROCESSING (Continued)											
Stamping and Extruding Industry											
Auld Co., D. L.	x						1868	1920	297	150	447
Banner Die, Tool and Stamping Co.						x	1918	1933	50	2	52
B and T Metals Co.		x	—		x		1938	1940	407	19	426
Buckeye Stamping Co.			—				1902	1910	30	25	55ª
Columbus Stamping and Mfg. Co.					x—		1946	1946	19	26	45
Capital Mfg. and Supply Co.			x—				1925	1937	230	20	250
Lilley-Ames Co. (U.S. Chromite)		x—	x—				1865	1950	30	130	160ª
National Aluminum Co.		—	x				1939	1948	43	6	49
United Seal Co.		—					1906	1915	15	4	19
Total									1,121	382	1,503
Structural Steel and Ornamental Iron											
Structural Steel											
Columbus Steel Industries, Inc.	x—						1920	1920	10	0	10ª
Dresser-Ideco Co.	x—						1921	1921	378	30	408
Edwards Co., J. T.					x		1932	1942	82	3	85
Federal Steel Fabricators, Inc.				x—			1942	1942	31	0	31
Morris, C. E., Steel Co.				x			1885	1905	47	1	48
Porcelain Steel Buildings Co.	x—		—				1934	1934	50	1	51
Total									598	35	633
Ornamental Iron											
Artcraft Ornamental Iron Co.	x—						1937	1945	13	0	13
Buckeye Wire and Iron Co.				—	x		1905	1935	12	1	13
Columbus Metal Craft Co.					x—		1946	1948	14	1	15
Total									39	2	41
Total Metal: Processing									7,537	947	8,484

TABLE 1—(Continued)

(x) = Present Area Site: (—) = Original Area Site

Industry Group and Company Name	Industrial Area						Year Located:		Number Employed—1953		
	North	South	Down-town	East	West	North-west	In Columbus	At Site	Male	Female	Total
SHOES AND TEXTILE PRODUCTS											
Shoe Industry											
Dickerson, The Walker T. Co.			x—				1930	1930	155	195	350
Godman, H. C. Co.			x—				1865	1923?	179	172	351
Hollywood Products, Inc.			x—				1945	1945	12	17	29
Jones Heel Mfg. Co.		x—					1916	1916	11	9	20
Joyce, Incorporated			x—				1941	1941	54	199	253
Julian and Kokenge Co.			x—		x		1932	1932	367	544	911
Leighton Heel Co.			—				1931	1938	23	18	41
Leighton Fiber Products Co.				x	x—		1938	1938	32	1	33
Prima Footwear, Inc.			—		x—		1940	1948	160	200	360
Total									993	1,355	2,348
Textile Products											
Barry Corp.			x—				1947	1950	30	150	180
Capital Bag and Burlap Co.			x—				1918	1936	5	15	20[a]
Central Ohio Bag and Burlap Co.				x—			1937	1950	4	6	10
Columbus Coated Fabrics Co.	x—						1900	1900	960	113	1,073
Columbus Glove Mfg. Co.				x—			1932	1946	45	1	46
Gordon, J. P. Co.				x—			1900	1932	21	57	78
Hercules Trouser Co.		x—					1921	1921	69	20	89
Joseph and Feiss Co.			—				1945	1945	14	124	138
National Glove Co.				x			1899	1901	32	24	56
Practical Burial Footwear Co.	x—						1915	1920	8	24	29
Rudolph Stern Dress Co.			x—				1931	1946	4	21	29
Simon & Haas Co.				x—			1917	1946	1	25	26
United Woolen Company			x—				1924	1924	275	75	350[a]
White-Bush Mfg. Co.			x—				1950	1950	10	90	100[a]
Total									1,478	746	2,224

TABLE 1—(Continued)

(x) = Present Area Site; (—) = Original Area Site

Industry Group and Company Name	Industrial Area						Year Located:		Number Employed—1953		
	North	South	Down-town	East	West	North-west	In Columbus	At Site	Male	Female	Total
WOOD AND PAPER PRODUCTS											
Caskets											
Advern Casket Co.	x—						1943	1943	10	4	14
Belmont Casket Mfg. Co.	x—						1916	1916	113	38	151
Boyerton Burial Casket Co.		x					1924	1924	61	16	77
Buckeye Casket Co.	x		—				1921	1933	69	29	98
Columbus Coffin Co.	x—	—					1880	1880	29	12	41
Total									**282**	**99**	**381**
Paper and Paper Containers											
Columbus Paper Box Co.	x—						1890	1920	34	58	92
Corrugated Container Co.		x—					1916	1946	106	34	140
Dobson-Evans Co.		x—				x	1902	1938	47	42	89
Frankenberg Bros., Inc.			x—				1895	1923	61	41	102
Hercules Box Co.					x—		1919	1919	157	43	200
Pollock Paper Co.			—				1946	1946	180	20	200
Puritan Products, Inc.			x—				1951	1951	15	7	22
Total									**600**	**245**	**845**
Showcases and Furniture											
Boss Display Fixtures, Inc.			—				1932	1932	13	2	15
Columbus Showcase Co.					x	x	1895	1923	236	11	247
Franklin Lumber and Fixture Co.	x						1901	1933	47	0	47
General Furniture Corp.			—				1948	1948	37	21	58
Josephinum Church Furniture Co.				—			1882	1912	26	0	26
Lerch Industries						x—	1951	1951	35	10	45[a]
MacLean Co., J. S.		x	x				1885	1925	27	1	28
Schwartz Showell Corp.						x—	1899	1920	69	2	71
Total									**490**	**47**	**537**
Total Wood and Paper Products									**1,372**	**391**	**1,763**

TABLE 1—(Continued)

(x) = Present Area Site: (—) = Original Area Site

Industry Group and Company Name	Industrial Area						Year Located:		Number Employed—1953		
	North	South	Down-town	East	West	North-west	In Columbus	At Site	Male	Female	Total
MISCELLANEOUS											
Pumps											
Weinman Pump Mfg. Co.	x				—		1877	1908	125	0	125
Sucker Rods											
Columbus Sucker Rod Co.		—				x	1900	1923	23	1	24
Glues and Adhesives											
Commercial Paste Co.	x		—				1900	1920	22	7	29
Franklin Glue Co.		—	x				1935	1945	21	6	27
Total									**191**	**14**	**205**

a Number employed as reported to interviewer.
b Figures as of May 1955. The plant was opened in 1953 with the expectation of employing 8,000.
c Approximate date. Could not be verified more accurately.
d Nearest approximate date available.
Source: Number employed from *Directory of Ohio Manufacturers*, Department of Industrial Relations, State of Ohio; All other data, from interviews with officials.

LIST OF REFERENCES

BOOKS

ALDEFER, E. B. and MICHL, H. E., *Economics of American Industry*. New York: McGraw-Hill Book Company, Inc., 1942.

ARMSTRONG, J. R., *The Columbus Business Directory* for 1843-1844.

BIDWELL, P. W. and FALCONER, J. I., *History of Agriculture in the Northern United States, 1620-1860*. Washington, D.C.: The Carnegie Institution, 1925.

BORTH, CHRISTY, *True Steel*. Indianapolis: The Bobbs-Merrill Company, 1941.

BROWN, RALPH H., *Historical Geography of the United States*. New York: Harcourt, Brace and Company, 1948.

BRUCE, ROBERT, *The Old National Road*. Clinton, N.Y., 1916.

FAILING, HENRY M., *The First Report of the Business and Prospects of the City of Columbus*. Columbus: The Ohio State Journal Commercial Printing House, 1873.

GLOVER, E. and HENDERSON, W., *Directory of the City of Columbus for the Years 1850 and 1851*.

GLOVER, JOHN G. and CORNELL, WILLIAM B., *The Development of American Industries*. New York: Prentice-Hall, Inc., 1946.

HOOPER, OSMAN C., *History of the City of Columbus, Ohio*. Columbus: The Memorial Publishing Company, 1920.

HOWE, HENRY, *Historical Collections of Ohio*. Cincinnati: C. J. Krehbiel and Company, 1898.

HULBERT, ARCHER B., *Red-Men's Roads: The Indian Thoroughfares of the Central West*. Columbus: F. J. Heer and Company, 1900.

. . . ., *Historic Highways of America*. Cleveland: A. H. Clark Company, 1902-1905, 15 volumes.

HUNTINGTON, C. C. and McCLELLAND, C. P., *History of the Ohio Canals: Their Construction, Cost, Use and Partial Abandonment*. Columbus: The Ohio Archaeological and Historical Society, 1905.

Industries of Columbus, The: A Resume of Mercantile and Manufacturing Progress of the Capital City of Ohio. Columbus: Enterprise Review Publishing Company, May 1887.

JORDON, PHILIP D., *The National Road*. New York: The Bobbs-Merrill Company, 1948.

KETCHAM, ALVIN, *Columbus Manufacturers*. Columbus: The Ohio State University Library, unpublished manuscript, 1906.

LEE, ALFRED, *History of Columbus, Ohio*. Columbus: Munsell and Company, 1892.

MARTIN, WILLIAM T., *History of Franklin County*. Columbus: Follett, Foster and Company.

Moore, Opha, *History of Franklin County, Ohio*. Topeka: Historical Publishing Company, 1930.

Noble, Henry C., *Historical Address*. Columbus: Ohio State Journal and Job Printing Rooms, 1876.

Peattie, Roderick, Editor, *Columbus, Ohio: An Analysis of a City's Development*. Columbus: Chamber of Commerce, 1930.

Sherman, C. E., *Original Ohio Land Subdivisions: Vol. iii of the Final Report of the Ohio Cooperative Topographic Survey*. Columbus: The Ohio State Reformatory, 1925.

Siebert, John, *Directory of the City of Columbus for the Year 1848. Story of Columbus, The*. Columbus: Johnson Publishing Company, 1898.

Studer, Jacob H., *Columbus, Ohio: Its History, Resources, and Progress*. Columbus: J. Studer, 1873.

Taylor, William A., *Centennial History of Columbus and Franklin County, Ohio*. Chicago: S. J. Clarke Publishing Company, 1909, Vols. 1 and 2.

Unstad, Lyder L., *A Survey of the Economic and Historical Development of Central Ohio With Special Reference to Columbus, 1797-1872*. Columbus: The Ohio State University Library, unpublished manuscript.

Wright, Alfred J., *Economic Geography of Ohio*. Columbus: Division of Geological Survey, 1953.

PERIODICALS AND NEWSPAPERS

Carney, Frank, "Geographic Influence in the Development of Ohio." *Popular Science Monthly*, November 1909.

Columbus *Dispatch*, The, "Salute to Curtiss-Wright," November 30, 1941, p. 3.

Columbus *Gazette*, The, February 13, 1857.

. . . ., June 4, 1858.

. . . ., June 11, 1858.

. . . ., September 17, 1858.

Dial, George W., "The Construction of the Ohio Canals," *The Ohio Archaeological and Historical Society Quarterly*, Vol. 13, 1904.

Finn, Chester E., "The Ohio Canals: Public Enterprise on the Frontier," *The Ohio Archaeological and Historical Quarterly*, Vol. 51, 1942.

Hulbert, Archer B., "The Indian Thoroughfares of Ohio." *The Ohio Archaeological and Historical Quarterly*, Vol. 8, 1900.

. . . ., "The Old National Road: The Historical Highway of America." *The Ohio Archaeological and Historical Quarterly*, Vol. 9, 1901.

Isard, Walter, "Interregional and Regional Input-Output Analysis: A Model of a Space-Economy," *The Review of Economics and Statistics*, Vol. 33, No. 4, November 1951.

Jackson, W. B., "Industrial Columbus," *The Ohio Illustrated Magazine*, Vol. 5, No. 6, December, 1907.

McKenzie, Roderick D., "The Neighborhood: A Study of Local Life in the City of Columbus, Ohio," *The American Journal of Sociology*, Vol. 27, No. 2, September 1921.

Monthly Industrial Review, June 12, 1928.

Ohio State Journal, The *"Columbus: The Hub of Ohio."* Columbus: *The Ohio State Journal*, 1890.

Randall, E. O., "The Beginnings of Columbus: Primeval and Capital," *The Ohio Illustrated Magazine*, Vol. 3, No. 6, December 1907.

Stoddards, Paul W., "The Economic Progress of Ohio: 1800-1840," *The Ohio Archaeological and Historical Quarterly*, Vol. 41, 1932.

Wright, Alfred J., "Joel Wright, City Planner," *The Ohio State Archaeological and Historical Quarterly*, Vol. 56, No. 3, July 1947.

Zimmerman, Carrie B., "Ohio, the Gateway to the West." *The Ohio Archaeological and Historical Quarterly*, Vol. 40, 1931.

CITY AND STATE AGENCIES

Board of Public Works, *Annual Reports,* 1837, 1841, 1844, 1845, 1851, 1856, 1861, and 1879: Columbus, Ohio.

............, *Special Report of the Board of Public Works Relative to the Rates of Tolls on the Canals of This State.* Columbus: 1845.

Bureau of Unemployment Compensation, *Labor Market Information.* Columbus: Ohio State Employment Service, 1953.

Columbus Board of Trade, *Annual Report of the Directors and Secretary for 1855.* Columbus: The Columbian Printing Company, 1886.

............, *Annual Report of the Directors and Secretary for 1890.* Columbus: Nitschke Brothers, 1891.

............, *Annual Report of the Directors and Secretary for 1895.* Columbus, 1896.

............, *The City of Columbus: The Capital of Ohio and the Great Railway Center of the State.* G. L. Manchester, 1885.

............, *Bulletin,* Vol. 2, No. 1, March 1900.

............, *Columbus, Ohio.* Columbus 1904.

Columbus Chamber of Commerce, *Monthly Bulletin,* Vol. 4, August 1917 and October 1917.

............, *Determining the Location of the Government Armor Plate Plant: A Brief for Columbus, Ohio.* Columbus: Schmidt Printing Company, 1916.

............*Annual Report, 1914.*

............, *Manufacturers Directory,* published annually.

............, *Columbus, Ohio: Industrially and Commercially,* 1914.

............, *Yearbook of the Columbus Chamber of Commerce, 1914-1915.*

Columbus City Council, *Remarks on a Water Supply for the City of Columbus,* by Joseph Sullivant, May 28, 1856.

Columbus Industrial Bureau, *Columbus: A City of New Materials and Management,* 1928.

Commissioners of the Canal Fund, *Annual Report of the Commissioners of the Canal Fund*. Columbus, 1843.

Commissioner of Statistics, *Annual Report*, Public Document No. 8, Nos. 1-5, 1858.

District Manufacturers Commission of Ohio, 1918.

Ohio Development and Publicity Commission, *Ohio: An Empire Within An Empire*. Columbus: Ohio Development and Publicity Commission, 1950.

GOVERNMENT REPORTS

United States Bureau of the Census, *United States Census Reports, 1860-1910*, U. S. Department of Commerce. Washington, D.C.: Government Printing Office, 1864-1913.

............,*United States Census Reports, 1880-1890*, U. S. Department of Commerce. Washington, D. C.: Government Printing Office, 1883-1901.

The Geographic Distribution of Manufacturing Facilities Expansion, July 1940-May 1944. Washington, D. C.: Government Printing Office, 1945.

UNPUBLISHED MANUSCRIPTS

BOWERFIND, E. S., *Notes on Early Columbus* (1939) In The Ohio State Archaeological and Historical Museum Library.

Franklin County Regional Sanitary Survey Committee, *Minutes of the Third Meeting*, April 1952. Copy of typewritten notes.

McGINNIS, ROBERT D., *The Columbus Produce Market*, Unpublished M.A. Thesis (The Ohio State University Library, Columbus, Ohio).

REYNOLDS, ESTHER C., *Settlement of Licking County to 1840*. Unpublished M.A. Thesis (The Ohio State University Library, 1951).

TAVENNER, ROBERT L., Ketcham, Alvin, Boesal, Walter J., Miller, B. Frank, and Murray, F. J., *Columbus Manufacturers*. Unpublished Seminar Paper, 1906-1907 (The Ohio State University Library).

UNSTAD, LYDER L., *A Survey of the Economic and Industrial Development in Central Ohio With Special Reference to Columbus, 1797-1872*. Unpublished Dissertation, 1937 (The Ohio State University Library).